Q&A Intellectual Property Law

Routledge Questions & Answers Series

Each Routledge Q&A contains questions on topics commonly found on exam papers, with comprehensive suggested answers. The titles are written by lecturers who are also examiners, so the student gains an important insight into exactly what examiners are looking for in an answer. This makes them excellent revision and practice guides.

Titles in the series:

Q&A Company Law
Q&A Commercial Law
Q&A Contract Law
Q&A Criminal Law
Q&A Employment Law
Q&A English Legal System
Q&A Equity and Trusts
Q&A European Union Law
Q&A Evidence
Q&A Family Law
Q&A Intellectual Property Law
Q&A Jurisprudence
Q&A Land Law
Q&A Medical Law
Q&A Public Law
Q&A Torts

For a full listing, visit www.routledge.com/cw/revision

Q&A
Intellectual
Property
Law

Janice Denoncourt

Routledge
Taylor & Francis Group

LONDON AND NEW YORK

Fourth edition published 2016
by Routledge
2 Park Square, Milton Park, Abingdon, Oxon, OX14 4RN

and by Routledge
711 Third Avenue, New York, NY 10017

Routledge is an imprint of the Taylor & Francis Group, an informa business

First edition published by Cavendish publishing 2007
Third edition published by Routledge 2012

British Library Cataloguing in Publication Data
A catalogue record for this book is available from the British Library

Library of Congress Cataloging-in-Publication Data
Denoncourt, Janice, author.
Q&a intellectual property law / Janice Denoncourt. – Fourth edition.
  pages cm. – (Routledge Q&A series)
   1. Intellectual property–Great Britain. I. Title. II. Title: Q and A intellectual property law.
  KD1269.D46 2016
  346.4104'8–dc23   2015029622

ISBN: 978-1-138-83100-1 (pbk)
ISBN: 978-1-315-73685-3 (ebk)

Typeset in TheSans
by Wearset Ltd, Boldon, Tyne and Wear
Printed by Ashford Colour Press Ltd.

Contents

Preface   vii
Table of Cases   ix
Table of Legislation   xv
Guide to the Companion Website   xix

Introduction   1

1   General Themes in Intellectual Property Law   3
2   Copyright and Moral Rights   17
3   Copyright Infringement   43
4   Computer Technology and Copyright Law   57
5   Design Right and Registered Designs   79
6   Patent Law   97
7   Passing Off   137
8   Registered Trade Marks   153
9   Confidential Information   177
10 Enforcement of Intellectual Property Rights   191

Appendix I Intellectual Property Law Exam Technique   201

Appendix II Intellectual Property Law Exam Methodology   203

Appendix III Intellectual Property Exam Cram Guide   207

Appendix IV Useful Resources   209

Index   211

Preface

A landmark survey of UK student attitudes to intellectual property confirmed that students increasingly recognise that understanding intellectual property is important for their education and future careers. The online survey of students in further and higher education was carried out by the National Union of Students in partnership with the Intellectual Property Awareness Network (IPAN) and the UK Intellectual Property Office (UKIPO). Over 2,000 replies were analysed, making this the first large-scale survey to provide insight into student attitudes to intellectual property and their need to be aware of the legal regime to protect human creativity.

Market research carried out by the Nottingham Law School, one of the largest law schools in the UK, also showed that there is increasing student demand to study IP law as part of the LLB and at postgraduate level. This is not surprising given that intellectual property is at the centre of the knowledge economy.

To help students succeed on their journey from university student to a professional career, this fourth edition of *Q&A Intellectual Property Law* is designed to make preparing for law exams easier, through a variety of IP law exam questions that students may face when they are assessed.

Forty-one problem and essay questions have been arranged topically. Each question comprises an answer checklist, tips on how to read and answer the question, followed by a comprehensive suggested answer and 'Up for Debate', 'Common Pitfalls' and 'Aim Higher' sections. New questions deal with the **Intellectual Property Act 2014** and the EU's Unitary Patent. There is advice on IP law exam technique, an 'Exam Cram' feature and a list of web links to additional resources for those students who wish to take their exam preparation further.

My involvement with both the European Intellectual Property Teachers Network (EIPTN) and the International Association for the Advancement of Teaching and Research in Intellectual Property (ATRIP) has informed my teaching. See my Amazon Author page and follow me on Twitter: @JanDenoncourt.

Learning and understanding intellectual property is important, not only for the successful completion of an academic course, but also to ensure students understand how ideas are recognised and protected, to prepare them for the growing world of enterprise and innovation beyond graduation. My hope is that this Q&A text provides students with a solid basis for tackling a broad range of topics and exam question formats that will enable them to achieve success in their IP law exams and assessments.

I have endeavoured to state the law as it stood on 1 May 2015. All errors are mine alone.

Dr Janice Denoncourt

1 May 2015

Table of Cases

Note: Where recent cases have not been widely reported, it is possible to read the judgment on the ECJ website, Go to www.curia.eu.int, select 'Proceedings' and 'case law'. Use the case number to search for the case you want to read.

A v B and C plc (2002) EWCA Civ
337 **197, 199**

A Fulton Company Ltd v Totes (Isotoner)
UK Ltd [2003] EWCA Civ 1514 **84**

A Levey v Henderson-Kenton (Holdings)
Ltd [1974] RPC 617 **142**

Actavis Ltd v Janssen Pharmaceuticals
NV [2008] EWHC 1422 **121**

AD2000 Trade Mark (1996) RPC168 **155**

Adam Opel AG v Autec AG (Case
C-48/05) [2007] ECR-I-1017 **165**

American Cyanamid v Ethicon [1975] AC
396; 1 ALL ER 504 **194, 197–199**

Amoena (UK) Ltd v Trulife Ltd (1996)
IPD19006 **85**

Ansul BV v Ajax Brandbeveiliging
C-40/01 [2003] ECR-I-2439, CJEU **173, 175**

Antec International Ltd v South Western
Chicks (Warren) Ltd [1998] EWHC
Patents 330 **140**

Anton Piller KG v Manufacturing
Processes Ltd [1976] RPC 179 **185**

Argyll v Argyll [1967] Ch 302 **185**

Arsenal Football Club plc v Mathew Reed
[2002] ECr-I10273, [2003] 1 CMLR345,
ECJ; Referred from [2001] ALL ER (D)
67 (Apr) **144, 164–166**

Attorney-General v Blake (Jonathan
Cape Ltd third party) [2001] 1 AC 268;
[2000] 4 All ER 385, HL; Affirming on
other grounds [1998] Ch 439; [1998]

1 All ER 833, CA; [1996] 3 All ER 903,
Ch D **183**

Attorney-General v Guardian
Newspapers Ltd (Spycatcher Case)
[1990] 1 AC 109; [1988] 3 All ER
545 **182**

Baby Dan AS v Brevi SRL and Trend
Europa [1999] FSR 377; [1998] EWHC
291 84 (Pat); All ER (D) 473 (Oct) **86, 88, 96**

Baigent and Lee v Random House Group
Ltd [2007] FSR 579 **20, 51**

BBC v British Satellite Broadcasting Ltd
[1992] Ch 141 **55**

BBC v Precord [1992] 3 EIPR D-52 **198**

BBC v Talksport [2001] FSR 53 **140**

Beloff v Pressdram Ltd [1973] 1 All ER
241 **50**

Bollinger (J) v Costa Brava Wine Co Ltd
[1960] RPC 16; [1960] Ch 262 **140**

Bongrain SA's Trade Mark Application
[2005] RPC 306 **171**

BP Amoco plc v John Kelly Ltd [2001] FSR
21 **141**

Bristol Conservatories Ltd v
Conservatories Custom Built [1989]
RPC 455 **137, 145**

Bristol-Myers Squibb Co. v Baker Norton
Pharmaceuticals [2001] RPC 1 **119, 121**

British Leyland Motor Corp Ltd v
Armstrong Patents Co Ltd [1986] 2
WLR 400 **84, 87**

British Medical Association v Marsh (1931) 48 RPC 565   **149**
British Steel Plc's Patent [1992] RPC 117   **132**
Brüstle v Greenpeace (C-34/10) [2012] 1 CMLR 41   **118**

C & H Engineering v F Klucznik & Sons Ltd (the Pig Fenders case) [1992] FSR 427   **84, 95**
Cantor Fitzgerald International v Tradition (UK) Ltd [2000] RPC 95   **58**
Celanese International Corporation v BP Chemicals [1999] RPC 203   **195**
Chelsea Man Menswear Ltd v Chelsea Girl Ltd [1987] RPC 189   **138–139, 142–143**
Chiron v Murex Diagnostics [1996] FSR 153   **105, 125**
Clark v Freeman (1848) Beav 112   **41, 149**
Clarke v Associated Newspapers Ltd [1988] 1 WLR 1558   **41**
Coco v AN Clark (Engineers) Ltd [1969] RPC 41   **179–181**
Colloseum Holding AG v Levi Strauss Case C-12/12 CJEU 18 April 2013   **173**
Confetti Records v Warner Music [2003] EMLR 35   **32, 40**
Consorzio del Prosciutto di Parma v Marks & Spencer Plc [1991] RPC 351   **140**
County Sound plc v Ocean Sound Ltd [1991] FSR 367   **140**
Cream Holdings and other v Banerjee and others [2004] Ch 650   **199**

'Das Prinzip der Bequemlichkeit' ['The Principle of Comfort'] (Case–64/02 P) [2004] ECR-I10031   **157**
De Maudsley v Palumbo and Others [1996] FSR 447   **181**
Designers Guild Ltd v Russell Williams (Textiles) Ltd (No 2) [2001] 1 All ER 700   **51**
Donoghue v Allied Newspapers [1938] 1 Ch 108   **19, 27, 71**
Dowson v Mason Potter (1986)   **183**

Dualit Ltd's (Toaster Shapes) Trade Mark Application [1999] RPC 304   **169, 171**
Dyson Ltd v Qualtex (UK) Ltd [2004] EWHC 2981 (Ch)   **86, 88–89**
Dyson Ltd v Vax Ltd [2010] EWHC 1923   **81, 83**

Electronic Techniques v Critchley Components [1997] FSR 401   **32, 52, 55**
EPI Environmental Technologies plc v Symphony Plastic Technologies plc [2004] EWHC 2945 (Ch); [2005] 1 WLR 3456   **182**
Exxon Corporation v Exxon Insurance Consultants International Ltd [1981] 3 All ER 241   **28**

Farmer's Build Limited v Carrier Bulk Materials Handling Ltd [1999] RPC 461   **86, 88–89, 95**
Fenty and others v Arcadia Group and another [2013] EWHC 2310 (Ch) (Rihanna v Topshop)   **148, 151**
Football Association Premier League v QC Leisure and Others C-403/08 [2012] EWCA Civ 1708   **54**
Francis Day and Hunter Ltd v Bron [1963] 2 All ER 16   **46**
Francis Day and Hunter v Twentieth Century Fox [1940] AC 112   **27**

GEC Avionics Ltd's Patent [1992] RPC 107   **132**
General Tire v Firestone Tyre Co Ltd [1975] RPC 457   **195**
Gilette v Anglo-American Trading [1913] 30 RPC 465   **129**
Green Lane Products Ltd v PMS International Group Ltd and others [2008] EWCA Civ 358   **82**

Harrods v Harrodian School (1996) unreported   **140–141**
Harvard College v Canada (Commissioner of Patents) (2002) 21 CPR (4th) 417 SCC   **117**

Harvard/OncoMouse, Re (1990) EPOR 501   **115**

HFC Bank v HSBC Bank plc [2000] FSR 176   **141**

Hubbard v Vosper [1972] 2 QB 84   **22**

Hyde Park Residence Ltd v Yelland [2000] RPC 604   **24**

Ibcos Computers v Barclays Mercantile High Finance [1994] FSR 275   **58, 60**

Improver Corp v Remington Consumer Products Ltd [1990] FSR 181   **129**

Independent Television Publications v Time Out Magazine [1984] FSR 64   **24**

Infopaq International A/S v Danske Dagblades Forening C-5/08 [2009] EUECJ C-5/08, [2012] Bus LR 102, [2009] ECR I-6569, [2010] FSR 20, [2009] ECDR 16   **77**

Inland Revenue Cmrs v Muller & Co's Margarine Ltd [1901] AC 217   **139**

IPC Magazines Ltd v MGN [1998] FSR 431   **28**

IPC Media Ltd v Highbury-SPL Publishing Ltd [2004] EEWHC 2985 (Ch); [2005] FSR 434   **28**

Irvine v Talksport [2002] EMLR 32   **148, 150–151**

J&S Davis (Holdings) Ltd v Wright Health Group [1988] RPC 403   **31**

James Duncan Kelly, Kwok Wai Chiu v GE Healthcare Ltd [2009] EWHC 181 (Pat) HL   **131**

John Richardson Computers Ltd v Flanders and Chemtech Ltd [1993] FSR 497   **60**

John Wyeth & Bros Ltd's Application (1985) RPC 545   **125**

Kelly and Chiu v GE Healthcare Ltd [2009] EWHC 181   **132–133, 135**

Kenrick & Co Ltd v Lawrence & Co (1890) 25 QBD 99   **20, 60**

Koninklijke Philips Electronics NV v Nintendo of Europe GmbH (2014) HC12E04759 (Ch)   **127**

KWS Saat AG v OHIM [2002] ECR II-3843   **160**

L'Oréal SA and others v Bellure NV and others (Case C-487/07/) [2010] All ER (EC) 28; [2009] All ER (D) 2225 (Jun)   **146, 163–164, 166, 168**

Ladbroke (Football Ltd) v William Hill (Football Ltd) [1964] 1 WLR 273   **29, 35, 45, 46, 51, 55**

Lawson v Dundas (12 June 1985) unreported   **36**

Leland Stanford Modified Animal [2002] EP 2   **125**

LengD'Or SA v Crown Confectionary Co Ltd (OHIM Ref ICD 000000370, 23 February 2005)   **82**

Libertel Group BV v Benelu-Merkenbureau (Case C-104/01) [2003] ECR I-3793; [2004] FSR 65   **155–156, 158–160**

Lindner Recyclingtech GmbH v Franssens Verstäder AB [2010] ECDR1 (OHIM)   **81, 83**

Lock International plc v Beswick [1989] 3 All ER 373   **181**

London Evening Mail: (1) Associated Newspapers, Daily Mail & General Trust v Express Newspapers [2003] EWHC 1322; FSR 51   **142**

Ludlow Music Inc. v Robbie Williams (No 2) [2002]FSR 271; [2002] EMLR 29   **51**

McCulloch v Lewis A May (Produce Distributors) Ltd [1947] 2 All ER 845   **149**

Mag Instrument v OHIM [2005] ETMR 46   **169, 171–172**

Mayfair Brassware Ltd v Aqualine International Ltd [1997] EWCA Civ 2560; [1998] FSR 138   **83**

Memco-Med Ltd's Patent [1992] RPC 403   **132**

Menashe Business Mercantile Ltd v William Hill Organization Ltd [2003] RPC 31A   **128**

Mirage Productions v Counter-Feat Clothing Co Ltd [1991] FSR 135   **145**

Morning Star Co-operative Society v Express Newspapers [1979] FSR 113   **141**

Morrison v Moat (1851) 9 Hare 241   **180**

Mothercare UK Ltd v Penguin Books Ltd [1988] RPC 113   **198**

MS Associates Ltd v Power [1988] FSR 242

Naomi Campbell v Mirror Group Newspapers [2004]   **180**

Navitaire Inc v EasyJet Airline Company [2004] EWHC 1725; [2004] All ER (D) 162 Dec, Ch D; [2006] RPC 111   **58, 61, 64, 75**

Nestlé France v OHIM [2004] ETMR 566   **169, 171**

Nestlé SA's Trade Mark Application (Have a Break) v Mars Ltd *see* Société des Produits Nestlé SA v Mars UK Ltd

Neutrogena Corp v Golden Ltd [1996] RPC 473   **141**

Newspaper Licensing Agency Ltd v Marks & Spencer plc (1999) *The Times*, 15 June   **24**

Nintendo v PC Box [2014] C-355/12   **68, 75**

Noah v Shuba [1991] FSR 14   **36**

Nottinghamshire Healthcare NHS Trust v News Group Newspapers Ltd [2002] EWHC 409 (Ch)   **195**

Nova Productions Ltd v Mazooma Games Ltd [2007] All ER (D) 234 (Mar)   **64, 73–75, 77**

Ocular Sciences Ltd v Aspect Vision Care Ltd [1997] RPC 289   **81, 84, 86, 88, 95**

Parker v Tidball [1997] FSR 680, Ch D   **85**

Pasterfield v Denham and Another [1998] FSR 168   **32, 40**

Peek & Cloppenburg KG v OHIM [2005] ECR II-4633 Case T-379/03   **169–170**

Perry v Truefitt (1842) 6 Beav 66   **137, 140, 144**

Phillips Electronics BV v Remington Consumer Products Ltd [1998] RPC 283   **156**

Phones 4u Ltd v Phone4u.co.uk Internet Ltd [2007] RPC 5   **141**

PLG Research Ltd v Ardon International Ltd [1995] FSR 116   **105**

Pozzolli SpA v BDMO SpA [2007] EWCA Civ 588   **129**

Prince Albert v Strange (1849) 2 De G & Sm 704   **180**

Pro Sieben Media AG v Carlton UK TV Ltd [1999] FSR 610   **24**

Procter & Gamble Company v Reckitt Benckiser (UK) Ltd [2007] EWCA Civ 936   **82**

Ralf Sieckmann vs Deutshes Patent-und Markenamt (Case C-273/00) [2003] Ch 487; [2002] ECR I-11737   **155, 158, 161**

Reckitt and Coleman Products v Borden Inc. [1990] All ER 1873, HL   **138–141, 145**

Reddaway & Co Ltd v Banham & Co Ltd [1896] AC 199   **140**

Rihanna v Topshop [2013] EWHC 2310 (Ch)   **148, 151–152**

Robb v Green [1895] 2 QB 315   **180**

Saltman Engineering Co Ltd v Campbell Engineering Co Ltd (1948) 65 RPC 203; [1963] 3 All ER 413   **180–181, 185**

SAS Institute Inc. v World Programming Ltd [2010] EWHC 1829 (Ch)   **58, 62, 63**

Schering and Wyeth's Application [1985] RPC 545   **112**

Scholes Windows v Magnet [2001] EWCA Civ 532   **86, 89**

Seager v Copydex Ltd [1967] 2 All ER 415   **180, 182–183, 185**

Series 5 Software Ltd v Philip Clarke and others [1996] 1 All ER 853; [1996] FSR 273   **197–199**

Shanks v Unilever [2014] EWHC 1647   **134**

Shell/Blood Flow [1993] EPOR 320   **112, 125**

Silberquelle GmbH Case C-495/07 [2009] ECR-I-137, CJEU   **176**

Sinanide v La Maison Kosmeo (1928) 44 TLR 371   **27**

Slater v Wimmer [2012] EWPCC 7   **35**

Smith Kline and French's Trade Mark [1975] 2 All ER 57 **160**

Société Des Produits Nestlé SA v Cadbury UK Ltd [2013] EWCA 1174 Civ **161, 169**

Solar Thomson v Barton [1977] RPC 357 **52**

Sony Computer Entertainment Inc v Edmunds [2002] EWHC 45 (Ch) **65**

Sony Computer Entertainment v Ball [2004] EWHC 1738 (Ch) **65, 66**

Spalding & Bros v AW Gamage Ltd [1915] 32 RPC 273 **140**

Stafford-Miller's Application [1984] RPC 239 **112**

Stennards Reay [1967] RPC 589; FSR 140 **140**

Stilltoe v McGraw-Hill Books [1983] FSR 545 **24**

Swizzels Matlow Ltd's Trade Mark Application [1998] RPC 244 **169, 171**

Synthon BV v Smithkline Beecham plc [2005] UKHL 59 **120**

Terrapin Ltd v Builders Supply Co (Hayes) Ltd (1967) RPC 375 **182**

Triomed (Proprietary) Ltd v Beecham Group plc [2001] FSR 583 **169, 171**

Total Information Processing Systems v Daman [1992] FSR 171 **59**

Ultraframe UK Ltd v Clayton [2003] EWHC 242 (Ch) **84**

Unilever (Davis's) Application [1983] RPC 219 **112**

Unilever's Application, Unilver plc's Trade Mark [1984] RPC 155 **160**

Universal Thermosensors Ltd v Hibben [1992] 3 All ER 257 **191**

University of London Press Ltd v University Tutorial Press Ltd [1916] 2 Ch 601 **26, 27, 29, 31, 35, 45, 59, 70, 71**

Upjohn's Application [1976] RPC 324 **113**

WARF/Stem Cells (G2/06) [2009] EPOR 15 (EPO EBA) **117**

Warnink BV v Townend & Sons (Hull) Ltd [1980] RPC 31 HL **141**

Williams v Hodge & Co (1887) 4 TLR 175 **149**

Windsurfing International Inc v Tabur Marine (GB) [1985] RPC 59 **105, 129**

Wombles Ltd v Wombles Skips Ltd [1975] RPC 99 **27–28**

Wrigley/Light Green [1999] ETMR 214 Board of Appeal of the OHIM **159**

Table of Legislation

■ Statutes

Copyright, Designs and Patents Act
  1988 **3, 17–23, 25–29, 31–37, 39–41, 44–47, 49–51, 54–55, 57–60, 65–66, 68–72, 74–76, 79, 81–88, 90–91, 93–95, 110, 195, 204, 207**
  s 1 **31**
  s 1(1) **26, 27, 31, 34, 58, 59, 69**
  s 1(2) **50**
  s 1B **82**
  s 3(1) **71**
  s 3(1)(b) **58, 59**
  s 31(1)(c) **58, 59**
  s 3(1)(d) **29, 35, 39, 49–50**
  s 3(2) **50**
  s 4 **34**
  s 4(1) **71, 76**
  s 4(1)(a) **26, 27, 31, 35, 44, 45, 70**
  s 4(2) **31**
  s 9(1) **31**
  s 9(2) **191**
  s 9(5) **19**
  s 10 **34, 35**
  s 11 **60**
  s 11(1) **35**
  s 11(2) **36, 50**
  s 12 **36, 50**
  s 16 **19, 31, 44, 49, 55, 71, 76**
  s 16(1) **49, 50**
  s 16(1)(a) **32, 45**
  s 16(2) **45, 50**
  s 16(3) **46, 50**
  s 16(3)(a) **51**
  s 17 **58**
  s 17(3) **32**

s 17(6) **46**
s 18 **58**
s 19 **58**
ss 28–76 **19, 22, 23, 47, 52**
s 29 **23, 54**
s 30 **54, 55**
s 30(1) **23, 24, 31**
s 30(2) **23, 24, 29**
s 30A **25**
s 31 **23, 47**
s 50 **58**
s 50A **58**
s 50B **58**
s 62 **33**
s 77 **39**
s 77(2)(a) **40**
ss 77–79 **20, 37, 39, 41, 47, 72**
s 80 **39, 40**
s 80(2)(b) **40**
ss 80–83 **20, 32, 37, 39, 40, 41, 47, 72**
s 84 **20, 32, 39, 40, 41**
s 85 **20, 32, 39**
s 86 **32**
s 94 **32, 34, 36, 39**
s 96(1) **195**
s 99 **34**
s 100 **195**
ss 107–110 **195**
ss 153–155 **50**
s 198 **195**
s 213 **81, 83–88, 91, 93–95**
s 213–264 **87**
ss 214–215 **95**
s 216 **85, 95**
s 217 **95**
s 229 **195**

s 263(1)(a)   **95**
s 296   **66, 68, 69**
s 296(2)   **66**
s 296(4)   **65**
s 296ZA(3)   **66**
s 296ZB   **66**
s 296D   **66**
s 296ZE   **65, 66**
s 296ZF   **66**
s 297   **195**
s 297A   **195**
s 297B   **195**
Digital Economy Act 2010   **74**
Freedom of Information Act 2000   **188**
Human Fertilization and Embryology Act
   2008   **125**
Human Rights Act 1998   **197–199**
Intellectual Property Act 2014   **3, 12, 13,
   14, 86–87, 89–93, 99–100, 207**
London Olympic Games and Paralympic
   Games Act 2006   **156**
Olympic Symbol etc. (Protection) Act
   1995   **155–156**
   s 3(1)(a)   **156**
Patents Act 1949   **122**
Patents Act 1977   **3, 13, 74, 76, 82,
   99–100, 103–104, 107–109, 111–113,
   115–117, 119–124, 128–129, 131–135,
   184–185, 195, 207**
   s 1   **119–120, 124**
   s 1(1)   **76, 103, 124–126**
   s 1(a)   **77**
   s 1(2)   **124–125**
   s 1(3)   **104, 115–117, 124–126**
   s 1(4)   **116**
   s 2   **104, 120, 124**
   s 2(1)   **105**
   s 2(2)   **120**
   s 3   **103–105, 120, 124**
   s 4   **104, 124**
   s 4(1)   **105**
   s 4A   **111–113, 124–125, 129**
   s 5(1)   **105–106**
   s 7   **133**
   s 16   **122**
   s 16(1)   **106**
   a 61(1)(c)   **195**

s 61(1)(d)   **195**
s 17   **106**
s 21   **122**
s 22   **122**
s 24   **122**
s 25   **122**
s 39   **133**
ss 39–41   **131**
s 40   **132–134**
s 41   **133, 135**
s 60(1)(a)   **127**
s 70   **128**
s 72   **121**
s 72(1)   **119–120**
ss 72–74   **122**
s 74(1)(a)   **129**
Schedule A2   **115, 117, 124–126**
Patents Act 2004   **99, 113, 124, 125, 131,
   134, 135, 207**
   s 1   **125**
   s 10   **131, 134–135**
Plant Varieties Act 1997   **126**
   ss 4–7   **126**
Registered Designs Act 1949   **3, 79, 81,
   83, 87, 90–94, 96, 195**
   s 1(2)   **81, 82**
   s 1B   **82**
   s 1B(2)   **82**
   s 1C(1)   **83**
   s 1C(2)   **83**
   s 9(1)   **195**
   ss 35ZA-C   **92**
Senior Courts Act 1981   **191, 197**
   s37   **197**
Trade Marks Act 1994   **70, 72, 74, 76,
   139, 144, 153, 155–159, 163–165, 168–171,
   173–176, 195, 207**
   s 1   **155, 168, 207**
   s 1(1)   **153, 156–159, 164, 170**
   s 3   **155–156**
   s 3(1)(a)   **170**
   s 3(1)(b)   **72, 170**
   s 3(1)(c)   **156–157, 170**
   s 3(1)(d)   **156**
   s 3(1)(e)   **169–171**
   s 4   **155–156**
   s 4(5)   **156**

s 5 **155**
s 5 (1)–(3) **165**
s 5(2)(a) **157**
s 9 **165**
s 10(1)–(3) **165**
s 10(1)(a) **165**
s 10(2) **76**
s 10(6) **163**
s 14(2) **191**
s 46 **173–174**
s 46(1) **174–175**
s 46(1)(a) **174**
s 46(1)(b) **173–174**
s 46(2) **175**
s 72 **173**
s 100 **174**

■ Statutory Instruments

Civil Procedure Rules 1988, SI
    1998/3132 **99, 194, 197**
    CPR 31 **194**
    CPR 35 **197**
    CPR 63 **100**
Copyright and Rights in Performances
    (Quotation and Parody) Regulations
    2014 **53, 54**
Copyright (Computer Programs)
    Regulations 2003, SI 2003/2498 **58,
    59, 62**
Patent Rules 2007 **13, 99**
Plant Breeders' Rights (Naming and Fees)
    Regulations 2006, SI 2006/648 **126**

■ European Community and EEA Legislation Regulations

Council Regulation 3295/94/EC On
    Stopping the Release of Counterfeit
    Goods into Free Circulation **195**
Unitary Patent Court Agreement **14**

■ Directives

Directive 89/104/EEC (Trade Marks
    Directive) **144, 153, 155, 161, 165, 167,
    173–175**
    Art 2 **161**
    Art 5(2) **167**
    Art 15 **173–175**
Directive 91/250/EEC (Legal Protection of
    Computer Programs Directive –
    Software Directive) **59**
    Art 1(2) **59**
Directive 98/44/EC (Biotechnological
    Inventions, Biotech Directive) **117, 126**
Directive 2001/29 (Database and
    Information Society Directive) **65**
    Art 6(3) **65**
Directive 2001/84/EC (Resale Rights
    Directive) **20**
Directive 2004/48/EC (Intellectual
    Property Rights Enforcement
    Directive) **191, 195**
Directive 2005/29/EC Unfair Commercial
    Practices Directive **146**
Directive 2008/95 (Registration of Trade
    Marks Internationally) **153**
Directive 2009/24/EC Software
    Directive **58, 62–63, 68, 75**
    Recitals 13 and 14 **62**
    Art (1) **62, 63**
    Art 1(2) **58, 62**
    Art 5(3) **63**

■ International Agreements, Conventions and Treaties

Berne Convention for the Protection of
    Literary and Artistic Works
    1886 **20, 22, 38, 39, 75, 207**
    Art 2 **75**
    Art 6 **38, 39**
    Art 9(2) **22**
    Art 14 **20**

European Agreement on a Unified
    Patent Court   **97, 101**
European Patent Convention 1973   **100,
    112**
European Patent Convention 2000   **76,
    100, 109, 112, 114–117, 125**
    Art 6(2)(c)   **117**
    Art 52(2)   **76**
    Art 53   **112, 114–116, 125**
Hague Agreement Concerning the
    International Registration of Designs
    1925   **93**
Madrid Protocol for the International
    Registration of Marks   **153**
Paris Convention of the Protection of
    Industrial Property 1883   **87, 137, 146**
    Art 10   **146**
Patent Cooperation Treaty 1970   **97,
    104, 106, 109**
Universal Declaration of Human Rights
    1948   **4, 6, 7, 32, 36, 39, 207**

Art 27   **32, 36, 39**
World Intellectual Property Organization
    on Copyright Treaty 1996   **22, 57, 65,
    66, 68**
    Art 4   **57**
    Art 10(1)   **22**
    Art 11   **66**
    Art 27   **207**
World Intellectual Property Organization
    Performers and Phonograms
    Treaty   **65, 66**
    Art 18   **66**
World Trade Organization Agreement
    on Trade-Related Aspects of
    Intellectual Property Rights 1994
    (TRIPS Agreement)   **3, 7–11, 35, 57, 75,
    87, 97, 99, 110, 112**
    Art 2   **20, 35, 75, 112**
    Art 4   **57**
    Art 41   **99**

Guide to the Companion Website

www.routledge.com/cw/revision

Visit the Law Revision website to discover a comprehensive range of resources designed to enhance your learning experience.

The Good, The Fair, & The Ugly

Good essays are the gateway to top marks. This interactive tutorial provides sample essays together with voice-over commentary and tips for successful exam essays, written by our Q&A authors themselves.

Multiple Choice Questions

Knowledge is the foundation of every good essay. Focusing on key examination themes, these MCQs have been written to test your knowledge and understanding of each subject in the book.

Bonus Q&As

Having studied our exam advice, put your revision into practice and test your essay writing skills with our additional online questions and answers

Introduction

The term 'intellectual property' is used to describe the various rights that protect innovation and creative endeavour. An optional law subject, intellectual property (IP) law arises in the curriculum towards the end of a law (LLB) degree. This is because it is regarded as an advanced and specialist subject due to its diverse content and the fact that it draws on core legal subject knowledge including contract, tort, land, common law and equity. The discipline became popular in the late 1980s and early 1990s and was included in curricula as a stand-alone course to accommodate the changing demands of the legal professional bodies and business.

Typically, at the undergraduate level, an IP law course will cover copyright, moral rights, design rights, patents, passing off, trade marks, confidential information and know-how, remedies and enforcement. Common themes across the different forms of IP include authorship or inventorship, ownership, requirements for the right to subsist, the extent and duration of the statutory monopolies granted, remedies and enforcement, especially in the digital age. IP law is never static and this is likely why students regard it as 'exciting new law' within the LLB curriculum.

Fortunately, the number of books and online resources on the subject of IP law has grown to support the increased level of study of the subject. According to Professor Ruth Soetendorp, a pioneer in IP law education and Professor Emeritus at Bournemouth University, 'there is growing evidence of criticality in the IP law syllabus'. In addition, with globalisation, cross-border issues and the harmonisation of some of the administrative aspects of international IP regimes, the focus of the IP curricula is increasingly European and international.

Although this book is aimed at helping students to successfully deal with their written exams through a selection of problem, essay and mixed topic questions, it is hoped that they will retain some knowledge of this fascinating subject – even once assessments are over!

1 General Themes in Intellectual Property Law

Essay-style questions are commonly used to invite the student to discuss a variety of themes in intellectual property (IP) law. We are surrounded in our everyday lives by intellectual property, but defining or describing it is no easy feat. The range of matter which falls within the scope of intellectual property is diverse and extensive.

Examples of things that can be protected by intellectual property include inventions, novels, works of art, photographs, musical scores, sound recordings, films, computer software, bio-engineered living organisms, trade secrets, know-how, invented characters and brand names. Examiners often set questions relating to the rationales or traditional justifications for the existence of IP protection.

Another theme running through IP law is that the systems are constantly adapting, whether in response to advances in technology or as a result of shifting perceptions about the appropriate reach of IP protection. In general, the subject matter that may be protected by IP law regimes is increasing as new innovations are created which are deserving of property rights. The statutes that mainly govern IP law include the **Copyright, Designs and Patents Act 1988**, the **Registered Designs Act 1949**, the **Patents Act 1977** and the **Trade Marks Act 1994**. Case law helps to clarify how the law is applied. The **Intellectual Property Act 2014** made important changes to copyright, design and patent law (to improve efficiency and cost-effectiveness) and all the provisions should be in force by the end of 2015.

Finally, a popular topic with examiners relates to the most important international agreement on the subject of intellectual property, the **Agreement on Trade-Related Aspects of Intellectual Property** (**TRIPS**).

Checklist

Students should anticipate the debate about the following:

- the nature and role of the IP legal regime to shape society;
- the most significant types of IP protection: copyright, design, patents and trade marks and the doctrine of confidential information;
- the impact of the **TRIPS Agreement** on domestic IP law regimes;
- the advantages and disadvantages of IP law protection over valuable intangible property;
- important new legislation such as the **Intellectual Property Act (UK) 2014**.

QUESTION 1

Critically analyse and discuss the traditional justifications for the existence of the systems of intellectual property protection.

How to Read this Question

The examiner has made a statement and the instruction is to critically analyse and discuss it. What the examiner is looking for is an exploration of the constituent elements of the statement. Students should demonstrate to the examiner their understanding of the philosophical 'justifications' that justify the granting of monopolistic intellectual property (IP) rights to protect intangible property. It is important that students set out the 'traditional' justifications as referred to in the question and then consider any new justifications that may now apply.

How to Answer this Question

Exploring the types of traditional philosophical theories that underpin IP rights protection will need to take place at the outset. This will enable the student to identify the key theories and then critically analyse and discuss them in turn. The insights from the discussion can be applied to the modern UK IP law protection system. The structure below highlights the kind of content that could be discussed.

Answer Structure

This question requires the student to demonstrate an appreciation of the various theories for justifying the granting of monopolistic IP protection rights:

- ❖ 'Natural rights': John Locke's Labour Theory (1632–1704);
- ❖ Natural rights and **Art 27(3)** of the **Universal Declaration of Human Rights**;
- ❖ Hegel's Personality Theory (1770–1831);
- ❖ Economic justifications and the utilitarian theory;
- ❖ Consumer protection, technology transfer and social well-being;
- ❖ Concluding remarks.

Up for Debate

In 2014, the year the World Wide Web celebrated its 25th birthday, over half the planet's population is connected to the Internet and 1.7 billion people are active smartphone and social media users. The increasing influence of electronic communication on human beings is undeniable. While the WWW is not subject to IP ownership, social media platforms, smartphones and apps are valuable forms of intellectual property. Currently, however, according to Professor Estelle Derclaye at the University of Nottingham,

> Any work, design or invention can be protected if it is new, inventive and/or original, even if it does not enhance well-being. While the Internet, smartphones and Facebook make us more connected and social ties enhance

well-being, empirical research however reveals that such technologies' effects are overall more negative than positive. The question is thus posed whether the IPR framework should embed a 'not-well-being-reducing' condition for this type of invention and works as they do not fall into the morality clause.

ANSWER

Legal and political philosophers have often debated the status and legitimacy of intellectual property. They ask, 'Why should we grant intellectual property rights?' The answer to this question is important, because society has a choice as to whether it chooses to grant such rights. It is also important because the decision to grant property rights in intangibles impinges on traders, the press and media and the public.

IP rights have three key features. First, they are property rights. Second, they are property rights in something intangible. Third, they protect innovation and creations and reward innovative and creative activity. All IP rights have one common feature: for any subject matter to be protected by an IP right, the minimum criteria for that form of property must be met.

On the one hand, the grant of private property rights in land and tangible resources is premised on the scarcity or limited availability of such resources and the impossibility of sharing. However, how can we justify the grant of exclusive rights over ideas and information – which are not scarce and can be replicated without any direct detriment to the original possessor of the intangible (who continues to be able to use the information)?

A central characteristic of IP rights is that they are negative monopolistic rights. They exclude others from the use and exploitation of the subject matter of the right. However, all IP rights expire at some point in time, except for confidential information, trade marks and geographical indications, which can be perpetual.

Intangible property rights are fundamentally different from rights attaching to tangible property such as a house, a car or a piece of jewellery. The subject matter of IP rights, creative endeavour and inventions, necessarily has a link with knowledge and ideas. In economic terms, such matter is a public asset not easily owned by one person or group. The ability to exclude others from use or copying arises due to an artificial legal regime which grants an intangible property right to the inventor or creator.

Philosophers have not always found IP rights to be justified in the form they currently take. Why are intangible property rights created? The existence of IP rights is usually justified by reference to one or more of the following philosophical theories.

(1) NATURAL RIGHTS

One of the most basic justifications for intellectual property is that a person who puts intellectual effort into creating something should have a natural right to own and control what he creates. This is derived from the Labour Theory by the seventeenth-century philosopher

John Locke. He argued that everyone has a property right in the labour of his own body, and that the appropriation of an unowned object arises out of the application of human labour to that object. There must remain objects of similar quality in sufficient quantity to supply others. In other words, 'He who sows shall also reap.' Such an entitlement is recognised in **Art 27(2)** of the **Universal Declaration of Human Rights**, which states:

> Everyone has the right to the protection of moral and material interests resulting from any scientific, literary or artistic production of which he is the author.

In addition, according to Georg Hegel's Personality Theory, 'Creation is an extension of its creator's individuality or person, belonging to that creator as part of his or her selfhood'.

(2) TO ENCOURAGE AND REWARD INNOVATION AND CREATION

Intellectual property rights serve as an incentive for the investment of time and capital in the research and development which are required to produce inventive and creative works. By providing the owner with exclusive property rights, he enjoys the benefit of the stream of revenue generated by exploitation of his intellectual property.

(3) TO ENCOURAGE DISSEMINATION OF INFORMATION AND IDEAS

The existence of IP laws encourages the disclosure and dissemination of information and widens the store of knowledge available in the community. This justification is commonly given for patents. The specification of patented inventions are published by patent offices around the world and form a valuable source of advanced technical information.

(4) ECONOMIC EFFICIENCY

Economic theorists justify the recognition of property rights in creative endeavour on the basis that it leads to more efficient use of resources. Innovation is an essential element in a competitive free market economy. Economists argue that if everyone was freely allowed to use the results of innovative and creative activity, the problem of 'free riders' would arise. Investors would be reluctant to invest in innovation. Competitors would just wait for someone else to create a product, which they would then copy at little up-front cost. Legal protection of intangible property rights creates a climate in which investors are stimulated to invest in research and development, as they will be guaranteed a competitive 'first to market' advantage for a period of time.

(5) CONSUMER PROTECTION, TECHNOLOGY TRANSFER AND SOCIAL WELL-BEING

Some IP rights offer protection for consumers by enabling them to make informed choices between goods and services from different sources (for example, trade marks and geographical indications).

In addition, IP systems facilitate the transfer of technology through foreign direct invest-ment, joint ventures and licensing, which brings economic prosperity to lesser developed regions and countries. As innovation and creative industries remain overwhelmingly the province of the developed nations, the importance of international technology transfer for fostering economic development cannot be overstated. Most developing countries rely on imported technologies as a source of new productive knowledge. However, consider-able follow-on innovation and adaptation take place over time, adding to the global body of knowledge.

In conclusion, all of the above theories are encapsulated in the **Agreement on Trade-Related Aspects of Intellectual Property Rights** (**TRIPS**), which attempts to set minimum standards of intellectual property law protection for World Trade Organization members. In essence, IP law attempts to strike a balance between the:

❖ conflicting interests of society as a whole in economic and cultural development; and
❖ interest of the individual to secure a 'fair' value for its intellectual effort or invest-ment of capital or labour.

However, in the twenty-first century with the advent of the Internet and social media the time is ripe to question whether the current approach to granting monopolistic property rights is effectively a barrier to desirable social development and goals. Some argue that the IP rights legal framework should embed a 'discretion' to exclude from legal protection inventions and works that reduce human well-being.

This continual tension is at the heart of the development of the various IP law regimes and leads scholars to constantly evaluate the philosophical, economic and ethical justifi-cations of the systems for granting IP rights.

Common Pitfalls

Students should avoid elaborating on the same argument repetitively, but rather try to cover several themes in order to show greater depth of knowledge and thus obtain more marks. The instructing words for the essay are 'critically analyse', so don't forget to consider the impact of the direction of the law, i.e. the broader picture.

Aim Higher

Where possible, add depth to your essay answer by referring to the relevant legisla-tion and international law such as the **Universal Declaration of Human Rights** and the **Agreement on Trade-Related Aspects of Intellectual Property Rights**.

QUESTION 2

One of the most significant modern intellectual property (IP) issues is the clash between the developing and the developed countries with respect to the level and effectiveness of monopolistic protection for intangible property. Critically discuss whether or not the international IP frameworks of the developed countries lean towards protecting the interests of the rich rather than the poor.

How to Read this Question

The examiner has made a statement and is looking for an answer that either agrees or disagrees with it. The two main components here are 'international legal frameworks' and the **TRIPS Agreement**. The examiner wants the student to explore the reasons why the international IP law framework is perceived to favour the Organisation for Economic Co-operation and Development (OECD) countries over lesser developed countries.

How to Answer this Question

This question is often asked in one form or another and is reasonably straightforward. It requires the student to consider why features of the international IP law framework, namely the **TRIPS Agreement**, should be maintained. It is important to explain that the **TRIPS Agreement** sets out minimum standards for the level of IP protection in World Trade Organization member states.

Answer Structure

This essay question enables the student to consider the impact of the current IP regime from a policy point of view. The student should write a composition in continuous prose demonstrating the depth of his or her knowledge of the wider IP global policy issues. The discussion should adopt a two-sided approach and present arguments for and against each particular view. The arguments should be based on evidence such as key treaties and domestic legislation.

- ❖ Explain how the international IP framework is perceived to promote the interests of the developed countries and in particular **TRIPS**.
- ❖ Set out the issues of concern of the developing countries.
- ❖ Consider the merit of possible solutions or policy responses to the issues identified.
- ❖ Reach a reasoned conclusion that supports the student's preferred view.

Up for Debate

Students should form their own opinion on the effectiveness of the international IP law framework in OECD and developing countries based on evidence. One starting point is reading Hiroko Yamane's *Interpreting TRIPS: Globalisation of Intellectual Property Rights and Access to Medicines* (2011, Hart Publishing Ltd). It appears that the apprehension over the **TRIPS Agreement** in most developing countries has waned, or, at any rate, their current apprehensions or demands are of a different nature due to liberalisation in their economic policies, the rapid pace of globalisation and multilateral trade rules to curb unfair practices.

ANSWER

Protection of intellectual property rights (IPRs) has become a global issue. The control of knowledge is a key concern in relation to the international IP law framework. Will knowledge be monopolised by the commercial interests of the developed countries, or will knowledge be within the public domain, readily able to be used to overcome poverty, hunger and disease? The World Trade Organization's **Agreement on Trade-Related Aspects of Intellectual Property Rights (TRIPS)**, introduced in 1994 after intense lobbying by developed countries, is at the centre of this controversy. It is the main international treaty determining rights over intellectual property, which includes patents, copyright and trade marks among other forms of intellectual property. **TRIPS** established enforceable global minimum standards for most IPRs. After over a decade of intense debate over global IPR protection, problems remain acute; however, there is evidence of progress and cooperation to share knowledge.

GLOBAL MINIMUM STANDARDS OF LEGAL PROTECTION

What is the role of IPRs as incentive for innovation against the backdrop of development and the transfer of technology between globalised, knowledge-based high-technology economies? **TRIPS** requires all member states to implement relatively high minimum standards of protection, irrespective of a particular state's level of development or social needs. It is felt that this one-size-fits-all approach may damage social welfare in the developing countries. Has the balance shifted too far towards the private interests of corporations in the developed countries, and away from the users of knowledge?

Many non-governmental organisations such as Oxfam fear that the damaging effects of international IP rules will be felt most acutely in poor countries, in that high standards of IP protection will exclude poor people from access to vital 'knowledge goods'. They claim that **TRIPS** will result in higher prices for knowledge-rich goods, further excluding poor people from access to vital medicines, seeds, computer software and educational materials. The high price of HIV/AIDS medicines has illustrated graphically the iniquitous effect that the temporary 20-year monopolies created by patents can have. Higher prices also limit the ability of developing-country governments to meet people's basic rights to food, health and development. On the other hand, supporters of **TRIPS** say that short-term welfare losses caused by higher prices are offset by longer-term benefits through increased innovation and technology transfer for poor countries. In addition, the developed countries argue that higher levels of IP protection in developing countries will prompt greater foreign direct investment or licensing by transnational companies, even in pharmaceuticals and chemicals.

THE TECHNOLOGY DIVIDE

There is a wide technological gap between rich and poor countries. Although developing countries are rich in informal knowledge, for example traditional medicine, they are net importers of the kinds of high-tech goods and know-how protected by **TRIPS**. Developed industrialised countries, on the other hand, account for 90 per cent of global research and development (R&D) spending, an even higher share of patents, and are the main export-ers of intellectual property.

Developing countries are concerned that the **TRIPS** provisions will exacerbate this divide by increasing the cost of knowledge-rich goods they import. Royalties and licence fees paid by developing countries to patent holders in the industrialised world have been increasing rapidly over the last two decades. Typically, the US, for example, receives a net surplus of billions of pounds from its IP exports.

RESEARCH AND DEVELOPMENT

Developing countries argue that global R&D is targeted at the markets of rich consumers, rather than at the basic needs of the poor. Less than 10 per cent of global spending on health research addresses 90 per cent of the global disease burden. Similarly, much agri-cultural research aims to improve the appearance and taste of produce for consumers in rich markets, rather than to support the sustainable farming of staple foods such as sorghum and cassava, on which many poor farmers depend. Developing countries are concerned that global IP rules will worsen this problem by further concentrating R&D into profitable areas such as cures for obesity or impotence.

Developing countries are apprehensive that the biological resources and traditional knowledge of their farmers and indigenous people are the subject of piracy by the developed world. **TRIPS** was designed to prevent so-called piracy by developing countries of the inventions and products of rich countries. However, the agreement does not deal with the systematic appropriation of biological knowledge and informal forms of tradi-tional knowledge from developing countries by the corporations of the developed countries.

TRIPS AND ESSENTIAL MEDICINES

Another concern of developing countries is their ability to access essential medicines subject to patent rights. Fortunately, however, the developed countries have taken positive steps in this regard beginning in 2001, when a declaration was made to the effect that the **TRIPS Agreement** does not and should not prevent member states from taking measures to protect public health. In 2002, the EU member states met to try to assist the TRIPS Council in finding a solution to help countries with little or no manufacturing abil-ities in the pharmaceutical sector make effective use of compulsory licensing, as agreed in the declaration on **TRIPS** and public health. In 2003, the WTO member states agreed to allow the making of medicines under compulsory licences for export to developing coun-tries within the terms set out in the decision. In 2005, WTO members agreed changes to the **TRIPS Agreement** to reflect this decision. This General Council decision was the first time a core WTO agreement was changed.

TECHNICAL ASSISTANCE PROVIDED TO DEVELOPING COUNTRIES BY THE UK

Article 67 of **TRIPS** requires developed country members to provide technical and financial cooperation to developing and least-developed country members. The UK Government's White Paper, 'Eliminating World Poverty: Making Globalisation Work for the Poor', published in 2000, pointed to the need for IP regimes to work better for poor people. In addition, the UK Government's response to the 2002 Report of the Commission on Intellectual Property Rights confirmed the need to tailor IP regimes to individual countries' circumstances within the **TRIPS** framework.

INITIATIVES TO ASSIST DEVELOPING COUNTRIES WITH IP ISSUES

A number of international programmes and resources exist to assist developing countries and there is a body of work promulgated by the World Intellectual Property Organization's (WIPO) Cooperation for Development Programme; the World Health Organisation's Commission on Intellectual Property Rights, Innovation and Public Health; the Integrated Framework for Trade-Related Assistance to Least Developed Countries; the World Bank's reports; the World Trade Organization; the United Nations Conference on Trade and Development (UNCTAD) and others to evaluate the impact of IPRs.

The most controversial issue surrounding **TRIPS** is its impact on the pricing and availability of new medicines. For example, if patent protection is obtained and enforced in developing countries, **TRIPS** could reduce the availability of generic medicines, thus adversely affecting a de facto price control on medicines in these countries. The manufacture of products that were unprotected by patents led to competition that played a key role in determining prices for HIV anti-retroviral medicines in Brazil, India, South Africa and other countries. However, public health safeguards such as the 'compulsory licensing' are provided under the **TRIPS Agreement** to address access to medicines in certain exceptional situations.

Conclusively documenting the benefits or costs of **TRIPS** for developing countries is difficult. This is because innovation is a dynamic process influenced by many external variables including but not limited to the level of government support for science and technology, government projects to promote trade and knowledge transfer, and the capabilities of national pharmaceutical regulatory agencies. Nevertheless, despite the difficulties of measuring the effectiveness of **TRIPS**, historical precedent confirms that strengthening IP law regimes tends to increase foreign direct investment and technology transfer subject to the existence of supportive research and development environments, effective judicial systems to enforce IP law and viable domestic and export markets.

ISSUES FOR THE REFORM OF TRIPS

Several non-governmental organisations have come together to form the TRIPS Action Network (TAN), with a view to campaigning for further reforms of **TRIPS** and to lobby the Group of Twenty (G20) developed countries.

The G20 is an informal but exclusive body founded in 1999, whose members set out to tackle global challenges through discussion and action. With no headquarters, budget or permanent staff, the G20 comprises many of the world's leading industrialised nations (e.g. France, Germany, Italy, Japan, UK, US, Canada and Russia). The leaders of these countries meet face-to-face at an annual summit that has become a focus of media attention and protest action. The G20 IPR experts group has also agreed that technical assistance plans are needed to help developing countries strengthen their efforts to combat trade in pirated and counterfeit goods. G20 members can agree on policies and can set objectives, but compliance with these is voluntary. The G20 has clout with other world bodies because of the economic and political muscle of its members.

In conclusion, the two ends of the spectrum in relation to the IP global framework established by **TRIPS** are: (1) reinterpretation and incremental changes to the articles of **TRIPS** versus (2) outright abolition of the agreement. It appears that the former approach to **TRIPS** is achieving long-term change, as evidenced by the progress with essential medicines and public health issues. These concrete gains have largely legitimised the **TRIPS Agreement** for developing countries. Despite it being an inherently pro-IP and protectionist agreement, the developing countries must think more deeply about the validation of the IP regime from the perspective of 'balance' rather than the IP theories put forward by the developed countries. The developing countries have the flexibility to design their own IP regime while reflecting some internationally workable common grounds. The reality in today's international IP policy-making is that too often the voices of the powerful industries and companies in the developed countries dominate in the evolution of IP policy, but as there is no coherent alternative to the **TRIPS Agreement,** the developing countries have no real alternative and must continue to press their concerns to achieve cooperation. In conclusion, the key issue in IP protection is not whether such property should be protected or whether the standards of protection are excessive, but how such protection is balanced or tempered with genuine public interest needs, when the protection granted comes into conflict with such needs.

Common Pitfalls

When critically discussing the **TRIPS Agreement**, try to use headings to signpost the relevant topics as well as change in topics.

Aim Higher

Use the language of your headings to thoughtfully add value to the discussion in your composition. Draft a substantial conclusion to elaborate on the recommendations to update and amend **TRIPS**.

QUESTION 3

Will the impact of the changes to UK patent law made by the **Intellectual Property Act 2014** be significant?

How to Read this Question

The main focus of this question is the operation of the **Intellectual Property Act 2014** and the reforms patent law (although the Act also covered amendments to copyright and design law). The purpose of a question like this is to test a student's understanding of law reform in the patent law field specifically.

How to Answer this Question

In answering this question, it should be borne in mind that there are numerous changes in the law and that the student should focus on the most significant changes to the UK patent law regime for analysis and discussion.

Up for Debate

One of the most controversial changes the Act introduces is the UK Intellectual Property Office's (UKIPO) ability to give opinions on patent issues and initiate patent revocation proceedings in clear-cut cases where it determines the patent is invalid. While controversial, the Act does include some safeguards, in that the patent owner will be able to challenge the UKIPO's advisory opinion and potentially amend the patent claims. Students may wish to refer to peer-reviewed, up-to-date law journal articles directly relevant to the IP law field, for example: *Intellectual Property Quarterly (IPQ)*; *European Intellectual Property Review (EIPR)*; and the *Journal of Intellectual Property Law and Practice (JIPLP)*.

Answer Structure

- ❖ Introduce the UK patent law protection framework;
- ❖ Focus on the most significant patent law developments in the Act;
- ❖ The Unitary Patent and Unified Patent Court;
- ❖ Patent backlogs and the UKIPO's patent examination work-sharing programme;
- ❖ The UKIPO's Patent Opinions Service;
- ❖ Concluding remarks to comment on significance of the provisions of the Act in the short, medium and long term.

ANSWER

The **Patents Act 1977** (as amended), the **Patents Act 2004**, the **Patent Rules 2007** and the **Intellectual Property Act 2014** represent the modern governing UK national legislation that create the UK's patent law framework. These derive from a hybrid of national, European and international agreements. The recent **Intellectual Property Act 2014** (the 'Act') strives to implement the recommendations of the Hargreaves Review of Intellectual Property and Growth 2011 with a particular focus on reforming patent and design law. The Act came into force in October 2014 and it is expected that all provisions will have been implemented by late 2015.

What are the most significant features of the Act with respect to patent law reform? Briefly, the Act streamlines parts of existing patent laws and lays the groundwork for much more significant change to the patent legal framework with the introduction of the Unified Patent Court. The provision in the 2014 Act will be important for particular industries and stakeholders in the innovation sector which rely heavily on patent protection for their commercial success.

THE UNITARY PATENT AND UNIFIED PATENT COURT

The most significant aspect of the Act is that it enables the UK to implement the Unitary Patent Court Agreement (UPCA). Although the European Patent Office (EPO) provides single patent grant procedures, the ability to enforce European patents is in the process of change with the advent of the UPCA. The UPCA introduces the Unitary Patent (a single patent that will have legal monopolistic effect in 25 of the 28 EU Member States) and the Unified Patent Court (UPC) to deal with disputes regarding the Unitary Patent. This reform is a decisive step towards the long-awaited introduction of a truly supranational patent system in Europe and is the most dramatic change in the patent landscape across most of Europe in the last 30 years. According to the EPO, the UPC was needed to address the problem of the high legal costs that ensue when patent litigation has to be undertaken in two or more national courts, with the risk of diverging decisions and lack of legal certainty. Forum shopping also occurred as the parties sought to take advantage of differences between national courts' interpretation of harmonised European patent law and procedure. The aim of the Unitary Patent is to streamline the procedure to obtain patent protection and enforce them across the EU Member States. The UPC should also simplify dispute resolution and third-party challenges, requiring only one court action to determine patent disputes that could potentially involve multiple jurisdictions within the EU.

PATENT EXAMINATION WORK-SHARING TO ADDRESS PATENT BACKLOGS

Technological pressures are at work in the patent system due to the high level of patent applications. In 2011 the World Intellectual Property Organization (WIPO) reported that global patent applications reached the two million mark, evidencing almost constant growth spanning more than two decades. In the UK and other patent-rich jurisdictions, this is leading to problems of patent office backlogs and the emergence of so-called 'patent thickets', which obstruct entry to some markets and so impede innovation. A 'patent thicket' is a strategy whereby a patent owner develops a thick, dense collection of overlapping patent rights which means that innovators need to license multiple patents to use the technology. From a strategic point of view, patent thickets are also used to defend against third-party competition who might otherwise design around a single patent. This is normal according to the Rt Hon. Professor Sir Robin Jacob, who wrote in his article 'Patents and Pharmaceuticals' (2008) that

> every patentee of a major invention is likely to come up with improvements and alleged improvements to his invention ... it is in the nature of the patent system itself that [patent thickets] should happen and has always happened.

The Hargreaves Review took the view that patent thickets could reduce technological development and innovation. Therefore a provision of the new Act permits the UKIPO to send a higher level of UK patent information to international patent offices around the world under condition of confidentiality. This should facilitate quicker patent granting by reducing duplication of patent examination work. Reducing the time to grant patents will clearly benefit business as it facilitates their ability to launch new products and enforce their patent rights against infringers.

THE UKIPO'S PATENT OPINIONS SERVICE

The Act also reforms the UKIPO's Patent Opinions Service (POS) and gives third parties the opportunity to request an opinion regarding patent issues, for example, validity. The opinion, though not legally binding, provides helpful information to inform business decisions. However, the Act empowers the UKIPO in clear cases to initiate patent revocation proceedings on behalf of the third party. This is a significant legal development in terms of enhancing access to justice in the patent law arena. Having said that, to safeguard the patent owner's rights, it can challenge the UKIPO's opinion or the patent claims can be amended to overcome problematic issues. These amendments have been implemented to ensure that patents which are on the register that shouldn't be are more likely to be revoked. However, patent owners may view the amendments unfavourably as it is potentially easier to attack weak patents under the Act. Those who have been kept out of a market by invalid patents, but who do not have the financial resources to bring costly and often lengthy patent revocation proceedings, will certainly benefit from these reforms.

In conclusion, the Act has made meaningful reform to the patent law framework which will enhance the UK's innovation ecosystem. Most of the changes make granting, enforcing and challenging patents simpler, faster and more cost-effective. Some of these changes will have an immediate and clear impact on the wider business community. However, although the process to ratify the UPC is ongoing and the system is not yet fully operational, when complete the new patent prosecution system has the potential to transform patent law practice in the UK and in the EU.

Common Pitfalls

Failing to focus on patent law amendments and identify those with the most significant potential to impact on the UK patent law framework.

Aim Higher

Students could also note that, overall, the provisions in the **Intellectual Property Act 2014** pave the way for positive development for the patent law regime in the EU in the long term, although there will be a period of uncertainty for the innovation sector vis-a-vis the Unitary Patent and the Unified Patent Court system in the short to medium term.

2 Copyright and Moral Rights

The purpose of copyright is to allow creators to gain financial rewards for their efforts with a view to encouraging future creativity and developing new material. Copyright material is usually the result of creative skill, significant labour and judgement. However, without legal protection such material would often be relatively easy for others to exploit without paying the creator. Copyright law protects things like books, art, songs, films, broadcasts, performances and computer software.

In the UK, there is no official copyright registry nor are there fees to pay as in some other countries. Copyright protection is automatic as soon as there is: (1) a permanent record in any form of the newly created material; and (2) the material conforms with the criteria set out in the **Copyright, Designs and Patents Act 1988** (**CDPA 1988**).

Copyright is a partial monopoly and the law allows a number of exceptions whereby a copyright work may be lawfully copied without infringing the rights of the author. The wide range of permitted acts, exceptions and the fair dealing defences limit the copyright owner's rights.

As copyright is statute-based, in every answer students should refer to the relevant sections of the **CDPA 1988** as well as to case law authorities. The majority of questions will deal with literary, dramatic, musical or artistic (LDMA) works under **Part I** of the Act.

Checklist

Students should anticipate the debate about the following:

- the types of creative works protect by copyright;
- how copyright comes into existence;
- duration of copyright;
- authorship vs ownership of copyright works;
- rights of the copyright owner;
- the relationship between copyright and the creator's moral rights.

QUESTION 4

Critically discuss the benefits of the copyright law regime and moral rights protection.

How to Read this Question

The examiner has made a statement and the instruction is to critically analyse and discuss it. What the examiner is looking for is an exploration of the constituent elements of the statement. Students should demonstrate to the examiner their understanding of the advantages of both the copyright law regime and the moral rights of the creator even if s/he sells or transfers the copyright.

How to Answer this Question

The student should aim to explore the benefits and advantages that underpin copyright protection from the outset. This will naturally lead to a discussion and critical analysis of the rationale for granting moral rights to the creator of a copyright work. The structure below highlights the kind of content that could be discussed.

Answer Structure

This is a mixed topic question that requires the student to describe the key features of the copyright protection system as well as the range of moral rights that exist. It is important to critically analyse how such protection assists author/creators.

❖ briefly summarise the origins and nature of copyright: the variety of subject matter afforded protection;
❖ **Part I** of the **CDPA 1988**;
❖ exclusive economic rights;
❖ automatic protection – no need to register;
❖ duration of the monopoly;
❖ personal property; and
❖ the origin and nature of the authors' moral rights.

Up for Debate

A key issue for debate in the copyright field is whether copyright owners have gained rights at the expense of consumers' (the public) legitimate rights. The impact of over-expansive copyright law is a hot topic and there is clearly tension between IP creators and owners and the future direction of copyright law in the public interest in light of the digital revolution.

ANSWER

Although copyright protection has existed in the UK for several centuries, in modern times the scope of copyright has expanded incrementally to encompass new forms of creative material as well as new ways of disseminating material, made possible by technological advances. Modern copyright law gives the creators the benefit of protection over a wide range of material, such as literature, drama, art, music, sound recordings, films, broadcasts, cable programmes, typographical arrangement of published editions, computer software and databases. In the United Kingdom, copyright law is governed by the **Copyright, Designs and Patents Act 1988** (**CDPA 1988**). Copyright protection provides benefits in the form of economic rights which entitle the creators to control use of their material in a number of ways, such as by making copies, issuing copies to the public, performing in public, broadcasting and use online: **s16 CDPA 1988**. Copyright also enables creators to obtain an appropriate economic reward such as royalties and licensing fees. In other words, copyright allows an author to protect his original material and stops others from using that work without permission. However, in order to balance the rights of copyright owners with the interests of the general public, the **CDPA 1988** permits certain uses to be made of works and subject matter without the permission of the copyright owner. The wide range of permitted acts, exceptions and the fair dealing defences limit the copyright owner's rights (**ss 28–76 CDPA 1988**).

Another economic benefit afforded to authors of copyright works is that they are entitled to compensation where their works are loaned by public libraries. This 'public lending right' compensates them for lost revenue from sales. This right is administered via a Public Lending Rights Scheme.

In the UK there is no need for an author to register or deposit the copyright work or pay a fee in order to obtain protection, which reduces the financial burden on creators. Copyright protection is free and automatic once the criteria set out in the Act are met. Nor is it necessary to put a copyright notice (© name of the copyright owner, year of publication) on a work, although it is advisable to do so.

The duration of copyright protection varies according to the material protected. But for published literary, dramatic, musical and artistic works, protection lasts for 70 years following the end of the calendar year in which the author dies. The length of copyright protection is a key benefit for authors/creators, as they are able to continue to financially control their work for a long period before copyright expires and the work falls into the public domain and is free to copy. It is interesting to note that even unknown authors are recognised by the **CDPA 1988**. An unknown author is one whose identity cannot be ascertained by 'reasonable enquiry' (**s 9(5)**). The copyright work is known as an 'orphan' copyright.

Copyright works are like any other form of personal property: all or part of the rights in a work may be transferred or assigned by the owner to another. This means that copyright can be inherited, so that the author's beneficiaries will continue to benefit from the author's economic rights after his or her death.

However, one of the fundamental concepts of copyright law is that copyright does not protect ideas, information or facts, but instead protects the form in which those ideas, information or facts are expressed: *Donoghue Allied Newspapers* (1938) Ch 106 at page 109. The idea–expression distinction has been accepted and applied by the courts in the

UK throughout the history of copyright, although it is not explicitly stated in the **CDPA 1988**. This concept is, however, explicit in **Art 2** of the **Agreement on Trade-Related Aspects of Intellectual Property** (**TRIPS**), which states that copyright protection extends to 'expressions and not to ideas, procedures, methods or operation or mathematical concepts as such'. Where an idea can only be expressed in one particular way, that expression will not be protected since to confer copyright protection would monopolise the idea: *Kenrick & Co Ltd v Lawrence & Co* (1890). So although copyright protection is broad, it is not without boundaries. At times, it is difficult to state with precision the extent of the creator's copyright. The most recent case to illustrate this legal principle is *Baigent and Lee v Random House Group Ltd* (2007) FSR 579.

Regardless of ownership of the copyright in various works, creators will have moral rights in the works they have created. Thus the creators of copyright works also enjoy the benefit of several moral rights included in the **CDPA 1988**. These are the:

❖ right to be identified as the author or director of a work (the paternity right) (**ss 77–79**);
❖ right of the author or a director of a work to object to derogatory treatment of certain types of work (the integrity right) (**ss 80–83**);
❖ right for everyone not to have a work falsely attributed to him (**s 84**);
❖ commissioner's right of privacy in respect of a photograph or film made in private and domestic purposes (**s 85**); and
❖ artist's resale right.

With respect to the artist's resale right, resale royalties are the rights of visual artists to receive a percentage of the revenue from the resale of their works in the art market. Artists will be able to receive a royalty when their work is bought and sold, thereby profiting from the growing market value of the work. The **Resale Right Directive** came into force on 1 January 2006 for living artists and from 1 January 2012 for their heirs. The Directive sets out the standard royalty rate to be paid to an artist on resale of his or her work (that is, after its first transfer by the artist). This means that when a living artist's work is resold on the UK art market for 1,000 euros or more, s/he will be paid a royalty of up to 4 per cent of the sale price. The Resale Right is an optional provision of the **Berne Convention** (**Art 14**), where it also applies to writers' and composers' manuscripts and scores. It is envisaged that the new laws will greatly benefit struggling artists, without placing heavy administrative responsibilities on the art market. It is important to note, however, that the right does not apply to resales between individuals acting in their private capacity without the participation of an art market professional, or to those acting in their private capacity selling to not-for-profit museums open to the public. This is a welcome legal entitlement that will provide significant financial benefits for artists.

By understanding the advantages of copyright protection an author can sell the copyright but retain the moral right to object if a work is distorted or mutilated. Moral rights cannot be assigned during the author's lifetime; however, they can be lost through waiver if the copyright is assigned. Others argue that the **CDPA 1988**, in requiring certain moral rights to be asserted, leaves creators in a worse position than before they were introduced.

Nevertheless, the benefits creators can potentially derive from their moral rights are theoretically just and desirable, given the contribution creators and artists make to society. Moral rights also help assure the public the works it associates with a particular author/creator are genuinely the work of that person.

It is clear that the benefits of copyright and moral rights protection are substantial, both for the public and to enable creators to earn a living from their work. It is widely held that strong intellectual property protection spurs creativity, which in turn opens new opportunities for businesses, governments and the general public. Finally, the development of copyright and moral rights protection has taken place during the digital revolution with a focus on digital and online free access of creative content. The question is, why have copyright and moral rights protection continued to expand in this digital environment? The expansion of copyright law represents the political will to protect established business models. Whereas the expansion of moral rights guides the development of open access resources and the focus is on attribution and integrity and helps to maintain the connection between human beings and their work. In conclusion, the end goal is to create a system of copyright and moral rights protection that is sufficiently flexible to provide a fair and satisfactory balance of benefits as between authors, rights owners and the public.

Common Pitfalls

It is a common problem to discuss benefits that are not the result of the copyright and moral rights regimes. Focus on the nature of the rights gained by the authors, creators, artists etc. Try to adopt a balanced discussion of both copyright and moral rights. Adjust your timing when writing your composition to ensure you have sufficient time to discuss moral rights effectively.

Aim Higher

Think about why copyright and moral rights law are needed and how the system benefits creators. Recognise that the relationship between creators, owners and the public has been transformed by the digital revolution.

QUESTION 5

Critically analyse the concept of fair dealing under the **Copyright, Designs and Patents Act 1988**.

How to Read this Question

The examiner is looking for the student to explore and comprehensively analyse the constituent element of the umbrella term 'fair dealing' that refers to over 50 fact-specific defences to copyright infringement set out in the **Copyright, Designs and Patents Act 1988 (CDPA 1988)**.

How to Answer this Question

The student needs to demonstrate a high level of understanding of the 'fair dealing' concept. It will be important to give examples to illustrate how the fact-specific statutory defences in the **CDPA 1988** are applied in the UK. So although the question directly refers to the **CDPA 1988**, it implies application and the need to discuss relevant case law.

Answer Structure

This is a straightforward essay question that requires a discussion of the 'fair dealing' concept and the principles the courts use to assess the strength of fact-specific defences to copyright infringement.

- ❖   Introduce the fair dealing concept;
- ❖   explain the nature of the defences provided in **ss 28–76 CDPA 1988**;
- ❖   note there is no definition of fair dealing in the Act: *Hubbard v Vosper* (1972);
- ❖   illustrate the discussion with critical analysis of select case law.

Up for Debate

The number of fair dealing fact-specific defences in the **CDPA 1988** could be contrasted with the other principle-based approaches. Both the **Berne Convention Article 9(2)** and the **WIPO Copyright Treaty 1966 Article 10(1)** provide a simple test whereby any limitations or exceptions to copyright should be confined to certain special cases which do not conflict with a normal exploitation of the work and which do not unreasonably prejudice the legitimate interests of the author.

ANSWER

People may wish to make use of someone else's copyright protected works. There are certain very specific situations where they may be allowed to do so without seeking permission from the copyright owner. These can be found in the fair dealing provisions of the **CDPA 1988**.

'Fair dealing' is a legal doctrine used to establish whether a use of copyright material is lawful or whether it infringes copyright. The concept was designed to protect the public. However, the **CDPA 1988** does not define the term 'fair dealing'. According to Lord Denning in *Hubbard v Vosper* (1972), 'fair dealing is impossible to define'. Accordingly, there is no statutory definition of fair dealing – it will always be a matter of fact, degree and impression in each case. Nonetheless, case law suggests that a wide range of factors should be taken into consideration when determining whether the acts fall within the scope of fair dealing. The question to be asked is: how would a fair-minded and honest person have dealt with the work?

It is clear that copyright is only a partial monopoly: the statutory law allows a number of exceptions whereby a copyright work may be lawfully copied without infringing the rights of the author. The wide range of permitted acts, exceptions and the fair dealing defences limit the copyright owner's rights. On the other hand, the concept of fair dealing allows the copying or other use of a work which would otherwise infringe (**CDPA 1988, ss 28–76**).

Sections 28–76 of the **CDPA** provide a system of general and specific rights. A few examples of the most important of the 50 or so types of fair dealing include the use of copyright material for purposes of:

❖ research and private study (**CDPA 1988, s 29**);
❖ criticism or review (**CDPA 1988, s 30(1)**);
❖ reporting current events (**CDPA 1988, s 30(2)**);
❖ incidental inclusion (**CDPA 1988, s 31**).

ASSESSING FAIRNESS

To answer the question 'How would a fair-minded honest person have dealt with the copyright work?', the courts have identified several factors as relevant in determining whether a particular dealing with a work is fair. These include: (1) does using the work affect the market for the original work? If a use of a work acts as a substitute for it, causing the owner to lose revenue, then it is not likely to be fair; and (2) is the amount of the work taken reasonable and appropriate? Was it necessary to use the amount that was taken? Usually only part of a work may be used.

In other words, the relevant matters taken into consideration by the courts are whether the copying deprives the copyright owner of a sale that otherwise would take place, the size and proportion of the work copied and whether the infringer will obtain substantial financial gain from the infringement. The relative importance of any one factor will vary according to the case in hand and the type of dealing in question.

Anyone can make copies of a copyright work for the purpose of their own research or private study provided that it is within the scope of fair dealing (**s 28 CDPA 1988**). As fair dealing is not clearly defined, the only way to determine if the copy is within its scope is to consider the whole circumstances of the case.

APPLYING THE FAIR DEALING DEFENCES

In *Hubbard v Vosper* (1972) the defendant, who was a Scientologist for 14 years, wrote and published a highly critical book about Scientology, containing extracts from the plaintiff's book. The Court of Appeal held that whether the defendant could rely on the defence of fair dealing was a matter of degree and impression. Lord Denning provided further clarification and held that the relevant factors to be considered when determining fair dealing include the number and extent of extracts and the use made of the extracts. If the extracts were used as the basis of research, study, criticism, comment and review as per **CDPA ss 29** and **30**, this could amount to fair dealing.

However, if used to convey the same information in a competitive manner this would be unfair and would amount to infringement of copyright. In the *Independent Television Publications v Time Out Magazine* (1984) case, where the defendants attempted to rely on the defence of fair dealing for criticism and review, this failed because the purpose was to provide a television programme listing and had nothing to do with criticism or review. The same point was considered in *Pro Sieben Media AG v Carlton UK TV Ltd* (1999) where the defendants used a 30-second clip from a programme produced and owned by the claimant featuring a subject who had given an exclusive interview to the claimant. The defendant argued in the Court of Appeal that they were protected under **s 30** by fair dealing for the purposes of news reporting, criticism and review. The Court of Appeal held that the degree to which the use of a protected work competed with exploitation of the copyright by the copyright owner was very important in assessing fair dealing.

The decision in *Pro Sieben* was later considered in *Newspaper Licensing Agency Ltd v Marks & Spencer plc* (1999). The facts concerned the copyright in a typographical edition of a literary work. Lightman J established a three-stage test for raising a **s 30(2)** defence:

(1)   reporting current events;
(2)   fair dealing with copyright work – not an actual exploitation; and
(3)   acknowledgement.

Another factor that should be considered is the status of the copied work – whether it is confidential or published. In *Hyde Park Residence Ltd v Yelland* (2000) a two-stage test was applied to determine whether the defence of fair dealing was available. First, it was necessary to ascertain the purpose of the act: for example, if the purpose of such publication was within the ambit of reporting current events and whether the acts fell within the scope of fair dealing. Second, the work had not been previously made available to the public, which was an important indication that the dealing was not fair.

A financial motive behind making a copy must be considered when determining whether or not a copy falls within the fair dealing defence, as to allow another to financially benefit from someone else's work would be utterly contrary to the justification for copyright and Locke's Labour Theory, where it is argued that the owner should benefit from the fruits of their work. In *Stilltoe v McGraw-Hill Books* (1983) the defendant published extracts of the claimant's books for sale to English literature students. The defence of fair dealing failed as the publication was for their own commercial gain and not for the benefit of the students, the only ones capable of raising a legitimate fair dealing defence.

THE EXPANSION OF FAIR DEALING DEFENCES

The publication of *Digital Opportunity* (2011), an independent report by Professor Ian Hargreaves, about how the national and international intellectual property system can best work, also focused on aspects of fair dealing in copyright works. The parallel concept in US copyright law is fair use and Hargreaves rejected the proposal that 'fair use' principles based on the US model should be incorporated into UK copyright law: Executive Summary p. 5. The Report recommended updating what it is lawful to copy and expanding the fair dealing defences to cover copying for private purposes (such as shifting music from a laptop to an mp3 player), copying to make parodies or pastiche and copying which does not conflict with the core aims of copyright, for example, digital copying of medical and other journals for computerised meta-analysis in medical research. In 2014, the **CDPA 1988** was amended to expand the fair dealing defences to more accurately reflect the needs of non-rights holders and consumers of copyright works. New copyright exceptions for research, education, libraries, museums and archives, for disabled people, public administration, quotation, parody (new **s 30A CDPA 1988**), personal copying and orphan works were introduced.

In conclusion, fair dealing is important because the doctrine is one of the traditional safety valves intended to balance the public's interest in copyright works with that of the creator and owner. The courts have often held that taking even a very small amount of work is sufficient for an infringement of copyright and this is a concern for members of the public in terms of free speech, the digital environment, for disabled people and to create new copyright works, for example parody. The courts' findings will rely on key considerations of 'fairness' such as the purpose of the use, the proportion of the use, its motive (if it was to compete with the original work it will amount to infringement) and the status of the other work as to whether it is confidential or published material.

Common Pitfalls

As students typically are able to bring un-annotated copies of the **CDPA 1988** into the exam, avoid copying out verbatim sections of the Act as no credit will be given. Rather cite the relevant section and discuss in your own words and further analyse case law concerning interpretation and application of the legislative section.

Aim Higher

Critically discuss developments to expand the fair dealing defence as recommended by the Hargreaves *Digital Opportunity Report* (2011) and recent amendments to the fair dealing defences in the **CDPA 1988**. State whether you agree with the expansion to the range of purpose specific fair dealing defences.

QUESTION 6

Richie Rich writes a monthly investment newsletter in which he includes a model investment portfolio ('the Rich Fund'). The front cover of the newsletter includes the title in logo form and the strapline 'Get rich with Rich!' The Rich Fund consists of 10–12 recommended stocks, which can and do change from month to month. In each issue of the newsletter, Richie includes the following information about the Rich Fund:

❖ the names of the recommended stocks;
❖ current price, 12-month high price and 12-month low price for each stock included in the portfolio, obtained from the live data provided by the London Stock Exchange; and

❖   analysis (narrative commentary) on each stock added to or dropped from the portfolio since the prior month's newsletter.

▶ **What elements, if any, of the Rich Fund newsletter are covered by copyright?**

How to Read this Question

An intellectual property law question sets you a task. Problem-based questions in law are
intended to test your ability to identify and apply the relevant legal principles, in this case
to a literary work, a newsletter. The key issue is whether copyright subsists: in the whole
or only parts of the newsletter? Carefully evaluate the facts to determine the specific elements of the contents of the newsletter that could potentially attract copyright protection. Go through the information in question line by line to do this.

How to Answer this Question

Achieving a good grade in answering a subsistence of copyright law problem question is
by demonstrating: (1) your knowledge of copyright law by identifying the actual copy-
right-protectable elements; and (2) your understanding of the law by applying the relevant law to each identified element and reaching conclusions as you progress with your
answer. Using a legal analysis, apply the law to assess whether copyright subsists in any
of the elements identified and explain why or why not.

Answer Structure

This question is concerned with determining which elements of a typical financial newsletter might attract copyright protection.

❖   Subsistence of copyright in a literary work;
❖   idea/expression dichotomy;
❖   copyright in the newsletter title, mastheads and straplines;
❖   copyright in the arrangement of information in databases.

Applying the Law

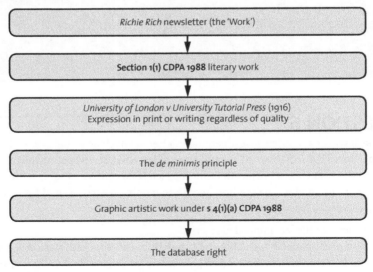

Richie Rich newsletter (the 'Work')

Section 1(1) CDPA 1988 literary work

University of London v University Tutorial Press (1916)
Expression in print or writing regardless of quality

The *de minimis* principle

Graphic artistic work under **s 4(1)(a) CDPA 1988**

The database right

ANSWER

Copyright is a negative right that aims to provide protection to authors such as Richie Rich for their creations. Such creations are usually designated as 'works'. There is no statutory definition of 'work' in the **Copyright, Designs and Patents Act 1988 (CDPA 1988)**, but case law suggests that its author must have expended a minimum level of effort. A similar principle is attached to the requirement of originality. The Rich Fund newsletter is typical of the genre of financial investment newsletters to which people subscribe in order to assist them to decide which shares or share funds are good investments. Many similar newsletters are published and Richie Rich will not have copyright in the idea for a financial newsletter. One of the fundamental concepts of copyright law is that copyright does not protect ideas, information or facts but instead protects the form in which those ideas, information or facts are expressed. This is known as the idea–expression dichotomy, which means that copyright will not be infringed when works based on the same ideas are independently created, provided the way in which those ideas have been expressed is not copied. The idea–expression distinction has been accepted and applied by the courts in the UK throughout the history of copyright, although not explicitly stated in the UK copyright legislation. What copyright protects is not the idea for the newsletter but 'the particular form of language by which the information which is to be conveyed is conveyed': *Donoghue v Allied Newspapers* (1938). Therefore, the key issue to be assessed here is which specific elements of the material in the Rich Fund newsletter are of the kind that will attract copyright protection. Problems arise when there is nothing substantive enough to be protected or it is not 'original'.

Section 1(1) CDPA 1988 provides that copyright will subsist in a literary work. A literary work is defined as any work, other than a dramatic or musical work, which is written, spoken or sung. As it is in writing, the Rich Fund newsletter will fall within this category of work. It would be wrong to think that the word 'literary' implies that an element of merit is required before a piece of writing can be treated as a copyright work. The case law establishes that this is not a qualitative standard, merely an indication that the work be recorded by means of letters or numbers. For example, in *University of London v University Tutorial Press* (1916) Petersen J explained that copyright existed in literary work 'expressed in print or writing, irrespective of the question whether the quality or style is high'. A commonplace work, such as a financial newsletter (or an exam paper, a lottery coupon or a tide table), will usually attract copyright so long as the author has expended sufficient labour, skill and judgement in creating the work.

THE TITLE 'RICH FUND', MASTHEAD AND STRAPLINE

Does copyright subsist in the newsletter's title, 'Rich Fund'? Titles and names have been refused copyright when they are not substantial enough to attract copyright in themselves. For example, no protection was given to the name of the song 'The Man Who Broke the Bank at Monte Carlo' in the *Francis Day and Hunter v Twentieth Century Fox* (1940) case. Nor was protection afforded to the 'Wombles' name in *The Wombles v*

Wombles Skips (1975). Therefore the title of the newsletter will not attract copyright protection. However, Richie Rich should be advised that if an unauthorised third party uses the 'Rich Fund' title, he could have an action for 'passing off' if the third party tries to persuade members of the public to buy another newsletter in the belief that they are choosing Richie Rich's newsletter.

Unfortunately, the strapline 'Get rich with Rich!' will be regarded as too trivial or small in terms of creative effort to attract copyright. This is known as the *de minimis* principle, an abbreviated form of the Latin maxim *de minimis non curat lex*, 'the law cares not for small things'. This is the legal doctrine by which a court refuses to consider trifling matters. For example, in *Sinanide v La Maison Kosmeo* (1928) the advertising slogan 'Beauty is a social necessity, not a luxury' was held to be too slight a work to found allegations of infringement by the rival slogan 'A youthful appearance is a social necessity'. The slogan is potentially registrable as a trade mark, nevertheless.

However, the masthead of the Rich Fund newsletter may attract copyright protection as a graphic artistic work under **s4(1)(a) CDPA 1988**. In *IPC Magazines Ltd v MGN* (1998) the 'Woman' masthead was regarded as, at least arguably, a copyright work. In *IPC Media Ltd v Highbury-SPL Publishing Ltd* (2004) IPC unsuccessfully alleged that a rival magazine publisher, Highbury, had infringed its copyright in *Ideal Home* because Highbury had copied the 'look and feel' of *Ideal Home*. The allegations related to the front covers and certain internal sections in four of its issues and focused on the copyright in artistic works. Laddie J assessed the elements of a design for a magazine cover including the logo (the name of the magazine), the straplines (lines of text immediately above and below the logo) and the hot-spot (so-called because, being just under the logo, it will be visible on racks of magazines for sale and would be important to attract buyers), but did not uphold IPC's claim of copyright infringement.

The names of the particular recommended stocks will not attract copyright as the courts will apply the *de minimis non curate lex* maxim. For example, a single word, EXXON, was refused copyright in *Exxon v Exxon Insurance* (1981) as it was held not to constitute an original literary work, the rationale being that it conveyed no information, provided no instruction and gave no pleasure. Further, the court noted that there was separate protection for names via the trade mark law. Indeed, Richie Rich would be advised to confirm whether or not the names of stocks he mentions in his newsletter are already protected as trade marks belonging to others.

THE STOCK PRICE INFORMATION OBTAINED FROM THE LSX

In his newsletter, Richie Rich reproduces the stock price information provided by the London Stock Exchange (LSX). He is not the creator of this information and as such cannot own or claim copyright in it. The LSX broadcasts all the activity of its markets live, in the form of data (information content) delivered by its LSX Infolect® electronic database systems. A certain level of information is publicly available; however, access to higher levels of data is by licence only. Accordingly, the LSX will have copyright in its original database as a literary work under **s 3(1)(d) CDPA 1988** or via a *sui generis* database right which lasts for only 15 years. Copyright protects the arrangement of the data. The LSX will have expended labour, skill and judgement in creating the database involving substantial monetary, technical and manpower investment. Richie is able to lawfully extract and re-utilise insubstantial parts of the database for any purpose. Exceptions are also made for fair dealing and in particular reporting current events under **s 30(2) CDPA 1988**, provided that it is accompanied by sufficient acknowledgement. However, if he is reproducing substantial LSX data content, he will require a licence, otherwise he will be infringing the LSX's copyright. Typically, a provision of the licence is that the licensee agrees to credit the source of the information as being the LSX.

Now we turn to the selection of the particular stocks to include in the Rich Fund newsletter. This would appear to involve the exercise of skill, judgement and experience and so will enjoy copyright protection: *Ladbroke (Football) v William Hill* (1964). In this analogous case, the House of Lords held that coupons for football pools constituted original literary works. It was accepted that the 'vast amount of skill, judgement, experience and work' employed in building up the coupon constituted an original work. This was so even though the effort and skill had gone not into the production of the literary work itself, but into the commercial selection of bets to offer, providing a remedy against unfair competition. This principle applies, however commonplace the sources used.

THE ANALYSIS AND COMMENTARY

The analysis and commentary on each stock will certainly attract copyright protection as it is clear that the skill, labour and judgement test is satisfied. Richie Rich will have no doubt exercised a sufficient degree of skill, use of knowledge, aptitude or ability, judgement or discernment in order to form his opinions by evaluating and comparing the different stocks. Copyright will subsist in this element of the newsletter, provided that the text originates from Rich and has not been copied from another source: *University of London Press v University Tutorial Press* (1916).

Finally, for those elements of the newsletter which will enjoy copyright, the exclusive rights will last for 70 years after the author's death. For those elements that will not attract copyright protection, Richie will have to consider other forms of IP protection such as trade mark law and should ensure he obtains the necessary licence from the LSX to ensure that he does not infringe their copyright.

Common Pitfalls

Students commonly fail to recognise and deal with the full range of copyright issues that arise in connection with the newsletter. Carefully consider each sentence of the problem question and identify each type of copyright that might potentially subsist in the newsletter.

QUESTION 7

In 2006, Anne Smith, a graduate of the prestigious Royal College of Art, wins that year's £25,000 Jarwood Sculpture Prize with her work *Tin* – a giant tin with the top left slightly ajar. Anne says the work reflects her notion that 'beyond literal legibility and metaphorical ideas, sculptures should be ambivalent in their meaning and identity'. The winning *Tin* sculpture will be sited in a park near Swindon. Judges praised its 'great intellectual depth and exceptional beauty' and said an aluminium sculpture would look 'outstanding' in the park.

Barry, a journalist, writes an article in *Arts Magazine* that is highly critical of Anne's sculpture. The article includes photographs of a series of four everyday tins and falsely claims that they are 'other works of genius by Anne Smith'. The sculpture is placed in the park, but when it is secured to the ground, the top of the giant tin closes and is no longer slightly ajar. Anne is devastated and claims that her work has been ruined.

Meanwhile, Carol, a local Swindon potter, having seen the *Tin* sculpture on display in the park, decides to recreate it in clay in a miniature version. She gives one of her clay 'Tin' sculptures to her new neighbour Deirdre as a housewarming present. Farrah, a buyer for Harrods, sees it while visiting the neighbour's house and places an order for 100 more for the London store.

▶ **Advise the parties as to whether or not any of them have infringed intellectual property rights, as well as any legal remedies that may be available.**

How to Read this Question

This is a detailed problem question. All problem questions test the students' ability to apply the law to a set of facts. On analysis it can be best approached by dealing chronologically with each event as it occurs in the question. Note that a discussion of legal remedies available is required.

How to Answer this Question

Students should take care to work out the impact of all the given facts before starting to answer the question. Essentially, the following areas should be covered: (1) subsistence of copyright; (2) moral rights; (3) copyright infringement and defences; and (4) remedies.

Answer Structure

This is a comprehensive problem question that cannot be fully answered with certainty in many respects. Nevertheless, the student should consider the following issues in his or her answer:

❖ does copyright subsist?
❖ artistic copyright work (**s 4(2) CDPA 1988**);
❖ moral rights;
❖ primary and secondary infringement;
❖ defences and remedies.

Applying the Law

Copyright?

Moral rights?

Anne's Tin sculpture

Infringement?

Possible remedies?

ANSWER --

In order to protect her work, a sculpture, Anne will have to show that copyright subsists in the work. Copyright comes into existence, or subsists, automatically when a qualifying person creates a work that is original and tangible. **Section 1** of the **Copyright, Designs and Patents Act 1988** (**CDPA 1988**) provides that literary, dramatic, musical and artistic works be 'original'. An artistic work such as Anne's *Tin* sculpture must be original in the sense that it originates from her: *University of London Press v University Tutorial Press* (1916). Expending skill, labour and judgement in creating the work is enough to deem the work to be original. Further, even though it looks like a commonplace tin, it will be protected as a sculpture because it has been made for the purpose of sculpture: *J&S Davis (Holdings) Ltd v Wright Health Group* (1988). A sculpture is protected as an artistic work under **s 4(2)** irrespective of its artistic merit (**s 4(1)(a) CDPA 1988**). Therefore, it is clear that copyright will subsist in prize-winning sculpture, as it is likely to be original and not copied from another source: **CDPA 1988 s 1(1)(a)**.

As creator of the artistic work, Anne will be regarded as its author and as the owner of the copyright in it (**s 9(1) CDPA 1988**). Accordingly, Anne has the exclusive right to do certain restricted acts in relation to her copyright work during her lifetime, and her heirs will benefit for a further 70 years following her death. The restricted acts are set out in **s 16(1) CDPA 1988** and include copying, issuing copies to the public, renting or lending the work, for example. Anne can prevent a third party from carrying out any unauthorised activities concerning her sculpture.

Barry has written an article in *Arts Magazine* criticising Anne's sculpture. Does writing an article about Anne's sculpture infringe her copyright? This is unlikely here because Barry will be able to claim that his dealing with the sculpture is fair in that he is using the work for the purposes of criticism and review. This is a permitted act under **s 30(1) CDPA 1998**. Barry does not require Anne's permission to refer to her work in the magazine article. Indeed, Barry probably has created a new work his own magazine article which attracts copyright as a literary work within **s 1(1)(a) CDPA 1988**).

However, **Art 27** of the **Universal Declaration of Human Rights** recognises that the creators of any scientific, literary or artistic production have both moral and 'material' rights, or 'economic interests', in their work which should be protected. Have any of Anne's moral rights been infringed?

Moral rights are personal rights conferred by **s 94 CDPA 1988** on the authors of primary copyright works and the directors of films. Moral rights are quite separate from the economic interests in the work. They are also distinct from the copyright in the work. Moral rights are concerned with protecting the personality and reputation of authors and creators. An author/creator's moral rights are protected as breaches of statutory duty, not as with copyright, as a property right. The aim of moral rights is to protect an author's artistic reputation and integrity. Before the **CDPA 1988**, authors in the UK mainly had to rely on their common law rights in contract, defamation, passing off, injurious falsehood and breach of confidence to protect their reputation and integrity.

Has Barry infringed Anne's moral rights? By falsely attributing work to Anne by publishing pictures in his article and claiming that they were 'other works of genius by Anne Smith', Barry has infringed Anne's right against false attribution. Anne has the right for the works in the photographs accompanying Barry's article not to be incorrectly attributed to her (**ss 84–86 CDPA 1988**). Here the false attribution is expressed by use of the caption. There is no requirement that Anne need have suffered any damage to assert the right: *Clark v Associated Newspapers* (1998). Anne may wish to consider bringing an action against Barry for infringement of this moral right.

The *Tin* sculpture is placed in the park, but when it is secured to the ground, the top of the giant tin closes and it is no longer slightly ajar. It would appear that Anne's moral right of integrity may have been infringed. Past cases have involved the removal of site-specific artistic works. **Sections 80–83** of the **CDPA 1998** provide that Anne can object to the derogatory treatment of her work if the work has been added to, altered or deleted (**s 80(2) CDPA 1988**) in such a way as to amount to a distortion, mutilation or otherwise prejudicial treatment. In *Pasterfield v Denham* (1998) Overend J held that distortion or mutilation must have harmed the honour or reputation of an artist, and that a subjective sense of grievance did not suffice. This was later affirmed in *Confetti Records v Warner Music* (2003). Here, as the *Tin* sculpture is a prize-winning sculpture, any change to its composition is likely to harm Anne's honour or reputation.

Meanwhile, Carol has recreated the *Tin* sculpture in a different material (clay) and in a smaller size. Carol has given one to her neighbour Deirdre as a gift. Only Anne, however, has the exclusive right to copy the work and issue copies to the public: **s 16(1) CDPA 1988**. Copying means 'reproducing the work in any material form'. Intention by the defendant is not relevant to finding infringement: Laddie J in *Electronic Techniques v Critchley Components* (1997). The facts show that there is a connection between the work and its alleged copy; and there is probably more than a passing resemblance to Anne's copyright sculpture. Changes to form or dimension of a copyright work may also constitute reproduction (**s 17(3) CDPA 1988**). Accordingly, Carol has infringed Anne's copyright in the sculpture, although there is no *mala fides* and she has not profited from doing so. There is nothing to suggest that Carol could rely on a fair dealing defence. However, **s 62** of the **CDPA 1988** concerns certain representations of artistic works on public display. A sculpture, for instance, if permanently situated in a public place open to the public, is not infringed by making a graphic work, photograph or broadcasting a visual image representing it. Would Carol's miniature sculpture fall into the category of graphic work and thus not infringe? In **s 4 CDPA 1988** 'graphic work' includes any painting, drawing, diagram, map, chart or plan, any engraving, etching, lithograph, woodcut or similar work. A sculpture is not included in the definition. Carol is not authorised by Anne to reproduce the *Tin* sculpture and should not accept the order placed by Farrah, the buyer for Harrods, otherwise she will infringe Anne's artistic copyright. In conclusion, Anne's best legal remedy, if she is interested in pursuing it, would be to apply for an order to have Carol deliver up all infringing copies of her work: **s 99 CDPA 1988**.

Common Pitfalls

Students need to remember that this question requires three key issues to be discussed: (1) subsistence of copyright in the sculpture; (2) Anne's moral rights in the sculpture; and (3) any infringement of Anne's artistic work copyright. It is important to structure your answer and devote your time to answering each of the three key issues. Students tend to focus on whether copyright subsists in the sculpture which is a good place to start and then rush through their analysis of moral rights and copyright infringement issues.

Aim Higher

A good answer will demonstrate knowledge of the appropriate statutory and case law that Anne may wish to rely on to enforce her copyright and moral rights. Advice concerning remedies adds value in a problem question as Anne is ultimately concerned with enforcing her legal rights in her sculpture.

QUESTION 8

Ariella and Bella are working together on a cookbook entitled *Top Tarts*. Ariella has developed the recipes and is writing the text and Bella is providing the graphics and taking still photographs of the food for the book. Ariella's daughter, Christina, has occasionally helped to test the recipes and has also offered suggestions to Bella on the sort of photographs that would be desirable. All three are employed as columnists by a national automotive magazine, *Top Wheels*. The book is to be published by another publisher, Cookery Editions.

▶ Evaluate and advise on the specific intellectual property rights that exist in the finished cookbook as well as any ownership issues arising.

How to Read this Question

Read the whole fact scenario through from beginning to end. Note the instructing phrase, which is to provide general IP advice including ownership issues. This is a clue that there are ownership issues arising on the facts. Go back and read each line of the question carefully, identifying the IP issues. Think about the relevant legal principles, statute law and case law that may apply to resolve the legal issues identified.

How to Answer this Question

Planning your answer is particularly important in copyright law because problem questions frequently contain a number of different issues and they can sometimes involve a number of potential copyright works, authors and owners. One approach that students find helpful is to use the IRAC mnemonic by following the steps listed below:

> **Identify** the legal issue(s);
> **Rule** – define and explain the legal rule and/or principle;
> **Apply** the rule/principle to the facts in question;
> **Conclusion** which sums up the advice to the party/parties.

It is important when answering problem questions to ensure that you *complete the task*. Here, the specific copyright law issues identified in the problem question should be resolved.

Answer Structure

This is a straightforward copyright law question that requires students to analyse:

- ❖ subsistence of copyright in literary and artistic works;
- ❖ the issue of authorship, joint authorship and ownership;
- ❖ asserting moral rights; and
- ❖ duration of copyright.

Applying the Law

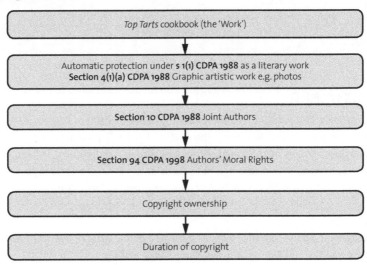

Top Tarts cookbook (the 'Work')

Automatic protection under **s 1(1) CDPA 1988** as a literary work
Section 4(1)(a) CDPA 1988 Graphic artistic work e.g. photos

Section 10 CDPA 1988 Joint Authors

Section 94 CDPA 1998 Authors' Moral Rights

Copyright ownership

Duration of copyright

ANSWER

In relation to the *Top Tarts* cookbook, copyright protection is automatic as soon as there is (1) a permanent record in any form of the newly created material; and (2) the material conforms with the criteria set out in the **Copyright, Designs and Patents Act 1988 (CDPA 1988)**. The **CDPA 1988** provides that a literary work such as the *Top Tarts* cookbook has to be 'original' to qualify for protection. This means that it has to be original in the sense that it originates from the author: *University of London Press v University Tutorial Press* (1916). Two types of copyright subsist in the work. First, the text is a literary work and Ariella is the author: **s 3(1) CDPA 1988**. The term author, however, is not limited to writers. Second, Bella's photos are artistic works capable of protection under the **CDPA 1988** irrespective of their artistic merit: **s 4(1)(a)**.

Section 11(1) CDPA provides that initial ownership of copyright vests in the 'author' of the work. Who are the authors of *Top Tarts*? This is the starting point for identifying the owner(s) of the work.

Under copyright law, a joint work is a work created by two or more people who share equal interests in the finished product. In order to be considered a joint work, the contributions of all of the authors must be interdependent and inseparable: **s 10 CDPA 1988**. Thus, if someone writes a foreword to a book written by someone else, this is not a joint work, but if a writer and illustrator collaborate to make a children's book, for example, they would be considered joint creators. Similarly, Ariella and Bella would be considered joint creators of *Top Tarts*. Books, journal articles, musical compositions and works of art can all be joint works. The size of a contribution does not matter. If someone contributed to a joint work, that person shares an equal part of the copyright and has equal rights. The contributions to a joint work are meant to be viewed as part of a seamless and interconnected whole. Without the work of one of the contributors, the piece would not be finished. Authors may choose to explicitly identify their contributions to the work, as when authors write alternating chapters of a book, but they are not required to. The contributors are usually named, but in the case of ghost-writers, a contributor's name may be publicly left off the finished joint work. The creators, Ariella who provided the literary content and Bella who provided the photographs, may wish to establish a contract to clarify certain points of their collaboration: see *Slater v Wimmer* (2012) EWPCC 7.

Should Christina be credited as co-creator of the recipes and author of the photos given her suggestions? The idea–expression distinction has been accepted and applied by the courts in the UK throughout the history of copyright, although it is not explicitly stated in the **CDPA 1988**. The concept is, however, explicit in **Art 2** of **TRIPS** which states that copyright protection extends to 'expressions and not to ideas, procedures, methods or operation or mathematical concepts as such'. In addition, the test for originality is the 'skill, labour, judgment' test: *Ladbroke (Football Ltd) v William Hill (Football Ltd)* (1964). Bella has applied her skill, labour and judgement to take the photos while Christina has merely provided ideas. Copyright does not subsist in ideas that have not been expressed in a permanent form. This is one of the fundamental concepts of copyright law. Accordingly, as Bella is the person who has 'fixed' the illustrations in a permanent form, it is highly unlikely that Christina will be regarded as a joint creator of the illustrations. Christina's contribution is unlikely to meet the strict definition of joint authorship: *Lawson v Dundas* (12 June 1985) unreported.

Authorship is relevant not only (a) as to whether the work attracts copyright in the UK; but also (b) to calculate the term of copyright protection; and (c) to determine whether moral rights arise.

Accordingly, as the authors, Ariella and Bella have the exclusive right to do certain restricted acts in relation to copyright in their literary work during their lifetime and their heirs will benefit for a further 70 years following their death: **s 12 CDPA 1988**. Authors have the right to assign non-exclusive rights to another party without consulting the other authors. Likewise, joint authors can transfer their interest in the work to someone else, as when someone bequeaths a share in a copyright work to heirs. Parties to a joint work cannot assign exclusive rights without the consent of the other author(s). They must also account for any profits they earn by exploiting the work.

In addition, **Art 27** of the **Universal Declaration of Human Rights** recognises that the author/creators of literary or artistic works have both moral rights and 'material' rights or 'economic' interests in their work which should be protected. In the UK, moral rights are conferred by **s 94 CDPA 1988**. Moral rights are separate from the copyright in the work and are not property rights, rather they are protected as breaches of statutory duty. The aim of moral rights is to protect an author's artistic reputation and integrity. Ariella and Bella should assert their rights in their cookbook contract with the publisher Cookery Editions to ensure that third parties are bound by the right and they should have express statements asserting the right on all copies of the cookbook. If moral rights are asserted, then Ariella and Bella will be able to rely on their statutory moral rights, if necessary. The paternity and integrity rights last for the same length of time as the copyright in the cookbook. Moral rights are, by their very nature, personal to the individual concerned and cannot be assigned. However, their exercise can be affected by waiver and consent and Ariella and Bella's moral rights can be transferred on death. For a waiver to be effective, it has to be in writing and signed by the person giving up the rights. Currently, there is little case law on breaches of moral rights and the issue of joint authorship.

Now, having identified the authors of *Top Tarts*, it is necessary to consider who owns the copyright. When a work is created by an employee in the course of employment, then copyright is automatically assigned to the employer by **s 11(2) CDPA 1988** except where agreed to the contrary. In the case of *Top Tarts*, has the cookbook been created in the course of employment with *Top Wheels*? First, the cookbook is a different genre of literary work to the automotive industry and their work as columnists with *Top Wheels*. It would be useful to review the pair's employment agreements to confirm their duties. This should confirm whether the pair could have been ordered to write a cookbook in the course of their employment. Ariella and Bella's case would be strengthened by providing evidence that they worked on the cookbook out of hours, from home and not using their employer's resources. For example, in the case of *Noah v Shuba* (1991) FSR 14 Mummery J held that a consultant epidemiologist who had, in his spare time, written a paper on good hygiene practices for tattoo parlours was the owner of the copyright.

In conclusion, the detailed provisions of the **CDPA 1988** as interpreted via case law regulate the issues of authorship, moral rights, ownership and duration of copyright. This makes it possible to evaluate the distinction between authorship and ownership and the role which each concept plays in the UK.

Common Pitfalls

First identify and deal with the relevant copyright works in chronological order. Write succinctly about the case law and copyright principles in relation to literary and artistic works. Additional marks will be gained through an illuminating discussion and analysis of the joint authorship issue and Christina's potential contribution and the copyright ownership issue.

Aim Higher

Credit will be given for confirming that in addition to copyright, Ariella and Bella will also acquire moral rights in their book. Cite the relevant international and national legislative authority to support your answer.

QUESTION 9

A well-known and distinguished author, Prissy Puritan, writes a serious and noble play, *Grey Pulp*, about the deepening relationship between a college graduate, Anna, and a young pulp and paper magnate, Chris, where love conquers adversity in the vibrant city of Seattle, USA. Prissy negotiates a six-figure sum and assigns the right to adapt the play for television to UK company, Channel Six. Channel Six rewrites the play and changes it into a 'pulsing erotic relationship' between middle-aged businesswoman Anna and university student Chris, set in Nottingham. When broadcast in the UK, it attracts 3.7 million viewers, a record for the Tuesday evening slot. Critical reception of the TV programme, however, has tended towards the negative, with the quality of the screenplay generally seen as poor. Prissy Puritan's name appears both in the publicity for the TV programme, and in the credits, as being associated with the writing of the screenplay adapted from the original work. Prissy is livid and seeks advice as to her IP rights and the nature of any cause of action she may have in respect of the changes to her story made by Channel Six and the damage to her reputation.

How to Read this Question

Problem questions are designed to get students to apply their knowledge of the law to a fact scenario. Identify the parties and the effect of any commercial transactions and/or conduct that may give rise to IP law issues. This involves issue-spotting: for example, can Prissy bring a claim against Channel Six for doing x. Failing to spot an issue is likely to result in a loss of marks.

How to Answer this Question

Avoid inventing facts you are not told. Similarly, avoid questioning the facts you are given. Is there a claim involving Prissy's IP rights? If so, decide on the relevant applicable law and proceed to apply it to the facts. This question really asks you to focus on one discrete area of IP law. Remember to apply the correct law (legislation and cases) to the facts and use your analysis of the law to assist Prissy, who you've been asked to advise.

Answer Structure

While the focus of this question is moral rights, students should not be penalised and indeed could be rewarded for briefly discussing copyright law issues such as the fact that the play is a literary work and will attract copyright protection and/or the possibility of copyright infringement as a cause of action, so long as they do not neglect moral rights issues.

❖ Define and explain moral rights as the rights of authors which are independent of the economic rights under copyright law (**Art 6** of the **Berne Copyright Convention**).

❖ The relevant moral rights in this problem are: (1) the right to object to modification and derogatory treatment of the author's work (the 'integrity' right) (**ss 80–83 CDPA 1988**); and (2) the right to object to being falsely attributed as the author (**ss 77–79 CDPA 1988**). Analyse each in turn with reference to the statute and relevant case law.

Applying the Law

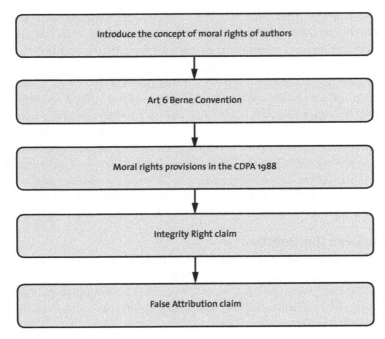

Introduce the concept of moral rights of authors

Art 6 Berne Convention

Moral rights provisions in the CDPA 1988

Integrity Right claim

False Attribution claim

ANSWER

Prissy is the author and first copyright owner of a play in which copyright subsists as a literary work according to **s 3(1) Copyright, Designs and Patents Act 1988** (**CDPA 1988**). She is appalled that, having sold the adaptation right to Channel Six, the company has rewritten her play transforming it into a vulgar farce and that her name is associated with this tacky new flipped version. Prissy is clearly concerned about the integrity of her work as well as her reputation. Fortunately, the law does provide some rights that she can rely on to protect these qualities, despite the fact that she has assigned the exclusive right to adapt her play (an economic right) to Channel Six. These rights are known as moral rights. Since 1988, the UK **Copyright, Designs and Patents Act 1988** has included the concept of protecting an author's personal integrity and reputation in relation to certain copyright works. **Chapter IV** of the Act is devoted specifically to the aim of protecting an author's artistic reputation and integrity. The concept of moral rights, that is, rights relating to the author of a work rather than the owner or licensee, was introduced to the UK fairly recently, although the concept of moral rights is well established in other European countries. An author of a copyright work, such as Prissy, now enjoys the benefit of several moral rights that have been enshrined in the **CDPA 1988**. These are:

❖ the right to be identified as the author or director of a work (the paternity right) (**ss 77–79**);

❖ the right of the author or a director of a work to object to derogatory treatment of certain types of work (the integrity right (**ss 80–83**));

❖ the right not to have a work falsely attributed to him or her (**s 84**).

The legal foundation for the moral rights of attribution and integrity is **Art 6bis** of the **Berne Convention for the Protection of Literary and Artistic Works 1886** which originally recognised the concept of moral rights. Further, **Art 27** of the **Universal Declaration of Human Rights** recognises that the creators of any scientific, literary or artistic production have both moral and material rights, or 'economic interests' in their work which require protection.

In the UK, moral rights are personal rights conferred by **s 94 CDPA 1988** on the author of primary copyright works (such as a play) and the directors of films. They exist independently of the economic rights afforded by copyright and continue to exist even after the economic rights have been assigned. This means that even though Prissy has licensed certain economic rights in the copyright of her play, she will retain moral rights and can enforce them if they are breached.

However, moral rights can be waived, or even fail for a lack of positive assertion on the part of the author, so it will be crucial to confirm whether Prissy asserted her moral rights as author of the play. Assuming she has done so, Prissy will be able to rely on her moral rights. These rights are important as they give the author some control over her work in the future (even once she, as author, no longer has any economic rights in the work), enabling her to control how it is used or modified in the future. The rights in **ss 77, 80** and **85 CDPA 1988** continue to subsist so long as copyright in the work subsists.

Breaches of an author's moral rights are protected as breaches of statutory duty and not as a property right. The relevant moral rights on the facts are:

(1) the right to object to modification and derogatory treatment of the author's work (the 'integrity' right) (**ss 80–83 CDPA 1988**);

(2) the right to object to being falsely attributed as the author (**s 84 CDPA 1988**).

THE INTEGRITY RIGHT

Turning first to the law surrounding Prissy's right of integrity, **ss 80–83 CDPA 1988** concern the right of an author to object when their work is added to, altered or deleted (**s 80(2)**) in such a way as to amount to a distortion, mutilation or otherwise prejudicial treatment. Further, in *Pasterfield v Denham* (1998), Overend J held that distortion or mutilation must be such as to harm the honour or reputation of an artist and that a subjective sense of grievance did not suffice. Some evidence that there has been damage to an author's reputation is required according to *Confetti Records v Warner Music* (2003). In that case, a 'garage' style music composer objected to the use of his single 'Burnin' by a rap group who added references to violence and drug use. Lewison J dismissed the case, in part because no evidence of damage to the composer's reputation had been adduced. He held that **s 80(2)(b)** provided a two-part test:

(i) adaptation that amounted to distortion, mutilation, modification or other derogatory action; and

(ii) that this would be prejudicial to honour or reputation.

The right to object to derogatory treatment of the work extends to treatment which distorts or mutilates the work (**s 80(2)(b)**). It would appear on the authority of *Confetti Records v Warner* (2003) that Prissy could successfully argue that Channel Six's adaption of her play fulfils the first element of the test as the original noble and serious qualities of the play have been undermined by the transformation into a vulgar farce, with the role of the characters interchanged and the action set in Nottingham. In addition, the sexually explicit nature of the adaptation is entirely different from the original serious and noble tone of the play. However, in order to succeed, Prissy will need to bring evidence as to how her honour and reputation have been prejudiced. This is more difficult but the negative critical reviews will support her claim and she could obtain survey evidence to confirm that her reputation as a serious literary author has been diminished. If this is necessary, it will be expensive for Prissy to enforce her right of integrity in connection with her play.

THE RIGHT AGAINST FALSE ATTRIBUTION

As Prissy's name appears in publicity and credits of the programme it may appear that her right to paternity has been respected. **Section 77(2)(a) CDPA 1988** specifically requires identification of the original author of an adaption as 'the author of the work, from which the adaptation was made'. However, Prissy is concerned at being described as being 'involved' with the writing of the Channel Six adaptation when she had nothing to do with this. As such, it may be that naming her as an author in connection with the Channel

Six adaption is a false attribution: **s 84 CDPA 1988** and *Clarke v Associated Newspapers Ltd* (1988) 1 WLR 1558.

Prissy's moral rights could also be protected indirectly because the act complained of might involve a copyright infringement. For example, she may be able to successfully argue that Channel Six, without her permission as a term of the adaptation agreement, has in fact made a 'parody' of her work rather than an adaptation. A parody is a work created to mock or trivialise an original work, its subject, author and style by means of humorous satiric or ironic imitation. Prissy might feel aggrieved because in her view the TV adaptation amounts to a parody which contains a substantial part of the original work. Prissy will have to review the relevant clauses in the adaptation for TV agreement to determine whether Channel Six's adaptation falls within the terms. If not, Prissy may be in a position to sue for breach of contract. Otherwise, in terms of her IP rights, she could rely on her moral rights. In particular, the claim for false attribution as the author of the screenplay for the Channel Six TV adaptation is the stronger claim as it is easier to prove on the balance of probabilities.

Common Pitfalls

It is important to plan your answer to deal relatively equally with the two key moral rights in the question: (1) the 'integrity' right (**ss 80–83 CDPA 1988**); and (2) the right to object to being falsely attributed as the author (**ss 77–79 CDPA 1988**).

Aim Higher

If time permits, consider the nature of any copyright infringement that may have occurred in connection with Channel Six's use of the work. This will lead to a discussion of whether the work has been parodied, which could be a breach of the scope of the right to adapt granted by Prissy to Channel Six.

3

Copyright Infringement

This chapter introduces copyright owners' exclusive rights and how these rights may be infringed. For example, if you wrote a book and it is copied rather than purchased from you, there has been a breach of copyright. This conduct was the historic starting point for the system of copyright protection. In fact, the law grants a series of *copy rights*. A copyright owner's rights have vastly expanded and include the right to display the work, perform it in public, translate it and adapt it, among many others. In the same vein, infringing conduct is no longer confined to direct copying but also includes appropriating some elements of the work and encouraging others to copy the work and so on. This interlocking system of rights and infringements is the subject of this chapter. We examine how copyright is infringed (primary and secondary infringement), the array of purpose-specific fair dealing defences and remedies.

Checklist
Students should anticipate questions about the following:
■ the copyright owner's exclusive rights;
■ copyright infringement – classes of prohibited acts;
■ the legal test for copying;
■ primary infringement;
■ secondary infringement;
■ copyright infringement in the digital age;
■ fair dealing and other defences to infringement.

QUESTION 10

Joe is a young freelance photojournalist who is becoming well known for his iconic photos of Special Olympic athletes with intellectual disabilities. Since the games were held in Athens, Greece in 2011 his photographs are increasingly historically significant. Joe is now regularly approached with requests to license the use of his photographs in domestic and international markets for a variety of uses. On other occasions Joe's images are copied. Joe is becoming more IP-savvy and uses online tools such as Internet search engine Google and TinEye Reverse Image Search to check the web to see how his photos are being used. He discovers that a YouTube user has taken 10 of his images and reproduced them as background for his music video clip which he uploaded to the website. The clip attracts 250,000 views.

What approach should Joe take to protect his valuable intellectual property rights yet continue to develop his reputation as a freelance photojournalist that may lead to new professional opportunities?

How to Read this Question

This is a fairly typical problem question. Students are asked to advise on a specific fact scenario that at first glance involves copyright and potentially moral rights infringement on the Internet.

How to Answer this Question

In terms of structure of the answer, it is important to briefly introduce the task at hand and the law, in particular whether Joe has artistic copyright to enforce. This should be followed by a detailed consideration of and application of the law to the facts, concluding with thoughtfully reasoned advice to Joe.

Applying the Law

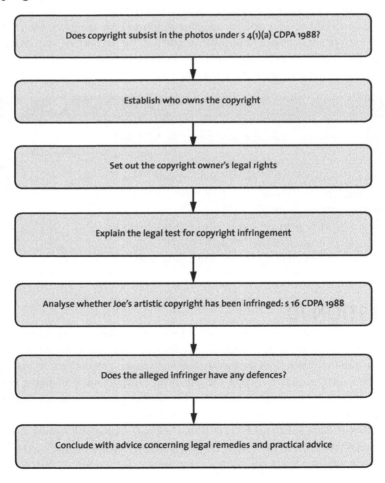

Does copyright subsist in the photos under s 4(1)(a) CDPA 1988?

Establish who owns the copyright

Set out the copyright owner's legal rights

Explain the legal test for copyright infringement

Analyse whether Joe's artistic copyright has been infringed: s 16 CDPA 1988

Does the alleged infringer have any defences?

Conclude with advice concerning legal remedies and practical advice

ANSWER

With the advent of the Internet, each day more than 500 million digital images are shared. This means that photographers such as Joe need to strike the right balance between making sure that his photos get visibility to enhance his professional reputation and keeping control of his intellectual property rights.

Still image photography is generally protected by copyright and moral rights law. As the use of photos is broad, so are the potential income streams for the 'use rights' of Joe's images.

The first issue is whether copyright subsists in Joe's photos such that there is a copyright work capable of being infringed. Copyright is automatic as soon as there is (1) a permanent record in any form of the newly created material, and (2) the material conforms with the criteria set out in the **Copyright, Designs and Patents Act 1988** (**CDPA 1988**). In other words, as soon as a photo is taken, copyright automatically protects the original work against copyright, reuse and dissemination to the public without permission. Accordingly, copyright subsists in an original photo (a recording of light or other radiation on any medium on which an image is produced, or from which an image by any means can be produced) which is not part of a film.

Photographs are classed as artistic works capable of protection irrespective of their artistic merit: **s 4(1)(a) CDPA 1988**. However, the Act provides that an artistic work has to be 'original' to qualify for protection. This means that it has to be original in the sense that it originates from the author, in this case Joe, a freelance photojournalist: *University of London Press v University Tutorial Press* (1916). In addition, the photos must be the result of Joe's skill, labour and judgement: *Ladbroke (Football Ltd) v William Hill (Football Ltd)* (1964). In summary, in the UK, for Joe's photos to be protected, they must represent his intellectual creation and show at least a small degree of mental effort.

As Joe is self-employed he will be the owner of the photographs. He does not need to register copyright in his photographs in order to take steps to enforce his artistic copyright.

As it has been established that copyright does subsist in Joe's photos, we will consider the nature of Joe's legal rights and how he can enforce them against infringers who use his work without permission. In essence, copyright owners such as Joe gain a negative right to prevent others doing certain acts in relation to their work. Copyright law specifies acts (the 'acts restricted by Copyright') which can only be performed lawfully by the owner. **Section 16(1) CDPA 1988** confers the following exclusive rights on the copyright owner:

(1)   copy the work;
(2)   issue copies of the work to the public;
(3)   rent or lend the work to the public;
(4)   perform, show or play the work in public;
(5)   communicate the work to the public; and
(6)   make an adaptation of the work, or do any of the preceding acts in relation to an adaptation.

Further, **s 16(2) CDPA 1988** provides that if a person (including a legal person such as a company) does any of these acts without authority in the UK, this will infringe the owner's copyright in the work. In other words, copyright means 'reproducing the work in a material form'.

Joe is concerned about a specific instance in which he believes the copyright in his photographs has potentially been infringed. Ultimately, his goal is to stop the unauthorised use of his images and/or receive appropriate compensation as well as attribution for their use. Joe can protect the creative content in his photographs by relying on his copyright and moral rights.

UNAUTHORISED USE OF 10 DIGITAL IMAGES ON A YOUTUBE VIDEO

Copyright in Joe's images subsist even if they are reproduced digitally on the Internet: **s 17(6) CDPA 1988**. Joe has the right to control what is made available to the public, and the Act refers specifically to communication via the Internet and the digital environment. **Section 16(3)(a) CDPA 1988** provides doing a restricted act involves the doing of it (a) in relation to the work as a whole or any substantial part of it; and (b) either directly or indirectly. Essentially, Joe's artistic copyright is infringed if his photos are directly copied in whole or in part (primary infringement) or by dealing in infringing copies of the photos (secondary infringement). However, Joe must show that there is a causal connection between his photos and the allegedly infringing work as well as substantial copying: per Lord Denning LJ in *Francis Day and Hunter Ltd v Bron* (1963). Whether the copying is substantial will be analysed on a qualitative rather than a quantitative basis: *Ladbroke (Football Ltd) v William Hill (Football Ltd)* (1964) per Lord Pearce. Piracy is the popular term for illegal copyright infringement activity.

In this case, 10 of Joe's photos have been digitally reproduced in full by the YouTube user so it is a clear case of direct copying. The TinEye Reverse Image Search report will provide useful evidence of copying on the balance of probabilities.

DOES THE FACT THAT THE PHOTOS WERE POSTED ON YOUTUBE MAKE A DIFFERENCE?

YouTube is a video-sharing website headquartered in California, United States. No, not in terms of the unauthorised use and copyright infringement, breach of moral rights defences and remedies. However, practically speaking, if Joe wants the images removed he will have to contact the user who posted them and ask him or her to remove them from the infringing video clip. If the user refuses, Joe can contact YouTube directly to request that the video containing his images be taken down. In addition, it may be in Joe's interest to obtain compensation from the infringing use and potentially generate a new revenue stream from the use. Joe may require the YouTube user to pay a licence fee if he agrees to permit the continued use of his images on the video clip, subject to proper attribution that he is the photographer in order to benefit from the publicity.

MORAL RIGHTS ISSUES

Moral rights are especially important for photographers and the moral rights arising on the facts are:

❖ the right to be identified as the photographer (the attribution or paternity right): **ss 77–79 CDPA 1988**;
❖ the right not to have the photo manipulated, mutilated or distorted (the integrity right): **ss 80–83 CDPA 1988**.

The attribution right (being credited as the photographer) is fast becoming more valuable than the copyright itself for photographers in terms of reputation and generating income.

Nonetheless, an alleged copyright infringer is lawfully able to carry out certain 'permitted acts' known as 'fair dealing': **ss 28–76 CDPA 1988**. Alleged infringers may also be able to rely on other statutory defences. However, on the facts it is unlikely that the YouTube user could rely on fair dealing given that he has made use of 10 of Joe's entire images and there are no facts to suggest that the use amounts merely to incidental inclusion: **s 31(1) CDPA 1988**.

In conclusion, how Joe chooses to react to the direct infringement of his artistic copyright may depend on the severity, ranging from ignoring occasional use in social media, through to asking for an image to be removed within 24 hours, right up to seeking a settlement for unauthorised use and loss of revenue. Many businesses have set aside money in their annual budget specifically to pay for copyright infringement claims. Joe could also join the National Union of Journalists (NUJ) as they offer legal advice and support on copyright matters. Joe could also join the Design and Artists Copyright Society (DACS), a not-for-profit rights management organisation to help with licensing and to potentially get a revenue stream from the secondary uses of his images such as photocopying. For photos that Joe may wish to share he could use a Creative Commons licence, specifically the CC BY-NC-ND licence which says anyone can use the photo, provided it is properly attributed, not changed and not used for commercial purposes. This option means that Joe can get his images seen and used, but still maintain control of the artistic copyright and license them for a fee if someone wants to use them commercially. Joe needs to develop an IP strategy for protecting his photographs that sits comfortably with his outlook and philosophy on life. Nevertheless, he recognises that the copyright in his photos are likely to earn him revenue over his lifetime and a further 70 years.

Common Pitfalls

Students commonly fail to recognise and deal with the full range of copyright and moral rights issues that arise in connection with photographs as a class of copyright work.

Aim Higher

In addition to the copyright and moral rights issues that subsist in the photographs, provide practical legal advice that will assist Joe to achieve his goals with respect to his valuable IP rights.

QUESTION 11

Jessica is an experienced Human Resources Officer for Trent University and her employer has asked her to draft a completely new Staff Handbook. When she drafted this, she used a template that she had from her previous employer, the University of Rutland ('UoR'), which was 100 pages long which she and two other UoR staff had drafted. She then made the following changes to the UoR template:

❖ deleted five pages which were not relevant to Trent University;
❖ included five new pages and added language required by statutes;
❖ added two pages from other agreements, some of which she had authored and which were publicly available on the Internet to other UK universities;
❖ created three new pages to cover complex new legal rights for employees over the age of 65 years;
❖ edited all of the above for style and consistency;
❖ made a large number of minor stylistic and grammatical revisions suggested by Mr Pickwick, the Head of Human Resources for Trent University.

The resulting Staff Handbook is about 105 pages long and is published on the University's intranet, accessible to all staff.

Several months later, Jessica's line manager Mr Pickwick calls her into his office for a meeting together with the university's in-house legal officer. Mr Pickwick informs Jessica that a letter has been received from her former employer claiming that Trent University has breached the copyright subsisting in the UoR Staff Handbook and must cease its use or agree to pay a licence fee.

Advise Trent University as to whether there is any basis for the claim of copyright infringement and any defences it may have.

How to Read this Question

Read the facts of the problem question in full. Then read it a second time and note the specific instances of potential copyright infringement (primary and secondary) and any facts that may give rise to potential defences.

How to Answer this Question

The focus of the question is an analysis of copyright infringement, so while it is helpful to confirm subsistence of copyright, authorship, ownership and duration of copyright, the student should centre the answer on copyright infringement analysis to provide the requested advice to Trent University on whether there is a basis for a claim for copyright infringement and any defences it may have.

Answer Structure

This is a practical problem question concerning copyright infringement.

❖ Analyse whether copyright subsists in the UoR Staff Handbook as a literary work under **s 3(1) CDPA 1988**.

❖ Establish who owns copyright in the UoR Staff Handbook and the nature of the UoR's exclusive rights in its UoR Staff Handbook under **s 16(1) CDPA 1988**.

❖ Examine whether Jessica (and thereby her employer, Trent University) has infringed any of the exclusive rights in the Staff Handbook.

❖ If so, consider any likely defences Trent University may have and any remedies available to UoR.

Applying the Law

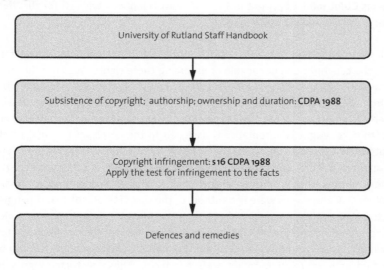

University of Rutland Staff Handbook

↓

Subsistence of copyright; authorship; ownership and duration: **CDPA 1988**

↓

Copyright infringement: **s 16 CDPA 1988**
Apply the test for infringement to the facts

↓

Defences and remedies

ANSWER --

Copyright law in the UK is governed by the **Copyright, Designs and Patents Act 1988** (**CDPA 1988**) and in particular, **Part I** of the Act sets out the substantive copyright law. This means that the University of Rutland ('UoR') Staff Handbook will only be a copyright work if it meets the statutory requirements. The Act identifies three categories of works in which copyright subsists:

❖ original literary, dramatic, musical or artistic works;

❖ sound recordings, films or broadcasts;

❖ typographical arrangements of published editions.

The first issue is whether copyright subsists in the UoR Staff Handbook such that there is a copyright work capable of being infringed. A 'work' is not defined by the **CDPA 1988** except to say that a 'copyright work' means a work of any of those descriptions in which copyright subsists: **s 1(2)**. **Section 1(1)(a) CDPA 1988** provides that copyright subsists in original literary works. Whether a work is a 'work' for copyright purposes is inseparable from whether it is 'original' since copyright will only subsist in an original work. The Act defines a 'literary work' as any work other than a dramatic or musical work that is written, spoken or sung: **s 3(1)**. It appears that the UoR Staff Handbook will fall within the scope of the definition of 'literary work' and as such is prima facie copyright material for several reasons. The handbook is original in the sense that it originates from the UoR's employee, Jessica (and perhaps other staff) and is the result of the authors' skill, labour and judgement: *Ladbroke (Football Ltd) v William Hill (Football Ltd)* (1964). Further, case law establishes that this is not a qualitative standard, merely an indication that the work be recorded by means of letters or numbers: *University of London Ltd v University Tutorial Press Ltd* (1916) per Petersen J. The UoR Staff Handbook is fixed in writing as required by **s 3(2)** of the Act and also qualifies for protection under the heads of authorship or place of publication in **ss 153–155 CDPA 1988**. Copyright in the UoR Staff Handbook will last for the life of the author plus 70 years: **s 12 CDPA 1988**.

As it is established that copyright subsists in the UoR Staff Handbook, the next issue is, who is the copyright owner capable of enforcing these rights? We are told that when Jessica drafted the new Trent University Staff Handbook, she used a template that she had from her previous employer, the UoR, which was 100 pages long. Jessica is a former UoR employee. When a work is created by an employee in the course of employment, then copyright is automatically assigned to the employer by **s 11(2) CDPA 1988** except where agreed to the contrary. In *Beloff v Pressdram Ltd* (1973) the court cited with approval the dictum of Lord Denning that an employee is employed as part of the business and his work is an integral part of the business. So even though Jessica and two other UoR employees were the authors of the UoR Staff Handbook, copyright vests with the UoR as the employer and not with the former employee Jessica, unless her contract of employment with UoR provided otherwise, which is unlikely in this case. Accordingly, as copyright owner, only the UoR has the exclusive right to carry out the 'restricted acts' in relation to its staff handbook. These restricted rights include copying the work or a substantial part of it and publishing it: **s 16(1)**, **s 16(3)(a) CDPA 1988**. Copying means 'reproducing the work in a material form'. If a third party has copied the UoR Staff Handbook, the UoR will have standing to sue in respect of copyright infringement.

Therefore the crux of the problem is whether copyright in the UoR Staff Handbook has been infringed by Trent University. There are two types of infringement. Primary infringement occurs when a person does, or authorises another to do, any of the restricted acts without the licence of the copyright owner: **s 16(2)**. Secondary infringement is mainly concerned with dealings in infringing works or facilitating their production. In this case, the concern is primary infringement. Can UoR stop Trent University using the copied portions of the UoR Staff Handbook without a licence? Two key elements are required in order to establish primary infringement. According to Denning LJ in *Francis, Day and Hunter Ltd v Bron* (1963), there must be:

(1)   a causal connection between the copyright work and the allegedly infringing work; and
(2)   copying of a substantial part of the copyright work.

In other words, the court will consider if there is objective similarity between the two works and whether there is a causal connection between them.

As to the first element, for a work to be infringing, it must derive from the copyright work – it must have been copied by someone. Here, the causal connection is Jessica, the former UoR employee, who had access to the UoR Staff Handbook which she did indeed refer to as a template for the Trent University Staff Handbook. The first element of the test for copying is satisfied.

Apart from a causal connection, in order to infringe, copying must be in relation to the work as a whole, or any substantial part of it: **s16(3)(a)**. The UoR's copyright will not be infringed unless a substantial part of its staff handbook has been used by Trent University via its current employee Jessica. Whether the copying is substantial will be analysed on a qualitative rather than quantitative basis: *Ladbroke (Football Ltd) v William Hill (Football Ltd)* (1964) per Lord Pearce. It is a question of fact whether the degree of similarity is sufficient to warrant the inference that there is a causal connection between the two works.

The way in which a court determines the issue of substantial taking is summarised in *Baigent & Lee v Random House Group Ltd* (2007) FSR 579. Is there more than a passing resemblance to the UoR Staff Handbook? In other words, are the two staff handbooks similar? The court will consider, first, the value and, second, the amount of the material that Trent University has repeated and how this has been used in the Trent University Staff Handbook. Every case is decided on its individual merits. For example, in *Ludlow Music Inc. v Robbie Williams* (2000) it was held that one refrain from a song could amount to substantial copying. On the other hand, where a work is not copied in extracts, but slight modifications are made to the whole of it, the question is whether the alleged infringer has misappropriated a substantial part of the claimant's labour, skill and judgement: *Designers Guild Ltd v Russell Williams (Textiles) Ltd (No 2)* (2001). In summary, a substantial degree of objective similarity, together with proof of access to the original work, is prima facie evidence of copying.

The court will assess whether the Trent University has created a new literary document of its own by evaluating Jessica's and Mr Pickwick's skill, labour and judgement, and/or whether the Trent University Staff Handbook infringes that of the UoR. On the facts, it would appear that there is some new material: five new pages which added language required by statutes; two new pages cut and pasted from other universities' staff handbooks which she found on the Internet (while potentially infringing, do not infringe the Rutland document); three new pages to cover complex new legal rights for employees over the age of 65 years; and minor stylistic and grammatical revisions. This means that only approximately 8 per cent of the materials have not been copied. Further, approximately 5 per cent of the UoR material was deleted. So the issue is whether the remaining 87 per cent of the Trent Staff Handbook was copied by Jessica from the UoR Staff Handbook.

Although the test for copyright infringement is a qualitative one and not a quantitative one, on balance the second element of the test for copying is satisfied. If Jessica has not made any changes to the text of the UoR Staff Handbook it is highly likely that a court would find that the Trent Handbook substantially infringes the UoR Staff Handbook both qualitatively and quantitatively. Intention by the defendant is not relevant to finding infringement: *Electronic Techniques v Critchley Components* (1997).

The facts show that there is a causal connection between the work and its alleged copy, namely Jessica a former employee of UoR: *Solar Thomson v Barton* (1977) RPC 357. Trent University derived a substantial part of its staff handbook from the source work, namely the UoR staff handbook. The evidential burden will then shift to Trent University to explain the similarities with a view to showing that it did not copy the UoR Staff Handbook. The permitted acts (the fair dealing defences) are set out in **ss 28–76** of the **CDPA 1988**. However, there is nothing to suggest that the Trent University could rely on a fair dealing defence as a staff handbook is not directly related to research, education, criticism or review.

If the action for primary copyright infringement is successful, UoR could take legal action to obtain an injunction (an equitable remedy) against Trent University (which is liable for the acts of its employee Jessica) from publishing its staff handbook on its website. UoR could also apply for an order that Trent University be required to deliver up all infringing copies and/or pay damages to the UoR.

Common Pitfalls

Many students typically launch into a discussion of copyright infringement without first analysing the issue of subsistence of copyright in the staff handbook as well as identifying ownership. These latter two issues need to be discussed initially in brief before a comprehensive discussion of primary copyright infringement can meaningfully take place. Discuss the relevant case law and then apply it to the facts of the problem as you go.

Aim Higher

Demonstrate your understanding of the 'quality versus quantity' debate with respect to primary copyright infringement.

QUESTION 12 --

Critically discuss the potential impact of the general qualified right to quote copyrighted works introduced by the **Copyright and Rights in Performances (Quotation and Parody) Regulations 2014** on the use of copyright-protected work in the digital environment. Refer to relevant legal authority to support your answer.

How to Read this Question

This is a very specific essay-style question. When specific questions like this are asked it is important to stay within the parameters set by the question and not to stray beyond them. This question clearly requires a focus on a particular aspect of copyright law, a new 'fair dealing' defence to copyright infringement in the context of the digital age involving computers and the Internet.

How to Answer this Question

Introduce the fair dealing defences to copyright infringement generally and then focus on critically evaluating the impact of the new qualified 'right to quote' copyright works. The answer should consider the impact of the new provision and its advantages and disadvantages, illustrated by examples that demonstrate its operation in the digital environment, for example on websites, social media etc.

Answer Structure

- ❖ Introduce the tensions that arise between the rights of copyright owners and the public.
- ❖ Illustrate the copyright issue with an example based on unauthorised use of copyright in the digital environment.
- ❖ Explain the legal test for copyright infringement.
- ❖ Introduce the new qualified right to use copyright material in quotations and how it operates.
- ❖ Evaluate the impact of the new law.

ANSWER --

Copyright law enables creators who have exercised a degree of skill, labour and judgement to gain financial rewards for their efforts with a view to encouraging future creativity and developing new material. However, without legal protection such material would often be relatively easy for others to exploit without paying the creator. Copyright infringement is against the law. Indeed, deliberate infringement on a commercial scale may lead to a criminal prosecution, so those who make use of copyright works need to do so either with the copyright owners' permission or in reliance on certain within the fact specific 'fair dealing' defences.

Intellectual property (IP) law has traditionally sought to balance monopoly protection with use access to copyright property. A key issue for debate in the copyright field in the digital age is whether copyright owners have gained rights at the expense of consumers' (the public) legitimate rights. Some argue that the impact of over-expansive copyright law is not in the public interest. There is clearly tension between IP creators and owners and the future direction of copyright law in the context of the digital revolution which is further addressed with the advent of the **Copyright and Rights in Performances (Quotation and Parody) Regulations 2014** which amends **s 30** of the **Copyright, Designs and Patents Act 1988** (**CDPA 1988**).

For example, technology has changed the way the public and consumers share and interact with sports media content. During the recent football World Cup in Brazil video clips of goals or other points of action from the matches were posted on social media platforms such as Twitter within seconds of the action being broadcast. In 2011, the Court of Justice of the European Union (CJEU) determined in that live sporting events do not of themselves qualify for copyright protection; however, broadcasts of those events and film, sound recording, graphics, music and other features included within such broadcasts attract copyright protection: *C-403/08 Football Association Premier League and Others*. This means that the unauthorised uploading of the key moments in a sports event such as goals, winning points, fights etc. gives rise to potential copyright infringement issues and inevitably leads to defences to infringement being put forward.

The law on these 'fair dealing' exceptions to copyright infringement has changed to enhance the UK's system of copyright to engage with the reality of the digital environment. These changes affect how copyright content online and in books, music, films and photographs can be used without infringing the copyright owners' monopoly rights in the work.

QUOTATION

A new qualified right to use copyright material in quotations is now one of the more than 50 'fair dealing' defences provided by **ss 29–30** of the **Copyright, Designs and Patents Act 1988** (**CDPA 1988**). Should a person use a copyright work or copy it, they usually have to obtain permission from the lawful copyright owner; however, there are exceptions whereby copyright material can be used in full or in part without permission. However, the existence of a copyright exception does not change who owns the copyright in a work. The majority of uses of copyright materials continue to require permission from copyright owners. In certain circumstances it is now possible to rely on the quotation fair dealing exception.

The quotation right allows copyrighted material to be used in a quotation provided that

> the work has been made available to the public, the use of the quotation is fair dealing with the work, the extent of the quotation is no more than is required by the specific purpose for which it is used, and the quotation is accompanied by a sufficient acknowledgement (unless this would be impossible for reasons of practicality or otherwise).

Similarly, quoting from a copyrighted performance or recording will also be a permitted Act, as long as the performance or recording has been made available to the public, the use of the quotation is fair dealing with the performance or recording, and the extent of the quotation is no more than is required by the specific purpose for which it is used.

This means that a user who quotes the copyright with the scope of the exception will be within the law and not infringe, even though they have not sought the authorisation or a user licence from the copyright owner. In short, copyright law has changed to give the public greater freedom to quote the works of others on the proviso that the quotation is accompanied by sufficient acknowledgement and the use is considered reasonable and fair ('fair dealing'). The exception only allows use of material where it is genuinely for the purpose of quotation, and only where the use is fair and reasonable (e.g. it does not replace a commercial sale).

Nevertheless, copyright is only infringed if the unauthorised use involves the whole or a 'substantial part' of the copyright work: **s16 CPDA 1988**. The legal test for copyright infringement is a qualitative one and not a quantitative one. This means that small parts of a copyright work can be said to constitute a substantial part: *Ladbroke (Football Ltd) v William Hill (Football Ltd)* (1964) per Lord Pearce. In the example mentioned above, the more significant the piece of broadcast footage that is uploaded, such as a goal or red card incident, the more likely it is to be deemed to be a 'substantial part' of the copy-righted work. In a dispute between the BBC and British Satellite Broadcasting, the latter's use of video clips of World Cup broadcasts which ranged in length from 14 to 37 seconds was held to infringe: *BBC v British Satellite Broadcasting Ltd* (1992) Ch 141. The defendant's intention is not relevant to finding infringement: *Electronic Techniques v Critchley Components* (1997).

WHAT IS MEANT BY SUFFICIENT ACKNOWLEDGEMENT?

Typically, this means the title and the author's name should be indicated. In the case of a broadcast, the title, channel, date and year. This is an extension to the existing law that already allows fair dealing with copyright materials for the purpose of news reporting, criticism and review: **s30 CDPA 1988**.

IMPACT ON THE DIGITAL ENVIRONMENT

While the exception applies to all types of copyright work, it would only be in exceptional circumstances that copying a photograph or digital image would be allowed under this exception. It would not be considered fair dealing if the proposed use of a copyright work would conflict with the copyright owner's normal exploitation of their work. For example, the ability to sell or license copies of photographs for inclusion in newspapers, other broadcasters or online content providers would be a normal exploitation.

In summary, the quotation exception could permit a short quotation that is necessary and relevant in an academic paper or a history book, but it would not permit a long extract.

However, the impact on the digital environment is less clear-cut. 'Fair dealing' is a legal term used to establish whether a use of copyright material is lawful or whether it infringes copyright. There is no statutory definition of fair dealing – it will always be a matter of fact, degree and impression in each case. The question to be asked is: how would a fair-minded and honest person have dealt with the work? Factors that have been identified by the courts as relevant in determining whether a particular dealing with a work is fair include the following:

❖ Does using the work affect the market for the original work? If a use of a work acts as a substitute for it, causing the owner to lose revenue, then it is not likely to be fair.

❖ Is the amount of the work taken reasonable and appropriate? Was it necessary to use the amount that was taken? Usually only part of a work may be used.

The relative importance of any one factor will vary according to the case in hand and the type of dealing in question. Anything that is not fair dealing will require a licence or permission from the copyright owner.

In conclusion, the new quotation exception allows a reference to a copyright work – in essence providing an opportunity to build on it. This means it is very unlikely that someone could copy a whole unchanged work without permission from the copyright owner. However, the change to the law highlights the pressure that copyright owners, who rely on copyright protection for their work for investment and to generate revenue, will face from the public, armed with increasingly sophisticated technology to instantly reproduce copyright material in cyberspace.

Common Pitfalls

Students fail to cite primary sources of law, namely, the legislation and case law to support their answer. This is an important aspect of formal legal writing style. In addition, brief conclusions that are vague do not attract marks.

Aim Higher

The best answers will tend to focus more immediately on the new fair dealing amendment and illustrate how it could apply with relevant examples. The conclusion to the answer presents an opportunity to reflect on the state of the law and is an important way to gain additional credit.

4 Computer Technology and Copyright Law

A theme running through copyright law is that it is constantly adapting, whether in response to advances in technology or due to shifting perceptions regarding the extent of intellectual property protection. Computer technology developments with which copyright law has had to grapple include, but are not limited to:

❖ computer software programs and computer implemented inventions;
❖ the circumvention of technological protection measures;
❖ databases; and
❖ the Internet.

Computer programs have been protected by copyright in the UK since 1988, when the definition of 'literary work' in the **Copyright, Designs and Patents Act 1988 (CDPA 1988)** was extended to include 'a computer program' and 'a database'.

An international consensus that computer programs should be protected by copyright emerged during the 1980s and was confirmed by **Art 4** of the **TRIPS Agreement** and **Art 4** of the **1996 WIPO Copyright Treaty**.

Since computer programs and databases are protected under the **CDPA 1988** as literary works, the copyright owner can exercise all the exclusive rights attaching to literary works. In practice, the most valuable rights are those of reproduction and adaptation.

This chapter considers the nature of the legal protection afforded by the copyright law to certain aspects of computer technology including infringement of copyright via the Internet. The patentability of computer software is also problematic but is not covered in the text.

Checklist

Students should anticipate questions about the following:

■ the idea–expression dichotomy and impact on computer programs;
■ copyright infringement – literal and non-literal;
■ the legal test for copying;
■ copyright infringement in the digital age;
■ fair dealing and other defences to infringement.

QUESTION 13 --

Critically discuss the extent and effectiveness of the copyright law mechanisms that exist to protect computer software.

How to Read this Question

In this essay question, the examiner is looking for an exploration of two issues: the 'extent' of legal protection for computer software and whether or not it is 'effective'. Students should include material on both aspects in their essay answer.

How to Answer this Question

It seems logical to begin exploring the current level of copyright law protection for software at the outset. This will allow key characteristics to be identified and focused on, which in turn can then be evaluated in terms of effectiveness, for example, is the current state of the law adequate or inadequate?

Answer Structure

This is a broad question that requires the student to deal with a lot of material. In answering this question, it is important to examine the legislation, specific regulations and reported decisions relating to computer software, and discuss any issues that arise in connection with infringement of software that may apply.

❖ Original literary works (**s 1(1) CDPA 1988**);
❖ **Section 3(1)(b)** and **(c) CDPA 1988**;
❖ **Copyright (Computer Programs) Regulations 1992**;
❖ Infringement by literal copying and *Ibcos Computers v Barclays Mercantile High Finance* (1994); *Cantor Fitzgerald International v Tradition (UK) Ltd* (2000);
❖ Infringement by non-literal copying and *Navitaire Inc v Easyjet Airline Company* (2004) and (2006);
❖ The scope of copyright protection afforded to computer programs under **Art 1(2)** of the **Software Directive** and the recent referral of nine questions to the European Court of Justice by Mr Justice Arnold in *SAS Institute Inc. v World Programming Ltd* (2010).
❖ Defences under **ss 50, 50A, 50B** and **50BA CDPA 1988**;
❖ **Sections 17, 18** and **19 CDPA 1988**.

Up for Debate

The relationship between intellectual property protection and computer technology is complex, and several theoretical and practical problems arise. Generally speaking, copyright protects computer software and patents protect computer technology hardware. The **CDPA 1988** is the starting point for analysis. The Act protects computer programs as a whole; it does not protect, as such, individual files or part of a program. However, copyright also only protects expression (the computer code lines) and does not protect ideas. This means that those parts of the program that can only be expressed in one way if a certain result is to be achieved, due to technical restrictions, are not original and do not attract copyright: *Total Information Processing Systems v Daman* (1992) FSR 171. However, **EU Directive 92/250** and the European interpretation of originality which has been implemented into UK law is vital. The Directive protects all forms of expression of a computer program and the preparatory design work capable of leading to the reproduction or the subsequent creation of such a program. Therefore both source code and the object code are forms of expression entitled to copyright protection: **Art 1(2)**. However, the functionality, the programming language or format of data files used to exploit functions in the program are not copyright protected as this would enable the idea and not the expression to be monopolised.

These copyright law principles are important when determining literal and non-literal copyright infringement and whether substantial copying has taken place. The computer software program as a whole must be considered when applying the legal test for substantial similarity.

ANSWER

It is now possible to say that computer software has been brought under the umbrella of copyright law relatively smoothly by way of a concerted effort on the part of the legislature and the courts to take the necessary steps to adapt copyright law to encompass this new form of expression. A piece of computer software comprises a program, which is a series of instructions expressed in code, intended to cause a particular result when used in computer hardware.

Computer programs are afforded copyright protection as a category of literary work and enjoy copyright protection under **ss 1(1)** and **3(1)(b) Copyright, Designs and Patents Act 1988** (**CDPA 1988**). Also protected is preparatory design material for a computer program under **s 3(1)(c)**. The **Copyright (Computer Programs) Regulations 1992** amended the **CDPA 1988** to apply to computer programs whenever created.

The normal copyright rules apply to computer programs. For example, in order to be an original literary work, the computer program must be the product of a substantial degree of skill, labour and judgement by the author: *University of London Press Ltd v University Tutorial Press Ltd* (1916). However, the **CDPA 1988** does not define computer programs and this allows for law to adapt to evolving forms of computer software and/or technology. Case law suggests that for 'originality' to be found in a computer program, the court is particularly concerned with certain aspects including the algorithms or operational sequences and the structure or architecture of the program.

Copyright only protects expression and does not protect ideas. For example, the idea for a program to electronically manage a dental laboratory and the functions the program is to achieve are not protected by copyright: *Whelan Associated Inc v Jaslow Dental Laboratory*

Inc (1987). However, the code lines of the program, its algorithms, operational sequences, file structure and architecture may be protected by copyright once it is 'recorded in writing or otherwise' (**s 3(2) CDPA 1998**). This principle was explained in *Ibcos Computers v Barclays Mercantile High Finance* (1994) when Jacob J stated that 'UK copyright cannot protect the copyright of a mere general idea, but can protect the copyright in detailed ideas'. Fixation on a hard or floppy disk or hard-wired in a microprocessor in the form of micro code or micro programs would meet the fixation requirement under the Act. However, where there is only one way for a computer program to be expressed so as to achieve a particular technical result, this will not be protected by copyright: *Kenrick v Lawrence* (1890), cited in *John Richardson Computers Ltd v Flanders and Chemtech Ltd* (1993). This part of the program can be freely copied.

However, copyright protection for software comes in many different forms. As we have seen, the code is a literary work. The onscreen display could be an artistic work; the soundtrack used on a website is a musical work; and moving images can also be protected as film. These are all types of copyright works. **Section 11** of the **CDPA 1988** provides that the author of a work is the first owner in any copyright unless the author is an employee who creates the work in the course of employment.

Turning to copyright infringement, cutting and pasting a digital work is an example of literal copyright infringement which is relatively straightforward to prove. However, it is in the area of non-literal copying that the extent and effectiveness of copyright protection is less clear-cut. Non-literal copying does not involve the wholesale lifting of one computer programme into another. Case law has emerged to provide some guidance.

INFRINGEMENT: LITERAL AND NON-LITERAL COPYING

As with other literary works, a three-stage test for copyright infringement is applied:

(1) Does the work attract copyright protection?
(2) Has there been copying of the elements protected by copyright?
(3) Was the copying substantial?

The computer program must be assessed as a whole when considering whether copyright infringement has occurred. The **CDPA 1988** protects computer programs, not individual files or parts of a program. Similarly, it is a journal article as a literary work that is protected, not each individual sentence or paragraph. This is essential for the purpose of analysing cases in order to determine whether substantial copying has taken place. Separate programs can be combined into one program and this will be treated as a compilation. In *MS Associates v Power* (1988) the court identified two issues in relation to proving copying:

(1) the claimant has to prove that the defendant had access to the software program; and
(2) there are similarities between substantial parts of the programs.

The fact that two screen displays are similar is not proof of copyright infringement – this is because the copyright protects the program itself, not the results obtained from it.

However, the legal protection for computer software raises two main concerns:

(a) literal copying defined as direct copying or duplication (e.g. games software, operating systems software and popular applications software);

(b) non-literal copying, usually of bespoke software for a business application (e.g. booking a holiday on the Internet) that is done by creating modified software to emulate the functions and operation carried out by the first software but in a different way.

It is (b) above that is the most troublesome for copyright protection law. The new software may have been created without access to the source code of the first software, but the first software has been relied on in order to gain an understanding of what it does and how it does it. This type of copying is known as non-literal or non-textual copying. It is possible to do this without infringing the copyright in the first computer software, by relying on some of the permitted acts that apply to computer software. However, it is also possible to indirectly infringe the first software's copyright if the infringer appropriates elements of the first computer program not explicitly contained in the first software.

In *Ibcos*, it was found that there were many instances of literal copying, for instance, common spelling mistakes, similar headings, redundant and unexplained bits of code that appeared in both programs; and that the allegedly infringing program contained a part of the original program in its source code while it did not actually use this part. Quantitative and qualitative issues were considered. It was held that substantial copying had occurred in relation to program structure, several individual parts of the computer program and in the file transfer programs.

However, in *Navitaire Inc v EasyJet Airline Company* (2006) (a case involving non-literal copying) the court decided that in certain circumstances there would be no protection for the functionality of a piece of computer software against a new program that set out to emulate it. The facts were that Navitaire had licensed its software for a ticketless booking system to EasyJet since 1996. In 1999, EasyJet asked BulletProof to write a piece of software to perform essentially the same functions as the Navitaire software. The new software system was nearly identical in appearance and function to the Navitaire version. EasyJet was, therefore, no longer dependent on Navitaire for a software licence, upgrades and maintenance. EasyJet could also try to license the new system to third parties in direct competition with Navitaire. Navitaire sued EasyJet for copyright infringement based on:

❖ the substantial similarity between the 'look and feel' and overall functionality of the Navitaire software;

❖ the detailed copying of individual keyboard commands entered by the user to achieve particular results; and

❖ the copying of certain forms of results in the form of screen displays and reports, including icon designs so that the user interface looked the same.

Navitaire failed in its claim for non-literal copying. Curiously, the judge compared the software program to a pudding and explained that a chef who, by trial and error, manages to emulate the pudding does not infringe the copyright in the written version of the recipe. However, Navitaire did succeed with its claim that sufficient skill, labour and judgement had been used to create the Navitaire screen layout and icons and that these had been infringed (as an artistic work). In summary, EasyJet was held to have infringed Navitaire's copyright by reproducing a substantial part of the screen layout, regardless of the fact that the underlying source code was not found to have been copied. The practical effect of this decision was that EasyJet simply had to design new graphic interfaces to replace the infringing screens. The legal effect of the case indicates that the UK courts have little sympathy for a claim by a software owner that the functional effects of their software have been copied where there has been no reproduction of the source code. It is the code that is protected by copyright, not the functioning of the software. Accordingly, the UK position as regards the extent and effectiveness of copyright protection for computer software is currently that copyright protection should not be artificially extended where there is no question of the source code being copied. However, in July 2010 the High Court reconsidered this issue in the case of *SAS Institute Inc v World Programming Ltd* (2010) EWHC 1829 (Ch) and followed the decision in *Navitaire* and *Nova v Mazooma* (2006) EWCA Civ 1044.

THE *SAS* CASE (2010)

In the *SAS* case it was alleged by the claimant (SAS Institute Inc.) that the defendant (World Programming Ltd) had infringed copyright by indirectly copying the programs comprising the various components of its software system. It was also alleged that the defendant had infringed copyright of the claimant's manuals. It was accepted that the defendant had not reproduced the claimant's source code or any of the design elements of the program. The claimant alleged that this still amounted to copyright and based their claim on the interpretation and application of the **Software Directive** under English law. The **Software Directive** was implemented in the UK by the **Copyright (Computer Programs) Regulations 1992 (SI 1992/3233)** which amended the **CDPA 1988**.

Article 1(2) of the Directive provides that the expression in any form of a computer program is protected, but that 'Ideas and principles which underlie any element of a computer program, including those which underlie its interfaces, are not protected by copyright under this Directive.'

Recital 13 of the Directive states that: 'only the expression of a computer program is protected and ... ideas and principles which underlie any element of a program, including those which underlie its interfaces are not protected by copyright under this Directive.' **Recital 14** provides that, in accordance with the principle set out in **recital 13**, 'to the extent that logic, algorithms and programming languages comprise ideas and principles, those ideas and principles are not protected'. **Recitals 13** and **14** have not been incorporated into English law under the **Copyright (Computer Programs) Regulations 1992**.

Justice Arnold upheld the decision in *Navitaire* that **Art 1(2)** should be construed as meaning that copyright in computer programs did not protect either: (1) the functionality of a computer program or its interfaces; or (2) its programming language. He decided that there had been no breach of copyright in this instance. However, this was not the end of the matter as, in light of the claimant's interpretation of the **Software Directive**, the High Court decided to refer nine questions to the European Court of Justice (ECJ) to determine the correct interpretation of the **EU Software Directive** into English law. Until this was done Arnold J was not able to make his judgment.

ECJ REFERRAL

The questions sent to the ECJ include whether programming languages, interfaces and functional aspects of software are excluded from protection under **Art 1(2)** of the **Software Directive** and the extent of the exclusion from infringement for acts of observation and testing under **Art 5(3)** which reads:

> the person having a right to use a copy of a computer program shall be entitled, without the authorisation of the rightholder, to observe, study or test the functioning of the program in order to determine the ideas and principles which underlie any element of the program if he does so while performing any of the acts of loading, displaying, running, transmitting or storing the program which he is entitled to do.

The ECJ identified a number of elements commonly found in computer programs which are not a protectable form of expression, such as a program's functionality, its programming language and the format of its data files. These are merely *elements* of a program as opposed to *expressions* that would enable it to be reproduced and they are thus outside the scope of protection afforded by the **Software Directive**. It also confirmed that a user does not infringe the copyright in a program by doing any of these acts that are either permitted under his licence or are necessary to use the program.

Finally, the ECJ held that the reproduction, in a computer program or a user manual for that program, of certain elements contained within a program *could* amount to a copyright infringement if that manual reflected an expression of intellectual creation by the author. However, because keywords, syntax, commands, options, defaults and iterations consist only of words, figures or mathematical concepts, they are not by themselves eligible for copyright protection.

The ECJ's reasoning indicates that copyright protection will not be granted under the **Software Directive** to anything other than a program's lines of code. The decision appears to be pro-competition as it means that software proprietors cannot prevent their licensees from observing and studying the licensed program in order to find out its underlying ideas and principles, and then expressing their own 'intellectual creativity'. This entitlement cannot be excluded by contract provided that the source and object code is not reproduced, the acts are covered by the licence and this so-called 'reverse engineering' is necessary for the use of the program.

As a result, on 25 January 2013 a decision was finally issued in the *SAS* case on referral back to the UK's High Court. Justice Arnold endorsed his initial judgment which he felt had been supported by the ECJ. In summary, in both *Navitaire* and *Nova*, the UK courts held that copyright in computer programs does not extend to the functionality, interfaces or programming language of a computer program. Therefore, developing a computer program that has the same or similar functionality and interfaces of another computer program would not amount to copyright infringement, but copying the underlying software code would.

The current position that copyright only protects the underlying source code of a computer program and not its functionality and interfaces continues to apply. In the UK, the access plus similarity test continues to have weight. Any infringement will still be assessed by applying the traditional substantial similarity test, following an analysis that copyright in the software program subsists. Maintaining the conventional legal test of substantial copying keeps the copyright infringement framework simple, supporting the concept of legal certainty in the copyright field, which is helpful in terms of uniformity in the effectiveness of copyright enforcement. For the software industry as a whole, the area of law involving protecting computer programs with copyright is now far more certain.

Common Pitfalls

Avoid computer technology jargon and focus on a legal analysis of the nature of copyright law protection afforded to computer software programs as a literary work.

Aim Higher

Critically discuss the impact of the developing case law on the scope of copyright protection of computer software and whether this development converges with the copyright protection of other literary works.

QUESTION 14

How does copyright law protect technological protection measures (TPMs) and has such protection adversely affected access to digital works?

How to Read this Question
Although this is a copyright question, it is narrowly focused and requires a good understanding of the issues relating to digital copyright and the practical measures copyright owners put in place to limit unauthorised user access.

How to Answer this Question
It will be important for students to explain the term 'technological protection measures' (TPMs) in the context of digital works at the outset of the answer, before addressing user ability to access (open, retrieve, use etc.) digital works.

Answer Structure

This question needs to be answered in two parts. First, by establishing the current protection regime and then critically analysing the beneficial and detrimental aspects of the legal protection afforded to TPMs.

- ❖ **WIPO Copyright Treaty** and **WIPO Performers and Phonograms Treaty**;
- ❖ **Part VII CDPA 1988**; devices designed to circumvent copy-protection;
- ❖ TPMs and computer programs;
- ❖ copyright infringement;
- ❖ *Sony Computer Entertainment Inc v Edmunds* (2002);
- ❖ *Sony v Ball* (2004);
- ❖ defences and exceptions (**s 296ZE CDPA 1988**);
- ❖ remedies.

Up for Debate

Technological protection measures (TPMS), also known as digital locks, are controversial. Access to copyright material in legitimate cases, but which is prevented by TPMs, is an increasingly important legal issue that arises in the public interest especially in relation to education purposes and access to knowledge.

ANSWER

With the introduction of legal protection for technological protection measures (TPMs), the WIPO Treaties created a unique new way of protecting copyright works as new digital and Internet-based uses continue to emerge. A TPM in the field of computer technology is a system put in place by the owner of copyright material designed to reduce access to and therefore the ability to copy a work. It is an additional form of copyright protection that exists in the digital environment. In other words, the law grants specific copyright protection for TPMs (that use software or hardware) as a result of **Art 6(3)** under **Directive 2001 29 EC**, known as the Information Society Directive. Note, however, that the **Copyright, Designs and Patents Act 1988 (CDPA 1988)** does not include regional coding on DVDs or computer programs in its definition of an access control TPM. TPMs are most commonly used on electronic literary works (e-books).

The various forms of TPMs act as technological barriers to control access to a work. A common way of controlling access is encrypting or scrambling the content. The user will receive the data but must unlock or provide proof of authorisation by way of a password to make the information useable. Other types of TPMs include digital watermarking and digital fingerprinting which impair the quality of the copies made. **Section 296(4) CDPA 1988** defines copy-protection to include any device or means intended to prevent or restrict copyright of a work or to impair the quality of copies made. Bypassing a TPM is an offence in addition to any copyright infringement that has taken place.

As it stands, the use of TPMs is part of the exercise of the copyright owner's rights and is also important for consumers. According to the World Intellectual Property Organization (WIPO), their use helps to deter piracy, encourage copyright owners to use new media such as the Internet and provide consumers with new ways of enjoying copyright works, but only if TPMs are meaningfully protected. The **WIPO Copyright Treaty (WCT)** and **WIPO Performances and Phonograms Treaty (WPPT)** require adequate protection and effective legal remedies against the circumvention of TPMs applied to protected works and phonograms (**WCT Art 11** and **WPPT Art 18**).

If a copyright work such as a computer program includes a TPM and the TPM is unlawfully circumvented, this may result in civil liability or criminal prosecution. It is the copy-protection techniques designed to prevent or restrict unauthorised acts in relation to copyright works that are protected by copyright law. Circumvention devices, such as pirate decoders, also must be controlled if they are primarily designed or adapted to circumvent TPMs. The law does this by providing a range of remedies. There are civil remedies against:

❖   the act of circumvention itself (**CDPA 1988, s 296(2)**);
❖   making and dealing in circumvention devices (**CDPA 1988, s 296ZA(3)**); and
❖   the provision of circumvention services (**CDPA 1988, s 296ZD**).

In order to remove illicit devices from circulation there are remedies that allow for their delivery up and seizure. There are also criminal sanctions against making and dealing in circumvention devices and the provision of circumvention services (**CDPA 1988, s 296ZB**).

CIRCUMVENTION OF TECHNICAL DEVICES RELATING TO COMPUTER PROGRAMS

Section 296 of the **CDPA 1988** deals with the circumvention of technical devices relating to computer programs separately from the circumvention of TPMs applied to other copyright works (**CDPA 1988, ss 296ZA–ZF**). The first important case in this complex area of copyright is *Sony Computer Entertainment Inc v Edmunds* (2002), which interpreted the un-amended **s 296**. The facts of the case were that Sony produced PlayStation 2 computer game consoles. CDs and DVDs made for use with the consoles carried authorisation codes. These elements of encrypted data also allowed Sony to prevent games bought from one area of distribution being used in a different region. The defendant imported a 'modchip' (Messiah 2) which bypassed the authorisation process. The defendant argued that as the chips had legitimate uses, they had not been 'specifically designed or adapted to circumvent the form of copy-protection employed', as **s 296** then provided. The court rejected this argument and held that having other uses did not prevent a device being 'adapted to circumvent'.

The law was further developed in *Sony v Ball* (2004), which interpreted the new wording of **s 296**. This case was brought on the same facts, but against different resellers of the hardware. Videogame console manufacturers commonly build technical 'locks' into their console hardware to stop console owners running 'unauthorised' software. Publishers of licensed software must include in their game discs or cartridges the correct encrypted key in order for that software to run on consoles. Modchips are devices, which can either be fixed to standard consoles internally or externally, that effectively disable those 'locks' allowing any software to run on the console. The 'unauthorised software' which modchips enable could be: pirated software; legitimate, but unlicensed, 'homebrew' software; or, software legitimately published in another territorial region.

It was held that the modchips continued to infringe Sony's copyright. Laddie J held that the 'sole intended purpose' of the Messiah 2 modchip was to circumvent Sony's copy-protection.

TPMS AND ACCESS TO DIGITAL WORKS

There is continuing debate as to whether TPMs will lead to excessive restrictions on access to works or even public domain materials. There are fears that TPMs have the effect of 'locking up knowledge'. Many library and documentation associations support the notion of free access to information, including digital information. Such organisations stress the importance of equality of access to information and education in British society. For example, the novel *Pride and Prejudice* by Jane Austen is in the public domain and no longer protected by copyright. Copyright law would not prohibit free copying of this work, but a TPM would. The public domain is meant to be the global library of knowledge and with each year that passes, its catalogue increases as copyright expires and more works pass into the public domain. If TPM technology can be used to prevent access, there is a risk of perpetual monopoly rights, leading to intellectual stagnation and reduced public education.

CONSUMERS AND TPMS

Other problems involving the use of TPMs are that they are said to reduce the functionality of copyright works, in that some forms of TPM prevent compact discs from being played on a computer. Access to digital works arises in connection with the distribution of free software, damage caused by TPMs to the overall security of a computer system, and reduced interoperability in computer systems – all of which affect consumers – are also being debated. Copyright owners employing the TPMs to protect their work from being copied still have a responsibility to properly label and use the TPMs sensibly.

PERMITTED ACTS AND THE S 296ZE MECHANISM

Section 296ZE CDPA 1988 provides a remedy where a TPM prevents a permitted act. The section creates a mechanism for the Secretary of State to intervene where permitted acts appear to have been prejudiced. This mechanism relies on a person or personal representative of a class issuing a notice of complaint to the Secretary of State. The Secretary of State may then issue directions to the owner of the copyright work to permit access to the copyright work. However, this mechanism is an impractical method of obtaining access (which should be lawful in the first place) and it is unlikely to be used widely by the public.

ECJ'S 2014 DECISION IN *NINTENDO V PC BOX*

The Court of Justice of the European Union handed down its judgment in Case C-355/12 *Nintendo v PC Box* on 23 January 2014. It is the first of two cases concerning the legality of modchips for videogames consoles to come before the Court (Case C-458 remains pending). The judgment does not finally decide on the legality of modchips, rather it sets out the factors that courts across Europe should address when deciding on an individual device's legality.

Nintendo brought proceedings in Milan against PC Box on the grounds that they marketed devices which circumvented the TPMs in Nintendo consoles. In its defence PC Box argued that Nintendo's purpose was not to protect copyright works, but to prevent the use of independent software which enabled users to 'fully use' their consoles; by, for instance, playing music or video files. The first question the ECJ had to decide was whether a videogame fell within the **Copyright Directive** or the, rather more liberal, **Computer Program Directive** (Directive 2009/24). The ECJ held that videogames:

> constitute complex matter comprising not only a computer program but also graphic and sound elements, which, although encrypted in computer language, have a unique creative value which cannot be reduced to that encryption. In so far as the parts of a videogame, in this case, the graphic and sound elements, are part of its originality, they are protected, together with the entire work, by copyright.

As a result, it is clear that a videogame is a single whole protected by copyright. It is therefore legitimate for the copyright holder to deploy TPMs to protect their work. Further, the ECJ clarified that the owner of the console should be permitted to make any use of the console they wish, and could only be restricted by a TPM when it is necessary to do so to protect copyright works. This creates an interesting challenge for platform owners, such as Nintendo who seek to 'lock down' their platform to support their business model and guarantee revenue streams. They will only be able to defend a TPM when it is clearly necessary to protect copyright works. The more a TPM restricts the user, the more likely it will potentially be seen as a disproportionate restriction. If a TPM system goes too far they may continue to be a technical barrier, but they will no longer be given legal protection.

Finally, the law has never granted copyright owners an absolute monopoly. The law attempts to strike a balance between granting a certain level of protection while at the same time providing a certain level of access and use. The law needs to protect the public against the use of TPMs that prevent lawful access to digital works. Nevertheless, the starting point is that EU and UK law protects copyright owners who use TPMs to protect their copyright works, and bypassing such technology is illegal unless one can rely on one of the exceptions to copyright infringement (fair dealing defences) in the **CDPA 1988**.

Common Pitfalls

Avoid technical jargon and write in plain English to describe the meaning and technical effect of a technical protection measure (TPM) in relation to computer software. In terms of the structure of your answer, good starting points are either the **WIPO Treaty** or s 296 of the **CDPA 1988** followed by a detailed discussion of the key case law.

Aim Higher

Students will gain marks by giving a thorough discussion of the relevant case law which interprets and applies **s 296 CDPA** and this includes decisions of the ECJ. Think about the stakeholders with respect to this issue and in particular the public versus private interests.

QUESTION 15

Jancie is an English literature graduate who recently established a vibrant high-quality content blog called 'What Jancie Did Next', to help her find her own voice, develop her writing skills and create a platform to showcase her work relating to travel, festivals, beauty and fashion. Within a couple of months of operation her website attracted readers from all around the world. These 150,000-plus visitors mainly live in the UK, Canada and Australia. Recently, the blog featured in other websites and social media including the BBC and ITV. Jancie designed the blog, writes the blog posts and takes the photographs she uses to illustrate her website. Her readers comment on her posts and she interacts by responding and furthering the discussion, offering her insight and advice. She is becoming a local celebrity. In light of her meteoric success, Jancie wishes to develop her business plan to ensure that she maximises the passive income she is able to earn from her blog, but is not sure what legal rights she owns.

▶ **Advise Jancie as to any intellectual property rights issues arising.**

How to Read this Question

This question concerns intellectual property for interactive media and protecting the fusion between creativity and technology that is now a feature of web-logs (blogs) in the digital environment. It asks the student to identify the variety of intellectual property (IP) rights that may apply to the blog that Jancie owns and can commercially exploit to earn a passive income.

How to Answer this Question

Identify each potential IP-protected element in the blog and then apply the relevant IP law in turn to determine the extent of intellectual property that subsists and is capable of ownership.

Answer Structure

❖ subsistence of copyright in literary and artistic works;
❖ protection of the blog name and logo; and
❖ personality and image rights.

Applying the Law

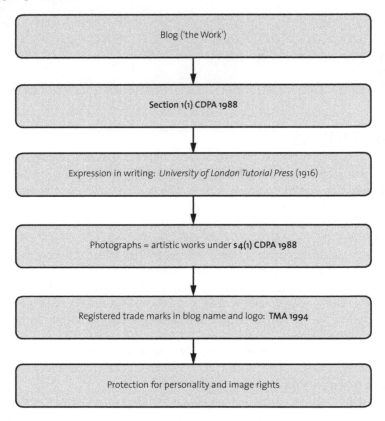

Blog ('the Work')

Section 1(1) CDPA 1988

Expression in writing: *University of London Tutorial Press* (1916)

Photographs = artistic works under **s 4(1) CDPA 1988**

Registered trade marks in blog name and logo: **TMA 1994**

Protection for personality and image rights

ANSWER

Interactive media, where cutting-edge creativity meets technology, is the fastest-growing creative content sector in the world. Intellectual property is at the heart of the interactive media business involving websites and web-logs (blogs). As Jancie is creating work in this field, she needs specific information regarding the various intellectual property (IP) rights that protect her work.

Interactive media means products and services on digital computer-based systems which respond to user actions by presenting creative content such as text, graphics, animation, video and audio. However, many interactive media developers, such as Jancie, are unaware of the legal and commercial implications of intellectual property when they create and publish content. It is essential for Jancie to understand the importance of IP rights when negotiating the terms of any contracts, as this determines ownership of the creative content. As Jancie is involved in the digital rights ecosystem she needs to ensure that appropriate IP protection is in place so that she is able to financially benefit from her work.

In effect, Jancie is a content developer who has conceptualised and realised (i.e. created) an interactive media project using the World Wide Web as the hardware platform and leading to a variety of commercially significant IP rights. These may include copyright and derivative works, moral rights, image and personality rights, trade marks and branding.

Initially, in respect of the online publishing platform for the blog, Jancie should review the terms and conditions of the blog-hosting site she uses to ensure that she has not waived her rights or rescinded ownership of her intangible work.

In terms of IP rights, Jancie has designed the look and feel of her blog, given it a name ('What Jancie Did Next'), written the posts and uploaded her digital photographic images. She has learned that every post looks better when accompanied by an image. Every blog is packed with IP-protected creative content including the text, the imagery, the layout and the name and logo for her brand. Each of these components attracts IP rights that Jancie owns.

Copyright protection which is governed by the **Copyright, Designs and Patents Act 1988** (**CDPA 1988**) is the most important form of legal protection for creative content. When Jancie writes a blog post she instantly creates a literary work: **s 3(1) CDPA 1988** as it will have met the requirements of the Act in that she has exercised skill, labour and judgement and has not copied it from elsewhere: *London University Tutorial Press* (1916). What copyright protects is not the idea for the blog but the particular form of language by which Jancie conveys information: *Donoghue v Allied Newspapers* (1938). As first creator and owner, Jancie has the exclusive right to reproduce, distribute, perform, broadcast, include in a cable programme and adapt her work: **s 16 CDPA 1988**. Her rights will last for her lifetime plus a further 70 years after her death. However, if a reader responds to a blog with a written comment, this is a separate literary work which attracts its own copyright. Jancie will not own these reader posts unless she makes it clear in the terms and conditions of accessing and posting on her blog that the reader agrees to assign Jancie the copyright in the post.

Similarly, her still image digital photos will be protected as artistic works under the Act: **s 4(1)**. To be protected by copyright, the photos must represent Jancie's intellectual creation and show at least a small degree of mental effort. There is no need to register copyright in the UK, it is free and automatic as soon as the work comes into existence and meets the requirements of the Act. In the digital environment, due to search engines, it is possible for people to see Jancie's images and pictures without the need to even visit her blog. To avoid this happening, Jancie could give each image she uses a random, numeric file name so that they cannot easily come up in the search engine results. In addition, she should digitally watermark each photo and link it to her blog. Copyright in a photo protects the photographer from their work being either directly copied (cut and pasted into another website) or indirectly copied (a substantial part reproduced). Jancie could periodically use tools like Google and TinEye to check the web to see if her images are being unlawfully used by others.

Fortunately, Jancie is using photographs she has taken herself. However, if in the future she does not create all the blog content herself, in other words, if she has used a substantial part of any third-party intellectual property, she will need to obtain the owners' permission and perhaps pay a reasonable licence fee for the privilege. It does not matter if Jancie gives attribution to the creator or links back to the creator's website, it is not fair use to use an entire image or substantial part of a literary work. It will not matter if an image is not full-size, nor if Jancie added commentary to the image or did not make money from it. The only way Jancie could be absolved of liability for copyright infringement is to get express permission from the copyright owner. Jancie could, however, use images that are subject to a creative commons licence and available for use for free. **Creative Commons** is a non-profit organisation that enables the sharing and use of *creativity* and knowledge through free legal tools such as copyright licences, providing a simple, standardised way to give the public permission to share and use *creative* work.

If, on the other hand, Jancie has merely used an insubstantial part of someone else's work, she may rely on the right to quote fair dealing defence, as long as she acknowledges the sources and gives attribution to the creator. Within the blogging community, bloggers adopt the etiquette of always attributing sources and the works of other writers, which is a good practice.

As the creator of literary and artistic works, Jancie will also have moral rights under the **CDPA 1988** which are personal to her, which she will have to assert in writing on her blog page. These include the right to paternity (**ss 77–79**) and the right of integrity (**ss 80–83**), which will last for the same period as the relevant copyright.

There is no global trade mark registration system and Jancie's brand protection strategy will depend on where her readers are located. The name of her blog, 'What Jancie Did Next' and her logo may be registrable as trade marks under the **Trade Marks Act 1994** (**TMA 1994**) in the UK, and equivalent legislation in Canada and Australia, to distinguish her blog from competing blogs. To be registrable, a trade mark must be distinctive and non-descriptive of the goods or services Jancie offers: **s 3(1)(b) TMA 1994**. A registered trade mark would give Jancie comfort knowing that no one else can lawfully use or trade on her blog name or logo without her permission. Owning a strong brand may help Jancie to market her blog, develop a loyal readership and lead to the option to license merchandise that she could sell online via her blog and enter the world of e-commerce.

In England and Wales, even though legal protection for image and personality rights does not exist per se, there is still a variety of laws that could be relevant to Jancie to protect her personal image rights. For example, the common law tort of passing off could apply if there was an impression of false endorsement by including Jancie's likeness in a way that would lead people to think she was endorsing a product when she has not given her permission. Likewise, Jancie should tread carefully when using someone else's image in her blog without their permission. As Jancie has a new celebrity status, she could consider registering her name and likeness as a trade mark under the **TMA 1994**.

In conclusion, Jancie is on her way from being a casual blogger to a professional blogger and is on a steep learning curve in terms of IP rights. There are two distinct ways that knowing what IP rights she owns will assist Jancie. First, copyright law will protect Jancie's blog content from being used without her permission. Second, she will be able to rely on her IP rights to commercially exploit her IP rights to generate revenue by, for example, entering into licensing agreements or selling goods or services online.

Common Pitfalls

Do not limit the discussion solely to copyright protection, as a blog attracts a variety of IP rights that protect different elements and aspects.

Aim Higher

It is important to advise Jancie as to intellectual property that she does not own, such as comments made by readers, and that she must take care not to infringe third-party intellectual property. The growth of the Internet has raised the level of exposure to copyright issues via linking, caching and framing, as well as unauthorised use of third-party content. Jancie will have to develop internal processes to minimise her risk.

QUESTION 16

An arcade game developer, Nemo, is concerned that a competitor, Zuma, has copied the look and feel of its skill-based coin-operated video arcade game *Easy Cash*, in which players could win cash prizes. Zuma has come up with its own game, called *Top Prize*, which also provides the opportunity for players to win cash prizes. Neither game includes a dramatic work, story or characters. Nemo is not sure where to begin in terms of analysing whether Zuma has copied software and other elements of the look and feel of *Easy Cash*. The Managing Director says he has spent in excess of £2 million on developing *Easy Cash* and wants to know what he owns and what he can do to stop Zuma.

How to Read this Question

Although this is a problem-style question, it is light on facts as between the similar elements between the two video arcade games. This invites the student to discuss the issue of videogame infringement issues more generally. This could potentially involve a rich variety of intellectual property (IP) issues including copyright, trade mark and patent law. The aim is to familiarise students with IP principles and methods as they apply to a particular type of creative digital work, the videogame.

How to Answer this Question

It is important to identify the elements of a videogame that are likely to attract IP protection. Students may recognise that the facts of the problem are similar to those in the case of *Nova Productions v Mazooma Games* (2009) EWCA Civ 219. It would be helpful for students to highlight this decision and discuss aspects of the judgment in their answer. Set out the relevant IP law principles that apply and explore how they may apply to interactive digital works, rather than try to resolve unambiguously whether there has been copying in this instance.

Applying the Law

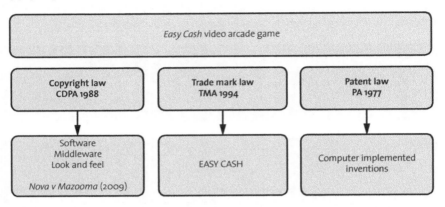

Easy Cash video arcade game

| Copyright law | Trade mark law | Patent law |
| CDPA 1988 | TMA 1994 | PA 1977 |

| Software Middleware Look and feel | EASY CASH | Computer implemented inventions |
| *Nova v Mazooma* (2009) | | |

Up for Debate

Interactive media, such as videogames, is the fastest-growing creative content sector in the world. However, knowledge of how IP rights protect this kind of work is less well understood. Are they software programs or audio-visual works? Some jurisdictions such as Canada, Israel, Italy, Russia and Singapore classify videogames as functional software with a graphic interface. Others such as the US, Japan, Germany, Sweden, Denmark and Belgium take a more pragmatic approach and protect each creative element of the game separately, depending on its nature. Korea and Kenya treat videogames simply as audio-visual works. Currently, there is no uniform international approach to IP protection for videogames. In reality, videogames are complex and a variety of IP rights arise to cover different elements of the work. Videogames are expensive to make, but relatively easy to copy. Copying and videogame piracy is a common problem in this industry. As a result, there is a heightened interest in policy formulation in the field of IP law and whether the law needs to be better shaped to protect videogames, a valuable sector within the digital creative economy. Is a rethink in relation to IP protection for videogames needed?

ANSWER

Nemo has developed *Easy Cash*, a popular and commercially successful video arcade game. As with any successful work it is at risk of being copied as others seek to benefit from the work without having to undertake the expensive and lengthy product development process. It is important for Nemo to understand the intellectual property it owns so that it can determine its enforcement strategy and how it deals with competitors such as Zuma, a company that Nemo alleges has used the look and feel of *Easy Cash* without its permission. However, the types of intellectual property (IP) right applicable to a videogame are not always immediately obvious, given the multilayered creative content that constitutes the end product. The potential IP rights most commonly involved in a videogame include the game design (an ordered sequence of events in designated order); copyright in the software, text, imagery, sound, audio, music and film as literary and artistic works under the **Copyright, Designs and Patents Act 1988** (**CDPA 1988**). There are potential trade mark rights in the game title, *Easy Cash*. In addition, patent law may protect any technological inventions Nemo has developed and the equitable doctrine of confidential information may protect Nemo's know-how. Each of these key forms of IP protection for *Easy Cash* and the allegedly infringing *Top Prize* video arcade game will be discussed in turn below.

COPYRIGHT PROTECTION FOR *EASY CASH*

Legal action against videogame developers typically focuses on copyright infringement. This is because **Art 2** of the **Berne Convention** provides a legal basis for the protection of videogames as copyright works (literary and artistic) and the **Software Directive 1991** makes it clear that copyright can subsist in a software program. As with traditional copyright law principles, the underlying idea for cash-prize games is not protected; rather it is the expression or representation of that idea that is protected: **Art 2 Agreement on Trade Related Aspects of Intellectual Property Rights**. The challenge of drawing this all-important distinction is important, as is considering the case law that has examined the legal nature of this distinction. The legal position is clear – Nemo does not own the right to the idea for an arcade video cash-prize game.

What about the software Nemo used to create the *Easy Cash* videogame? At present, firms such as Nemo typically do not create software, rather they license in the use of 'middleware' (third-party-created and -tested software) as the technical basis for the game. Therefore, only a small proportion of the code Nemo used would have been customised to develop the *Easy Cash* game. This makes the game development process less expensive and more efficient. Accordingly, many games will share the same source code. The distinctive elements of each game are created through 'code customisation' and creative audio-visual elements resulting in literary and artistic works.

On the facts the videogame concept is similar, but the legal question is whether the later work, Zuma's *Top Prize*, is substantially similar so as to infringe, leading to a court order for damages or an account of profits. In a case on point, *Nova Productions v Mazooma Games* (2007) EWCA Civ 219, Justice Kitchin carefully evaluated features of the game alleged to have been copied. He found that although Mazooma had copied certain features, these were at a high level of generalisation or abstraction and had no meaningful connection with the artistic nature of the Nova original. He determined that no exact code or architecture had been substantially copied and only generalised ideas had been used. He decided that many of the comparable features were obvious, commonplace or functional, but not substantial. In arriving at this decision, Kitchin J relied on *Navitaire Inc. v EasyJet Airline Company* (2004), which has been endorsed by the ECJ in Case C-355//12 *Nintendo v PC Box* on 23 January 2014. In the end, Justice Kitchin concluded that Mazooma's game was the subject of considerable independent creative effort. This case demonstrates that software using only generalised ideas of an earlier program or game is not enough to infringe copyright. Applying this case to Nemo, the company and its advisers will be in a better position, first, to carefully evaluate each element of the *Easy Cash* videogame to confirm whether copyright subsists. This will enable Nemo to gauge whether literal or non-literal copying of the software (literary work) has taken place, and whether the copying is substantial, bearing in mind that Zuma may have permission to use the same middleware. This detailed evaluation will be necessary to confirm whether any reproduction has occurred.

In terms of the look and feel of Nemo's *Easy Cash* game, this gives rises to an artistic works infringement claim. In the *Nova* case, the court accepted that frames of the game could be works capable of copyright protection. A court would need to assess whether the visual appearance of the games are similar. We are told that the look and feel is similar, so if the court finds substantial similarity Zuma may be held to have infringed the artistic works inherent in the visual identity of the *Easy Cash* videogame: **s 4(1)** and **s 16 CDPA 1988**.

TRADE MARK PROTECTION FOR *EASY CASH*

We are not told whether Nemo has registered the name *Easy Cash* for its video arcade game. If not, it should take steps to register the mark under the **Trade Marks Act 1994 (TMA 1994)** or as a **Community Trade Mark (CTM)** for pan-European trade mark protection. This is an important part of protecting the brand which will be a key value driver to enhance the commercial success of the game and is preferable to relying on the common law tort of passing off.

One of the central legal arguments in a trade mark case is confusion in the mind of the public. However, it is clear that the names *Easy Cash* and *Top Prize* for the video arcade games are unlikely to give rise to trade mark infringement as there is no aural, visual or conceptual similarity or likelihood of confusion. **Section 10(2)** of the **TM 1994** provides that an infringement occurs where there is use of an identical or similar sign for similar goods or services, or a similar sign for identical goods or services, if there is a likelihood of confusion. Confusion must be as to the trade origin of the goods.

PATENTS AND CONFIDENTIAL INFORMATION

Videogames draw on the worlds of both technology and creativity. Patent protection for computer technology hardware is possible under the **Patents Act 1977 (PA 1977)**. A computer-implemented invention is one which involves the use of a computer, computer network or other programmable apparatus, where one or more features are realised wholly or partly by means of a computer program. Under the **European Patent Convention (EPC)**, a computer program claimed 'as such' is not a patentable invention: **Arts 52(2)(c)** and **(3)**. Patents are not granted merely for software programs. Software 'as such' is protected by the law of copyright. For a patent to be granted for a computer-implemented invention, a technical problem has to be solved in a novel and non-obvious manner. In the UK patents are granted for computer-implemented inventions that comply with strict criteria on patentability laid down in **s1** of the **PA 1977**. If Nemo has solved a technical problem through the creation of its video arcade game software this may be potentially patentable. However, it is a strict legal requirement that the invention is new and has not been disclosed anywhere in the world: **s1(a) PA 1977**. In other words, if Nemo has disclosed its computer-implemented invention to the public, it will not be eligible for patent protection under the Act.

In the analysis, reliance on trade mark law is unlikely and reliance on patent law will depend on whether Nemo has created a computer-implemented invention. With respect to copyright protection for Nemo's *Easy Cash* game, the position of the English courts to date is that it is not an infringement of the copyright of a computer program to replicate its functionality without copying its source code or design. This involves a subtractive approach which begins by looking at the whole work and then takes it apart element by element. After separating out the protectable elements from the unprotected, the court considers whether the protectable parts are substantially similar. This approach would tend to favour Zuma, the alleged infringer. If Nemo has licensed in middleware, it must prove on the balance of probabilities that any new 'customised' software program elements have been substantially copied by Zuma: *Infopaq International* (2009) ECJ. However, the courts in *Nova Productions v Mazooma* (2009) recognised that copyright law could apply to the look and feel of computer software. This might involve the look and feel approach whereby the court doesn't dissect a work into protected and unprotected; rather, it reasons that a work should be looked at as a combination of its parts. A legal issue that remains untested is whether a computer game with a dramatic narrative would be protected as a dramatic work, although this is expressly excluded on the facts. There appears to be no reason why a computer game involving a dramatic narrative should be treated differently from a traditional literary or dramatic work. However, whether the dramatic narrative of a videogame would have sufficient unity and certainty to make it capable of reproduction given the unpredictability of user actions has not yet been judicially considered. In conclusion, even though IP rights are the lifeblood of the gaming industry, proving Zuma's *Top Prize* video arcade game infringes Nemo's *Easy Cash* game will be an uphill battle.

Common Pitfalls

Effective time management can be critical. Although the student needs to discuss copyright, trade mark and patent law, in this problem question it is reasonable to spend more time evaluating the issue of copyright protection for a videogame.

Aim Higher

Demonstrate in-depth knowledge of IP law by considering the boundaries of IP protection as it applies to a videogame. Critically discuss how court decisions have affected the videogame industry and whether the law adequately protects the look and feel of a videogame.

5 Design Right and Registered Designs

Designs play a vital role in marketing and consumer choice. Considerable resources and expense go into creating design features that provide a competitive edge in the marketplace. Many products are neither inventive nor constitute copyright works, but are marketed with features that have an artistic, aesthetic value. It is these features, either of appearance or arrangement of a commercially exploited article, which are the subject of design protection. Accordingly, legal protection for design falls between copyright and patent law. Examples of products which fall into the design sphere include jewellery, textiles, white goods, sunglasses, cars, aircraft. Design law protects the appearance of an article, not its function (the way it works).

Traditionally, intellectual property (IP) rights in designs have been regarded as the least important IP right after copyright, patents and trade marks. However, this perception is changing. First, commercial designs are gaining considerable economic importance in the marketplace. Second, as a result of the implementation of new design laws, the level of legal protection afforded to designs has increased. Finally, the owners of registered design and unregistered design rights appear to be more active in enforcing their rights through the courts.

UK design law legislation is over 200 years old. Currently, designs are protected via a combination of a system of:

❖ registered designs under the **Registered Designs Act 1949** (as amended);
❖ unregistered 'design right' under **Part III** of the **Copyright, Designs and Patents Act 1988 (CDPA 1988)**; and
❖ a residual role for copyright protection under the **CDPA 1988**.

Designs that meet the requirements of the **Registered Designs Act 1949** (as amended) may be registered at the Designs Registry, part of the UK Intellectual Property Office (UKIPO). Owners of new registered designs that have 'distinctive character' acquire a monopoly over making products with the same appearance. Knowledge of design law will provide an appreciation of the choices available to a designer who wishes to acquire protection for the appearance of an article under UK law or in the EU. European Community design law will not be covered separately as the principles are harmonised at the EU level. However, note that an application for a registered design that will cover the whole of the EU should be made at the Office for Harmonization in the Internal Market (OHIM).

QUESTION 17

Prosthetics UK Ltd have designed a new flesh-coloured breast prosthesis with a silky soft texture to assist breast cancer sufferers following surgery. In creating the design, the shape of the breast prosthesis was influenced but not dictated by the shape of a bra and would have fitted a number of different bras. The company seeks your advice on legal protection for the design.

▶ **Advise Prosthetics UK Ltd as to the registrability of the design or any other protection that may be available for the breast prosthesis design.**

How to Read this Question

This problem concerns the application of design law principles to a new article and is based on the unreported case of *Amoena (UK) Ltd v Trulife Ltd* (1996) IPD19006.

How to Answer this Question

Students need to identify the relevant forms of design protection that will best apply to protect the new 3-D breast prosthesis. These are registered and unregistered design.

Applying the Law

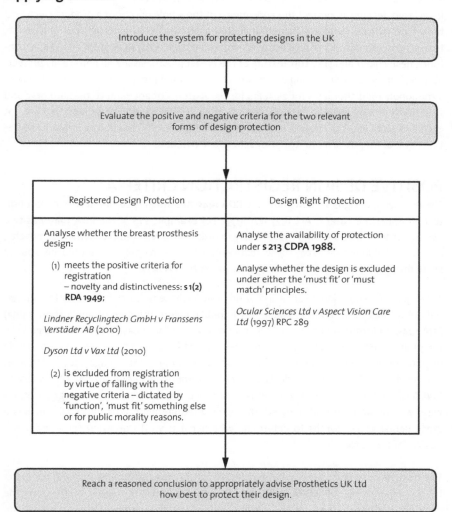

Introduce the system for protecting designs in the UK

Evaluate the positive and negative criteria for the two relevant forms of design protection

Registered Design Protection	Design Right Protection
Analyse whether the breast prosthesis design: (1) meets the positive criteria for registration – novelty and distinctiveness: **s 1(2) RDA 1949**; *Lindner Recyclingtech GmbH v Franssens Verstäder AB* (2010) *Dyson Ltd v Vax Ltd* (2010) (2) is excluded from registration by virtue of falling with the negative criteria – dictated by 'function', 'must fit' something else or for public morality reasons.	Analyse the availability of protection under **s 213 CDPA 1988.** Analyse whether the design is excluded under either the 'must fit' or 'must match' principles. *Ocular Sciences Ltd v Aspect Vision Care Ltd* (1997) RPC 289

Reach a reasoned conclusion to appropriately advise Prosthetics UK Ltd how best to protect their design.

ANSWER

The nature of design law is that it exists to protect the appearance of articles such as the breast prosthesis rather than the article itself and how it functions. There are two key forms of design protection to be considered in relation to protecting the breast prosthesis design from unauthorised copying. The principal means available under UK law to protect the appearance of a product is registration under the **Registered Designs Act 1949** (**RDA 1949**) or the unregistered design right under the **Copyright, Designs and Patents Act 1988** (**CDPA 1988**). Determining the best form of protection for the new breast prosthesis will depend on the nature of the product and whether the legal requirements under the respective legislation are met.

PROTECTION AS A REGISTERED DESIGN

Registered design can protect the appearance of the whole or part of a product, such as a breast prosthesis, resulting from the features of the lines, contours, colours, shape, texture or materials of the product or its ornamentation: **s1(2) RDA 1949**. The shape, contours, flesh colour and silky soft texture of the breast prosthesis are all potentially protectable design features. Obtaining a registered design would provide Prosthetics UK Ltd with a monopoly right that lasts for 25 years for the features of appearance that are new and give a different overall impression to an informed user (positive criteria), and that are not excluded from legal protection because they are dictated by function, or must fit something else or for public morality reasons (negative criteria).

POSITIVE DESIGN REGISTRATION CRITERIA

The registered designs system under the **RDA 1949** has much in common with patent protection under the **Patents Act 1977 (PA 1977)**. For example, **s1B** of the **RDA 1949** has two positive criteria that a design must satisfy in order to be registerable, namely (1) novelty; and (2) individual character. These requirements are separate and should be applied sequentially, like novelty and inventive step under the **PA 1977**.

A design is new if no identical design or no design whose features differ only in immaterial details has been made available to the public before the date of application: **s1B(2) RDA 1949**. Determining novelty will involve comparing the breast prosthesis design with the prior art features of appearance in other products in the sector potentially worldwide or photographic representations of them in, for example, trade magazines, catalogues and brochures: *Green Lane Products Ltd v PMS International Group Ltd and others* (2008) EWCA Civ 358. As the breast prosthesis is new and there are no facts to suggest otherwise, we will assume that it meets the novelty requirement. Prosthetics UK Ltd has a grace period of 12 months to determine whether it is worth applying for a registered design for their product.

The next issue to consider is whether the breast prosthesis also has individual character as required by **s1B CDPA 1988**, taking into account the degree of freedom the designer had when creating the design. Individual character involves a comparison between the prior art and the registered design, through the eyes of an informed user. According to Jacob LJ in the Court of Appeal, this comparison is broader and less precise, leaving the court with a considerable margin for judgment: *The Procter & Gamble Company v Reckitt Benckiser (UK) Ltd* (2007) at [34]. Here we have no specific factual information on whether the breast prosthesis has the required degree of individual character but would advise Prosthesis UK Ltd that the UKIPO's Design Examiner will compare it to other designs taking into account the nature of the product and the relevant industrial sector to ensure that the impression on the informed user is sufficiently different: *LengD'Or SA v Crown Confectionery Co Ltd (OHIM Ref ICD 000000370, 23 February 2005)*. The 'informed user' is a customer for the products who is 'interested in the products concerned and shows a relatively high degree of attention when using them': see *Grupo Promer Mon Graphic SA v OHIM* (2012) CJEU. In terms of design freedom, small details can be significant if they help the product to look good and work well. The flesh colour and silky smooth texture may uniquely provide the breast prosthesis with individual character.

In summary, the breast prosthesis design must satisfy both positive requirements (novelty and individual character) in order for a UK registered design application to be successful.

NEGATIVE DESIGN REGISTRATION CRITERIA

However, more importantly in the context of the breast prosthesis, the **RDA 1949** excludes two types of design features from protection. **Section 1C(1)** excludes features 'solely dictated by the product's technical function' to ensure there is no design monopoly over how something works. This interpretation of the section was confirmed in *Lindner Recyclingtech GmbH v Franssens Verstäder AB* (2010) ECDR1 (OHIM) and by the UK High Court in *Dyson Ltd v Vax Ltd* (2010) EWHC 1923.

Section 1C(2) RDA 1949 provides that a registered design will not subsist in features of appearance of a product that must necessarily be reproduced in their exact form and dimensions to be connected to, around or against another product in order for either to perform its function. In other words, there is no registered design protection for 'must fit' features – these are excluded. There is presently no case law on **s 1C**, but the interpretation given to the exclusion in **s 1C(1)** together with that of the parallel provision in **s 213(3) (b)(i) CDPA 1988** with respect to the unregistered design right suggests that it will have a narrow scope.

This will probably make it difficult for the breast prosthesis to gain registration given that we are advised that in creating the design, the shape of the breast prosthesis was influenced but not dictated by the shape of a bra and would have to fit inside a number of different bras.

PROTECTION BY UK UNREGISTERED DESIGN RIGHT

It may be a better option to consider protecting the breast prosthesis under the design right created by **Part III** of the **CDPA 1988** which introduced an important new form of intellectual property – the unregistered design right – to replace copyright as the basic vehicle for the protection of functional designs. The new UK unregistered design right has much in common with copyright, but offers a lower level of protection than a registered design.

The UK unregistered design right subsists in original designs, just as copyright does in original works. There is no need for there to be a design drawing or other document, as with copyright, although the design does have to be fixed in some form: **s 213(6) CDPA**; see also *Mayfair Brassware Ltd v Aqualine International Ltd* (1997) EWCA Civ 2560, (1998) FSR 138.

Section 213(2) defines 'design' to mean the shape or configuration of the whole or part of an article. This means the overall appearance or form of an article, or any part of it. Registered designs, by contrast, are largely concerned with particular features of a design. In *Ocular Sciences Ltd v Aspect Vision Care Ltd* (1997) RPC 289 Laddie J observed:

> The proprietor can choose to assert design right in the whole or any part of his product. If the right is said to reside in the design of a teapot, this can mean that it resides in the design of the whole pot, or in a part such as the spout, the handle or the lid.

The UK unregistered design right may therefore protect component parts that together make up an article, either individually as articles in their own right or collectively: *Baby Dan AS v Brevi SRL and Trend Europa* (1998) EWHC 291 (Pat), (1999) FSR 377. This may be advantageous to Prosthetics UK Ltd as component parts of the breast prosthesis may be eligible for protection even if the whole article is not. Indeed, the company can choose which features of their breast prosthesis design they put forward as qualifying for protection: *A Fulton Company Ltd v Totes (Isotoner) UK Ltd* (2003) EWCA Civ 1514.

Section 213 CDPA 1988 provides that original designs attract unregistered design right protection; however, a design is not original if it is commonplace in the design field in question. The basic test for originality is that the design must be independent in the sense that it is not a copy, although it need not necessarily be novel. In *C & H Engineering v F Klucznik & Sons Ltd (the Pig Fenders case)* (1992) FSR 427 Aldous J held that the same test as imposed in copyright law would be appropriate: that the design was not copied but the independent work of the designer. Originality is first assessed in the copyright sense and then commonplace designs are discarded. Designs features are unlikely to be commonplace if no or only few others include those design features. Thus, those design features that remain after this exercise may be asserted for protection. We will assume that Prosthetics UK Ltd has a fixed version of its breast prosthesis design and that it is original as there are no facts to the contrary.

A METHOD OR PRINCIPLE OF CONSTRUCTION

The UK unregistered design right does not subsist in certain situations: **s 213(2) CDPA 1988**). A key issue is whether the breast prosthesis design is excluded from design right protection because it is based on either a method or principle of construction (**s 213(3)(a) CDPA 1998**) or a 'must fit' and 'must match' requirement: **s 213(3)(b) CDPA 1988**. The underlying policy for the two exclusions is derived from the decision in the House of Lords in *British Leyland v Armstrong*. It has the objective of leaving the manufacturers of spare parts free to compete by making articles which are compatible with the design.

The UK unregistered design right does not subsist in those parts of the design of an article which enable an article to fit or connect to another so that either article may perform its intended function. The 'must fit' exclusion is primarily concerned with the 'interface' between two articles or 'things': *Ultraframe UK Ltd v Clayton* and *Dyson Ltd v Qualtex*. Some cases have observed that parts of the human body are an 'article' for this purpose, so that in *Ocular Sciences Ltd v Aspect Vision Care Ltd* (1997) RPC 289 the need for a contact lens to fit the eyeball was held to fall within the 'must fit' exclusion. In particular, the radius on the rear face of a contact lens was therefore a must fit feature. In *Parker v Tidball*, the shape of a mobile phone was dictated by the need to fit comfortably within the user's hand. However, in *Amoena (UK) Ltd v Trulife Ltd* (1996), a case on point as it also involved a breast prosthesis design, the exclusion was held not to apply. In its reasoning, the court added that the **s 213(3) (b)** exclusion is concerned with 'a much more precise correspondence between two articles'. In other words, to construe the provision as meaning that any article which is shaped to cover or contain another article cannot qualify as design right would be unhelpful. To clarify further, it is not the design for the spare part itself which is excluded from protection, but only the design of those features of shape or configuration of the article which enable it to fit. A competitor who wishes to produce an article will still be prevented from copying the free-standing parts of the design but will be able to copy the connecting or 'must fit' features. These may be applied to the second design to produce a competing article which will fit and function. The 'must fit' and 'must match' exceptions are intended to prevent design right conferring a monopoly and thereby to preserve competition. They permit copying where design constraints compel it.

In conclusion, where there is a possibility of a valid registered design being obtained, it should be pursued. However, the 'must fit' exclusion must be overcome. This will be an easier task with respect to the UK unregistered design right, as the decision in *Amoena* is particularly helpful as the 'must fit' exclusion in **s 213 CDPA 1988** was held not to apply. However, the reasoning in this case could be advanced if necessary when making an application for a registered design. An advantage for Prosthetics UK Ltd is that the UK unregistered design right protection for the breast prosthesis design is free and will begin when it is first recorded in a material form or when articles made to the design are first made available: **s 216 CDPA 1988**. The monopoly will generally expire 10 years after the end of the year in which articles to the design are first made available for sale. To avoid perpetual protection for unmarketed designs, **s 216(1)(a) CDPA 1988** provides for an overall period of 15 years from the end of the calendar year in which the design is first recorded.

Common Pitfalls

One common failing is not reading the question carefully. As the facts of the problem question do not suggest that the breast prosthesis design is unoriginal or commonplace, it is best to concentrate on resolving the issue of whether the breast prosthesis design is excluded from protection due to the 'must fit' and 'must match' exceptions. Ignore pre-2001 case law in relation to registered designs as the 'eye appeal' concept/legal test is no longer relevant.

Aim Higher

The focus of the question lies in evaluating the negative criteria for protection and whether the design is excluded from registration. Ensure that the majority of your essay is devoted to this issue.

QUESTION 18

The two concepts of 'originality' and 'commonplace' in design law have caused considerable difficulty in interpretation and application. It is not surprising that these two concepts have taken up a considerable amount of court time in providing guidance as to their meaning and ambit. Critically discuss with reference to relevant legislation and case law.

How to Read this Question

The word 'two' is repeated twice in the essay-style question, which indicates that the student should clearly discuss both concepts raised in equal measure. The reference to 'court time' suggests that important case law will need to be critically discussed in the body of the essay.

How to Answer this Question

This question requires knowledge of the relevant case law to set out how two key concepts in the UK unregistered design right created by **s 213 Copyright, Designs and Patents Act 1988** (**CDPA 1988**) have been interpreted by the courts.

- ❖ Subsistence of the design right under **s 213 CDPA 1988**;
- ❖ Discussion of the terms 'original' and 'commonplace';
- ❖ *Farmer's Build Limited v Carrier Bulk Materials Handling Ltd* (1999);
- ❖ *Baby Dan AS v Brevi SR* (1999);
- ❖ *Dyson Ltd v Qualtex (UK) Ltd* (2006) EWCA Civ 166;
- ❖ *Ocular Sciences Ltd v Aspect Vision Care Ltd* (1997);
- ❖ *Scholes Windows v Magnet* (2001) EWCA Civ 532.

Up for Debate

The UK unregistered design right is derived from copyright law principles. Recently, the **Intellectual Property Act 2014 (IPA 2014)** has only made minor amendments to **Part III CDPA 1988**. The definition of a design to which UK unregistered design right may apply has been slightly narrowed by the **IPA 2014**. Previously, for the purposes of UK unregistered designs, a design was defined as '*any aspect* of the shape or configuration (whether internal or external) of the whole or part of an article'. The reference to 'any aspect' has now been removed. This means that while a UK unregistered design right may still exist in the design of a whole item, or a particular part of that item, it will no longer exist in a 'part of a part', i.e. some small and trivial detail of that part.

In addition, UK unregistered design right is only available if a design is not 'commonplace in the design field in question at the time of its creation'. This definition has been refined and will now refer to 'commonplace *in a qualifying country*'. This will include the UK, EU and certain other countries which have reciprocal arrangements with the UK for protection of UK rights under their own laws.

ANSWER

The UK's unregistered design right protection attaches to the shape and configuration of an article and does not involve any formal application procedure. This form of protection is generated upon creation of a design document or article embodying the design. A design that is considered original insofar as it is not commonplace in the design field in question can qualify for design right to protection. The concepts of 'originality' and 'commonplace' in design law are of key importance to the practical application of design law to protect the appearance of an article in the UK. The court has been called upon in several design law cases to provide guidance as to the meaning of these two concepts. However, before considering the judicial interpretation of 'originality' and 'commonplace' in design law it is helpful to provide some background regarding the development of these concepts within the design law regime.

By way of introduction, the **Paris Convention** and the **TRIPS Agreement** require their signatories to provide protection for industrial design, but only in general terms. In the UK, designs are protected through the system of registered designs under the **Registered Designs Act 1949** (as amended) **(RDA 1949)** and via the design right under **s 213 Copyright, Designs and Patents Act 1988 (CDPA 1988)**, with a residual role for copyright.

The historical basis for the UK's design regime began with copyright as an important source of protection; however, copyright was abused in the design field in relation to non-aesthetic designs in the motor vehicle industry: *British Leyland v Armstrong* (1986). This led to the reform of the registered design regime in the 1980s and the introduction in 1989 of the new unregistered design right in **Part III, ss 213–264 CDPA 1988**. The new unregistered design right protects functional designs (designs lacking eye appeal) and aesthetic designs. It was intended that the introduction of the new design right would prevent copyright protection being used in connection with industrial products in an anti-competitive way. Functional, industrial designs would no longer be protected by copyright except in very limited circumstances. 'Artistic' industrial designs could still qualify for copyright protection, but if used 'industrially', the term of protection was reduced to 25 years.

The UK unregistered design right is defined in **s 213(1) CDPA 1988** simply as 'a property right which subsists in accordance with this Part in an original design'. In particular, according to **s 213(2) CDPA 1988**, a design right will subsist in any aspect of the shape or configuration (internal or external) of the whole or part of an article that is original. The term 'original' means original in the sense that it is not 'commonplace' in the design field in question at the time of creation: **s 213(4) CDPA 1988**. However, uncertainties arise in relation to the requirements under **s 213(4) CDPA 1988** which has recently been amended by the **Intellectual Property Act 2014 (IPA 2014)**.

THE ORIGINALITY REQUIREMENT

Originality is most likely to be an issue where the claimant's design is based on an earlier design. Alternatively, the originality in the later design relates to improvements or variations to the earlier design(s). The case law provides some insight into the courts' approach to assessing originality. *Farmer's Build Limited v Carrier Bulk Materials Handling Ltd* (1999) and *Baby Dan AS v Brevi SR* (1999) are cases where the designs in question were improvements over their own earlier designs.

In relation to the originality requirement in *Farmer's Build* it was held that a design has to be original in the sense that it is the independent work of the designer. This is akin to the requirement of originality in UK copyright law. The court set out a restrictive approach to the concept of 'commonplace', but nevertheless confirmed that it is not a test of novelty.

David Young QC (sitting as deputy judge) in *Baby Dan AS v Brevi SR* (1999) reached the conclusion that if the features giving originality represent a small change from earlier designs, the scope for infringement of any design right subsisting is likely to be narrow.

In *Dyson Ltd v Qualtex (UK) Ltd* (2004) the defendants admitted copying but sought to prove that some of Dyson's designs were not original because they were based on earlier Dyson designs and therefore a new design right did not subsist. Justice Mann determined that if a later design is created using skill and effort and is an interpretation of an earlier design on which it is based, it is likely to be an original design in which UK design right can subsist. He qualified this by stating that a design is unlikely to be original where the skill and effort really is in reproducing, in the 'tracing' sense of copyright, the previous design and making minor modifications which are not visually significant.

DESIGN MUST NOT BE 'COMMONPLACE'

A design which is original in the 'copyright sense' as referred to above, may nevertheless still lack originality for UK design right purposes if the design is commonplace: **s 213(4) CDPA 1988**. However, there is no legal definition of 'commonplace'. Its meaning is imprecise, vague and ambiguous.

It is important to remember that an original design may only be an 'aspect' of the whole of an article or part of an article. It is that particular aspect which must be assessed for originality and whether or not it is 'commonplace'. If the aspect is commonplace, then no UK design right will subsist.

Farmer's Build (1999) is the leading authority as to the meaning of 'commonplace'. Mummery LJ stated that the concept 'commonplace' in **s 213(4) CDPA 1988** should be construed narrowly rather than broadly. He reasoned that many designs of functional articles that fall within the definition of a 'design' are likely to be 'commonplace' if that term is construed broadly in the sense of 'well known'. In his judgment, Mummery LJ quoted from the parliamentary debate on the Bill that introduced the design right and noted that it was Parliament's intention to avoid giving design right to 'mundane, routine designs of the kind which are common currency in the particular field in question'.

Other relevant case law enables us to further clarify the meaning of 'not commonplace'. For example, in *Ocular Sciences Ltd v Aspect Vision Care Ltd* (1997) Laddie J stated that the flavour of the word [commonplace] is along the lines [that] any design which is trite, trivial, common-or-garden, hackneyed or of the type which would excite no peculiar attention in those in the relevant art is likely to be commonplace.

In *Dyson Ltd v Qualtex* it was held that the term 'commonplace' did not depend on marketing in the UK. The court explained that the design must be commonplace in the UK in the sense that UK designers in the field would have to be aware of the design to an extent sufficient to make it commonplace if the statutory exemption is to operate.

When carrying out a practical analysis in the *Farmer's Build* case to determine whether or not the particular design of an article was commonplace, Mummery LJ adopted the following approach. The first step is to determine if the design is taken from or copied from an earlier article. Step two involves a comparison of the claimant's design with the designs of other contemporaneous articles in the same field (including any infringing article) in an objective manner in light of all the evidence in order to confirm any similarities. Has the claimant's design been copied from any other design in the design field? If it has not been copied, then the claimant's design is original. Step three is to consider if the claimant's design is 'commonplace'. This comparative exercise is one of fact and degree. It is common sense that the closer the similarity of the design features, the more likely it is that the design is commonplace and therefore not original. If aspects of the claimant's design are only to be found in the defendant's design (and not vice versa), the court may rule that the claimant's design is original.

An example of the court's reasoning with respect to whether a design is 'commonplace' or not occurred in *Scholes Windows v Magnet* (2001) EWCA Civ 532. The claimants were the first to create sash windows in u-PVC. Many of the design features were commonplace in older wooden sash windows. The court held that designs could be commonplace by being in use, even though products being made to the design were no longer produced. Further, they held that the design field should not be limited by the purpose of the article, nor its material of construction. Ultimately, however, it was held that the design field was 'windows' and not 'u-PVC windows' so Scholes u-PVC window designs were found to be commonplace and not original.

NEW REQUIREMENT THAT THE DESIGN MUST NOT BE 'COMMONPLACE' IN A QUALIFYING COUNTRY

Part III CDPA 1988 previously provided that the UK unregistered design right is only available if a design is not 'commonplace in the design field in question at the time of its creation'. This definition has been refined by the **IPA 2014** and will now refer to 'commonplace *in a qualifying country*'. This will include the UK, EU and certain other countries which have reciprocal arrangements with the UK for protection of UK rights under their own laws and potentially make it easier for applicants to search and confirm their design is not commonplace.

In conclusion, in the UK, exclusive rights to designs can be established for free without formality in reliance on the law of unregistered design protection. Design owners who want to enforce their UK design right are advised to highlight the aspects of their designs which are unique or seen only in few other designs by reference to evidence of the design field in question in a qualifying country. Designs that are commonplace, so well known, ordinary or routine, will not acquire the UK unregistered design right.

Common Pitfalls

Make sure you keep your answer relevant to the UK unregistered design right under the **CDPA 1988** (and not the registered design under the **RDA 1949**). Ensure there is an appropriate balance between the critical discussion of the concepts of 'originality' and 'commonplace'.

Aim Higher

This essay-style question encourages discussion of the theoretical aspects of the UK unregistered design right. Accordingly, the ability to demonstrate a thorough under-standing of the difference between the concept of 'originality' and 'commonplace' supported by a discussion of the key case law will be to your credit.

QUESTION 19

Critically examine whether or not the UK's design law regime is now more 'designer-friendly' as a result of the **Intellectual Property Act 2014**.

How to Read this Question

The question refers to the changes that arise as a result of the introduction of the new piece of legislation that will impact on aspects of design law. The examiner is looking for an answer that either agrees or disagrees with the statement. Explore the reasons why the changes will make the design law legal framework more user-friendly than in the past.

How to Answer this Question

This question is reasonably straightforward. It requires the student to identify and focus on the most significant changes brought in by the Act with respect to both registered and unregistered design monopolies. The student should form a view as to whether the changes are an improvement from the designer's point of view.

Up for Debate

Do the changes to the design law regime introduced by the **Intellectual Property Act 2014** create any particular challenges? The introduction of criminal penalties will be of concern to those whose business model relies on intentionally copying all or part of a registered design. However, inconsistent approaches to design cases by the English and European courts mean that drawing the line between material and immaterial design features is difficult. This is important because if the infringing design has 'material' differences to the registered design, there will be no criminal liability. The line between civil infringement and criminal infringement will only become clear after cases have been brought to court and judgments rendered.

ANSWER

The UK design law regime is arguably now more 'designer-friendly' as a result of the new **Intellectual Property Act 2014** (**IPA 2014**). What do the amendments mean for designers trying to navigate the dense UK design law jungle? The new Act, which came into force on 1 October 2014, has made design law easier to understand and use. This is great news for entrepreneurial designers and small to medium-sized enterprises (SMEs) who have limited financial resources to devote to protecting and policing their valuable creative and innovative designs from blatant copying. The **IPA 2014** makes it easier to both obtain and enforce legal rights in designs.

Designers have an array of decisions to make when seeking legal protection. Should they register a design under the **Registered Designs Act 1949** (**RDA 1949**) or choose not to register and rely on their UK unregistered design right provided under **Part III** of the **Copyright, Designs and Patents Act 1988** (**CDPA 1988**)? Should the owner of a design seek protection in the UK, the EU or elsewhere in the world? The new **IPA 2014** helps designers answer these questions.

THE DEFINITION OF UK DESIGN HAS BEEN CLARIFIED

First, the legal definition of an unregistered UK 'design' is simpler: **s 213 CDPA 1988**. The focus is on protecting the overall design (the three-dimensional appearance of an article or product). A design is original if it is not 'commonplace' in any qualifying country. Trivial features of an 'aspect' of the design will not acquire legal protection. This makes the unregistered design right less complex and should reduce design infringement litigation. For example, it is less likely an action would be brought if a design appears to have copied a trivial part of someone else's design or a 'part of a part'. However, it remains an infringement to copy a part of an unregistered design.

DESIGNER IS THE FIRST OWNER

Further, the **IPA 2014** clarifies that the designer is now the first owner of the registered or unregistered design, even if it was commissioned by someone else. This means that if a commissioner seeks ownership of the design, they would have to take steps to obtain the designer's agreement to transfer (sell) or license the design on commercial terms. This will create greater legal certainty for both parties and reduce the likelihood of misunderstandings and disputes over who owns the legal rights in design. The position for employed designers remains unaffected – the employer will own the design.

NEW CRIMINAL OFFENCES FOR 'INTENTIONAL' COPYING OF A REGISTERED DESIGN

Arguably, the most important new provision is the introduction of a criminal offence for 'intentional' copying of a UK or Community-wide registered design. New **ss35ZA** to **C** of the **RDA 1949** provide that it is an offence for a person in the course of business to intentionally copy a registered design so as to make a product exactly to that design or only immaterially different. An important proviso is that the person must know or have reason to believe that the design is registered in the UK or in the EU. A court will have the power to award a hefty penalty of up to 10 years' imprisonment or a fine. This is because intentional or deliberate copying is the most serious type of design infringement, in contrast to innocent infringement. While a designer can still be inspired from another's design, the new law is aimed at preventing the deliberate direct copying and commercialisation of a design. The introduction of a criminal penalty for infringement brings the design law regime in line with infringement of other types of intellectual property such as copyright, patents and trade marks. However, the new criminal offence will not apply to *unregistered* design rights, only to registered designs acquired by meeting the requirements set out in the **RDA 1949**.

Further, there is a new 'good faith' exception to registered design infringement in that the **IPA 2014** allows a third party who, in good faith, started to use a design before it was registered by another, to continue to do so without fear of infringement.

NEW DEFENCES TO UNREGISTERED DESIGN RIGHT INFRINGEMENT HAVE BEEN INTRODUCED

To provide balance to the designer's monopoly in the design, several new defences to design infringement have also been created in the public interest. Certain specific activities will no longer infringe the UK unregistered design right. For example, it is not a crime to use a design privately, or for non-commercial, experimental or teaching purposes. In other words, the designer's permission is not needed for those types of design use. This is on the provision that use is fair, the source of the design is quoted and the use does not compromise the ability of the owner to exploit the design.

THE UKIPO'S NEW DESIGN OPINIONS SERVICE

A beneficial new service will also be launched by the UK Intellectual Property Office (UKIPO) to assist designers. A designer needing low-cost impartial advice will be able to contact the Design Opinions Service, which will be able to provide opinions on various issues including: ownership, validity or infringement of a registered design. The low-cost impartial advice will not be legally binding but should assist to clarify the strength of the designer's legal position. This will significantly improve the designer's ability to make decisions as to whether to pursue potential design litigation.

REGISTRATION OUTSIDE THE EU IS MORE EFFICIENT

The **IPA 2014** authorises the UK to sign the **Hague Agreement** – an international design registration system that provides designers with the option of registering their designs in countries outside the EU, using one application form. This reduces the administrative burden on designers and gives them more time to focus on what they are good at, design innovation.

ONLINE AVAILABILITY OF DESIGN REGISTRATION DOCUMENTS

Finally, design registration documents will become publicly available online. This will improve design searches carried out by a designer to confirm whether a design has already been registered with the UKIPO. The improved online system will also make it easier for a designer to confirm whether a potentially registrable design is novel and has individual character as required by the **RDA 1949**; and if an unregistered design is original and not commonplace as required by **s 213 CDPA 1988**.

In conclusion, the Government's stated primary aim for the **IPA 2014** is that it will 'make it easier for business to understand what is protected under design law'. The changes made by the **IPA 2014** to both registered and unregistered design monopolies tidy up rather than radically change the system. The improvements to the design law framework make the system more user-friendly and should increase designers' confidence in using design protection. Simply put, the legal environment has been enhanced to make it more accessible by creative designers who currently struggle to navigate the system without expensive legal advice. Designers will be better positioned to use design law to their commercial advantage more often, especially to deal with intentional infringers who blatantly copy. Overall, the impact of the **IPA 2014** on the UK's vitally economically important design sector is positive and has made several steps in the right direction.

Common Pitfalls

It is a better approach to focus attention on the changes that will have the most significant impact on designers who use the design law framework to protect their work, rather than give a section-by-section account of each change made to design law by the **IPA 2014**.

Aim Higher

A discussion of certain relevant practical implications of the new design laws could be made here. For instance, the impact of imposing criminal liability on intentional design infringers.

QUESTION 20

During a period of unemployment in 2010 Christian made an original design of a milk-shake maker for use in cafes. He kept a copy of his design on his home computer and also had hardcopies of the design in his portfolio folder. In 2014 he accepted a position as a designer with CaféSupplies Ltd. In this role he produced three new versions of the milk-shake maker. It was clear that these subsequent milkshake makers were evolved from Christian's original 2010 designs. In other words, all subsequent designs were derivatives of the original master design. Unfortunately, Christian never applied to register his original design. CaféSupplies Ltd has since made over £500,000 profit from UK sales of the new design of the milkshake maker. Does Christian have any intellectual property rights he can rely on in order to negotiate to license CaféSupplies Ltd for its use of his design? Advise Christian.

How to Read this Question

This problem question requires:

❖   a knowledge of the unregistered design right under **s 213 CDPA 1988**;

❖   the ability to analyse whether design right subsists in Christian's 2010 milkshake maker design so that he is in a position to negotiate a licence for its use by his employer CaféSupplies Ltd;

❖   critical discussion of the ownership issue of derivative designs created by Christian while he is employed by CaféSupplies Ltd.

ANSWER

Design is all about the way an object looks: its shape, its visual appeal. Design law pro-tects the physical appearance and visual appeal of products such as Christian's milkshake maker. Although Christian hasn't registered his milkshake design under the **Registered Designs Act 1949** (**RDA 1949**), he may still have some automatic protection from unregis-tered rights under **s 213** of the **Copyright, Designs and Patents Act 1988** (**CDPA 1988**). **Section 213** of the Act creates free automatic legal protection for three-dimensional (3-D) shapes only. Design right provides automatic protection for both the internal and exter-nal shape or configuration of an original design. The milkshake maker will have a 3-D shape and therefore may be eligible for protection under this regime. If Christian's design meets the criteria under **s 213 CDPA 1988**, the UK unregistered design right will allow him to stop anyone from copying the shape or configuration of the product, including his new employer CaféSupplies Ltd ('CSL'). The design right lasts either 10 years after the first mar-keting of products that use the design or 15 years after creation of the design, whichever is earlier. For the first five years the owner of the design right can stop anyone from copying the design. For the rest of the time the design is subject to a licence of right. This means that anyone is entitled to a licence to make and sell products copying the design. Naturally, the design right will only protect Christian's milkshake design in the UK.

The question arises then as to whether a design right subsists in the original 2010 milk-shake maker design made by Christian on his home computer. This will involve an analysis of **s 213(2)**, **(3)** and **(4) CDPA 1988**. One must consider whether the milkshake maker design is 'commonplace' in any qualifying country and thus not 'original' for the purpose of the Act. Any design which is 'trite, trivial, common-or-garden, hackneyed or of the type which would excite no peculiar attention in those in the relevant art' is likely to be 'commonplace'. It is important to note, however, that a design which has become very familiar does not necessarily become 'commonplace'. For example, if a design is applied to an article made by one manufacturer which sells in large numbers, that does not necessarily mean it is commonplace. In *C&H Engineering v F Klucznik & Sons Ltd* (1992) FSR 421 Aldous J stated that the word 'commonplace' was not defined by 'appears to induce a consideration akin to novelty ... and that for a design to be original it must be the work of the creator and that work must result in a design which is not commonplace in the field'. See also the court's pronouncements in *Ocular Sciences Ltd v Aspect Vision Care Ltd* (1997) RPC 289. Applying the law, there is no evidence on the facts that the design was created by anyone other than Christian, therefore we can assume it is an original design and not copied from another source. An assessment of whether the milkshake maker design is 'commonplace' is assisted by the decision in the *Farmers Build Ltd v Carrier Bulk Materials Handling Ltd* (1999) RPC 461 case where it was held that if there are aspects of an original design (e.g. for a milkshake maker) that cannot be found in any other milkshake maker designs, 'the court would be entitled to conclude that the design in question was not "commonplace" and that there was a good reason for treating it as protected from misappropriation'. Note that evidence of commercial success is irrelevant in determining whether a design is commonplace or not, so it will not benefit Christian to show that CSL has made £500,000 profit on the sales of its milkshake makers.

The next issue to consider is ownership of the 2010 milkshake maker design. According to **ss 214–215 CDPA 1988**, Christian is the first owner of the design which he created in 2010. Christian's design has been duly recorded as either a model or design document on his home computer and in hardcopy form. A design document is defined as 'any recording of the design, whether in the form of a drawing, a written description, a photograph, data stored on a computer or otherwise': **s 263(1) CDPA 1988**. Thus Christian's unregistered design right in his 2010 milkshake maker design continues to subsist (**s 216**) and is a qualifying design (**s 217**). As the unregistered design right lasts either 10 years after the first marketing of products that use the design or 15 years after creation of the design (whichever is earlier), Christian's 2010 design is still protected by the design right monopoly until the relevant term expires.

However, we are told that Christian has also made derivative designs while an employee employed to design with CSL. In the circumstances, CSL will own the derivative designs made while they employed Christian by virtue of the employment relationship, unless anything to the contrary was agreed between them. There is no suggestion of any alternative agreement on the facts. A similar analysis of subsistence of design right ensues. Are the derivative designs owned by CSL original and not commonplace, bearing in mind that they are derivatives of Christian's original 2010 design? Or, potentially, is CSL infringing the unregistered design rights in Christian's original 2010 version? This is difficult to answer without further factual detail. However, where improvements have been made to a design, originality may still exist in the later design. But if the differences between the original and the derivative designs are so minor that the extent of originality is negligible, originality will subsist in the earlier design: *Baby Dan AS v Brevi SR* (1999) FSR 377.

This means that Christian will nevertheless have unregistered design right in his original 2010 version of the milkshake maker as it is well within the term of 10 years from first publication. Since Christian's original design is still less than five years old, the UK design rights are still exclusive, meaning that Christian has the exclusive rights on the design of the product in the UK, irrespective of any later variations of the design made by CSL. Christian should consider negotiating with CSL to license his design right to his employer in return for a reasonable royalty payment. He should advise CSL that if he grants them an exclusive licence, they will then be in a position to control the UK market using the design right in the original earliest design of the milkshake maker. In this way, Christian will be able to assist his employer to successfully leverage its position into a controlling position in the UK and internationally for the niche milkshake maker product, by tracing the product back to its origin and establishing that Christian is the original designer of the earliest milkshake maker from which all subsequent milkshake maker variations derived. This would be a win–win situation for the parties. From 2011, Christian's milkshake maker design is subject to a 'Licence of Right'. This means that anyone, including CSL and other parties, will be entitled to a licence to make and sell products copying the design. Finally, CSL should ensure that it takes steps to apply to register all future variant designs under the **RDA 1949** in order to protect the registrable design features for each variant of the design as it is created and, over time, build up a portfolio of registered design rights on the subsequent variants of the milkshake maker product.

Common Pitfalls

Avoid simply restating the legislative provisions and summarising the facts of design case law. It is better to apply the law to the facts as you go and reach conclusions at each stage of the legal analysis. Ensure the focus of the discussion is the UK unregistered design right. Don't forget that there are clearly two layers of analysis required by this question, the 2010 design and the later derivative designs made while Christian was a CSL employee.

Aim Higher

Demonstrating a good understanding of the difference between registered design and the design right is important, but here the focus of the question is subsistence of the design right in the milkshake maker design and its later derivatives. Another key issue is ownership of the designs. Students can add value to their answer not only by applying the relevant law, but also by adopting a commercial approach to the relationship between Christian and CSL with regard to a licensing strategy.

6

Patent Law

The patent law system recognises that innovation and technological developments, both crucial tools for a country's financial and social wealth, cannot be motivated solely by market competition. A patent grants a monopoly over new technological knowledge (an invention) for 20 years from application, but may be revoked at any time if it is later found that the invention did not meet the legal requirements for patentability.

The basic legal requirements for a patent to be granted in Europe and the UK are that it must:

❖ be novel (new);
❖ possess an inventive step (non-obvious to a person skilled in the field);
❖ be capable of industrial application (be put into practice);
❖ not be excluded by law as being 'un-patentable' subject matter.

If an application does not satisfy each of these conditions, a patent will not be granted. Patents over methods of doing business, computer programs, biotechnology and medical methods of treatment and diagnosis are contentious and pushing the boundaries of existing patent law.

Patents are territorial rights and to date there is no such thing as a global 'international patent'. However, there are efforts to improve the global patent system to make it more effective and efficient. Harmonisation of laws between countries is a gradual process, yet remains a high priority. The only international treaty that provides for harmonisation of substantive patent law is the **TRIPS Agreement**. However, administrative procedures for filing patent using a single application to cover multiple international jurisdictions have been streamlined under the **Patent Cooperation Treaty**. At the European level, the harmonisation of the patent system is nearing completion but will not come into effect until the EU Member States have ratified the **European Patent Litigation Agreement**. Once this happens, a European Patent Office application will result in a single EU Unitary Patent being granted, providing EU-wide protection for an invention. A Unified Patent Court system has been created to enforce those patents. In the UK, the **Intellectual Property Act 2014** and the **Patents Act 2004** have amended the key piece of national legislation, the **Patents Act 1977**, in certain respects.

QUESTION 21

It is commonly said that patent rights are only as valuable as the ability to enforce them. Critically discuss this statement addressing the potential impact of the UK's Intellectual Property Enterprise Court and the new EU Unitary Patent on the ability to enforce patent rights.

How to Read this Question

This question focuses on a particular aspect of the patent system, namely how patent rights are enforced in the UK and the EU. The underlying issue is the ease with which patent holders can access the legal system to enforce their patent monopoly rights. Further, the question is asking the student to consider the impact of two new developments in the system. The student should explain each new development in turn and then consider whether they will have a positive, negative or neutral impact.

Up for Debate

In a headline-grabbing stunt in 2012, UK-based inventor, Michael Wilcox, burnt a copy of his patent in front of the Houses of Parliament, protesting that the high cost of litigation prevented him from enforcing his rights and allowed infringers to continue using his technology unabated and without paying him compensation. Nevertheless, in 2014 the *Taylor Wessing Global IP Index* judged the UK to have the best IP regime in the world. This was confirmed recently in the *US Global IP Center International Index* which ranked the UK number one for enforcement. Nevertheless, patent holders, especially small businesses, still face significant difficulties enforcing their valuable patent rights in terms of adequate enforcement mechanisms, court resources and the high cost of patent litigation in the High Court. How should the UK's IP framework continue to develop in order to meet the needs of its users and remain at the forefront of world-class IP systems?

ANSWER

Patent infringements are often difficult to identify, involve considerable expense to gather evidence of infringement and are arduous to litigate. Patent disputes present an enormous business risk for patent holders. At stake is the ability to sell, market share, damages and costs orders, possible future licensing royalties and the validity and thus the commercial value of the patent itself. Prudent management of patent assets is essential for patent holders, but knowing how to proactively enforce patent rights is far from intuitive. The ability to enforce patent rights is a key legal factor that impacts on patent value. This is why it is commonly said that 'patent rights are only as valuable as the ability to enforce them'.

The **Patents Act 1977** (as amended), the **Patents Act 2004**, the **Patent Rules 2007** and the **Intellectual Property Act 2014** represent the modern governing UK national legislation creating the patent law framework. These derive from a hybrid of national, European and international agreements such as the **1994 Agreement on Trade-Related Aspects of IP** (**TRIPS**), part of the World Trade Organization's founding treaty. As a minimum, the UK is required to ensure its patent rights enforcement system complies with **Art 41** of **TRIPS**, which describes the principles of an effective patent enforcement system. **Article 41** provides that its members shall ensure that enforcement procedures are available under their law so as to permit effective action against any act of infringement of intellectual property (IP) rights, including expeditious remedies to prevent infringements and remedies that constitute a deterrent to further infringements. **Article 41** states further that procedures concerning the enforcement of IP rights shall avoid the creation of barriers to legitimate trade and provide for safeguards against their abuse as well as be fair and equitable. **Article 41** concludes by confirming that enforcement procedures shall not be unnecessarily complicated or costly, nor entail unreasonable time limits or unwarranted delays.

Patent holders decide whether to take advantage of the patent system to enforce their rights. Enforcing these rights is an expensive and often drawn-out process, which many are unable to afford. Enforcing patent rights is a major concern for patent-owning businesses, big or small. In 2000, the EU study entitled *Enforcing Small Firms' Patent Rights* found that every single valuable EU invention that an innovating small to medium-sized enterprise (SME) held had been copied at least once, yet not one EU innovating SME had been able to successfully enforce their patent. Fortunately, in the UK recent legal reforms level the playing field for patent holders who wish to take enforcement action in the specialist Intellectual Property Enterprise Court (IPEC), the High Court and the new Unified Patent Court (UPC).

INTELLECTUAL PROPERTY ENTERPRISE COURT (IPEC) AND THE HIGH COURT, CHANCERY DIVISION

As of 1 October 2013, the Patents County Court (PCC) was reformulated as a specialist list of the High Court as the Intellectual Property Enterprise Court (IPEC): see **Civil Procedure (Amendment No 7) Rules 2013 (SI 2013/1974)**. The **Civil Procedure Rules** (**CPR**) are designed to improve access to justice by making legal proceedings cheaper and quicker, as well as easier to understand for non-lawyers.

Thus, currently in the legal system of the Courts of England and Wales, IPEC in London (previously the PCC) is an alternative venue to the High Court for bringing legal actions involving IP matters including patent rights: **CPR 63**. The IPEC provides access to justice for litigants who are unable to afford the costs of litigation in the High Court.

Revitalised rules of procedure require more detailed particulars of claim, no disclosure, no examination-in-chief of expert witness and tight control by the judge of the issues that go to trial. Financial ceilings were introduced to both the damages (at £500,000) and the legal costs (at £50,000, with an additional cap per stage) recoverable. Trials should last no more than two days. IPEC judges have specialist IP and patent knowledge and can order the full range of IP remedies, including financial compensation/damages, an account of profits, final injunction to prevent future infringements, search and seizure and freezing assets. Although the IPEC is now part of the High Court, patent attorneys retain their rights of audience and litigation.

Within IPEC there are two systems: the multi-track described above and the small claims track for claims of less than £10,000 with restrictions on costs orders; however, the latter is not appropriate for patent claims.

The creation of IPEC is a positive development supporting access to justice by patent holders in respect of their patent rights. IPEC deals with smaller, less complex, lower-value actions with procedures specifically designed for these type of cases, aimed at ensuring patent owners are not deterred from enforcing their patents due to potential litigation costs. Longer, more complex, higher-value actions, as is often the case with patent litigation, are heard in the High Court. IPEC aims to strike a balance between swift, low-cost, streamlined litigation and ensuring a proper investigation of the claim in an informal courtroom environment. Patent holders should take comfort in the high quality of the specialist IP courts and judges available in the UK to enforce patent rights and resolve disputes. Further, the UK's EU membership has had a huge impact, in particular the **Patents Act 1977** which harmonised UK patent law with the *European Patent Convention* (EPC) which came into force in 1974. Consequently, there is now a fusion of UK and European patent law and practice which has been largely positive in practical terms, resulting in a solid degree of legal certainty in the patent legal framework.

THE EUROPEAN UNIFIED PATENT COURT (UPC)

Although the European Patent Office (EPO) provides single patent grant procedures, the ability to enforce European patents is in the process of change with the advent of the UPC. Consequently, the UK's **Intellectual Property Act 2014** (**IPA 2014**) streamlined parts of existing laws, including improvements to the patent law regime. The Act provided the foundation for the UK to sign the UPC Agreement and lays out the groundwork for introducing the UPC.

'Patent prosecution' refers to the interaction between patent applicants, their representatives and the relevant patent granting office and is divided into: (1) pre-grant prosecution which involves negotiating with the patent office for the patent to be granted; and (2) post-grant prosecution which relates to post-grant amendments to the patent or responding to opposition to the patent by third parties. This is distinct from 'patent litigation' which is legal action taken to enforce the patent monopoly against an infringing third party. The *Agreement on the UPC*, signed by 24 EU Member States on 19 February 2013, creates a specialised patent court with exclusive jurisdiction for litigation relating to European patents and European patents with unitary effect. According to the EPO, the UPC was needed to address the problem of the high legal costs that ensue when patent litigation has to be undertaken in two or more national courts, with the risk of diverging decisions and lack of legal certainty. Forum shopping also occurred as the parties sought to take advantage of differences between national courts' interpretation of harmonised European patent law and procedure. The new court system paves the way for the implementation of a unitary patent system in Europe. The signing of the UPC agreement is a decisive step towards the long-awaited introduction of a truly supranational patent system in Europe. Following the endorsement of the unitary patent package by the European Parliament and Council in December 2012, the creation of a European court specialised in patent matters will be a tremendous boost for the completion of the European patent system. This is the most dramatic change in the patent landscape across most of Europe in the last 30 years. A unified patent system should reduce the cost of acquiring patents in Europe. It will be similar to the existing system in that one can apply centrally to the EPO in Munich, but rather than choosing to acquire a bundle of single national patent monopolies, the applicant will acquire a single monopoly covering the relevant EU Member States. Existing UK national patent rights will not change.

For the patent owner, the new system means that in the near future, when filing a UK patent application, the applicant will obtain a single European patent that will stand or fall across the whole of Europe. There will be a transition period for the first seven years during which the applicant can choose to opt-in its existing portfolio, or not opt-in for strategic reasons: for example, uncertainty as to implementation of the new system with the patent owner preferring to remain in the existing more predictable national-based UK system.

The UPC will be one court but will sit in a number of different locations and will hear disputes pertaining to the Unitary Patent. It will be composed of a central division with its main seat in Paris, with further seats in London and Munich. The London court will hear patent disputes relating to chemistry and pharmaceutical patents, with the German court hearing mechanical engineering cases. The UPC system aims to reduce complexity and increase legal certainty for the patent owner; however, this remains to be seen as it has yet to be fully implemented, although the Preparatory Committee published the UPC's seventeenth draft of the Rules of Procedure in November 2014 (which are to be agreed by May 2015). Judges may only be formally appointed once the UPC is established.

For patent holders who choose to file a Unitary Patent, it appears they will obtain an advantage through simpler administration processes for patent prosecution.

Finally, the value patent rights create is directly affected by the ease or difficulty with which they are able to be enforced. In recent years significant reforms have affected IP litigation in the UK and in the EU, with the aim of promoting access to justice at proportionate cost. Since the EU patent system was formulated in the 1970s, there has been a desire to have a single EU patent and single European court for resolving patent disputes. It has taken four decades to create such a system, largely due to the key stumbling block, language. Overall, the development is a positive step for the EU in the long term, although there will be a period of uncertainty for business (and therefore lenders) in the short term. A key decision for patent holders in the short term is whether to opt-in or opt-out. At the moment it is still not possible to apply for a unitary patent, although this option is not far off once the UPC goes live. After the UPC Agreement comes into force, there will be a transitional period of seven years that may be extended to 14 years. In terms of enforcing patent rights, on balance, a pan-European approach should create greater certainty (single system, single patent, single court, single renewal fee) and thus value in the medium to long term. This should be viewed as a positive development by the patent community; however, it will be an evolving process with many procedural issues to be ironed out along the way. However, a unitary patent will be vulnerable across Europe to a single unfavourable UPC decision which is a new risk to patent enforcement that patent holders will need to take into account. Expectations are also high that in the years ahead in the legal system of England and Wales, IPEC will deliver timely access to justice at affordable cost to SME patent holders. This means that in high-value cases we are not likely to see much difference in terms of the procedure followed and the cost of litigation in the UK, but a real difference has already been seen at the lower end of the value spectrum.

Common Pitfalls

Do not confuse the issue of the legal system for enforcing patent rights with patent infringement. It is not necessary to discuss the law on patent infringement in any detail in order to answer this essay question.

Aim Higher

Ensure that both IPEC and the UPC, specialist courts which are the result of law reforms to facilitate patent enforcement, are addressed relatively equally. Law reform is the process of advocating and implementing changes in a legal system, usually with the aim of enhancing justice or efficiency.

QUESTION 22

Frank Fysch, a keen fisherman and inventor (in his spare time) from the East Midlands, consults you regarding his latest invention, a new type of reel-release mechanism to be used with a standard fishing rod.

Frank sold his rights to a previous invention to an international company for a flat fee of £20,000 but feels he didn't get as much as he could have for it because he sold after having only produced a working prototype. The company has since gone on to sell thousands and made substantial profits from his earlier invention.

This time around, Frank, who feels he has established his reputation as an inventor in the field, wishes to apply for a patent in the UK and offer it to several companies to bid on. In doing this, he hopes to achieve a higher up-front fee for licensing his invention, as well as future royalties.

▶ **Advise Frank as to the patentability of his reel-release mechanism and the steps involved in the patenting process.**

How to Read this Question
This is a common practical problem question requiring the student to be broadly familiar with the key aspects of the UK's patent law system.

How to Answer this Question
The question requires the student to evaluate the 'patentability' of Frank's invention and explain the procedural process for filing a patent application in the UK and potentially in the EU and beyond.

Applying the Law

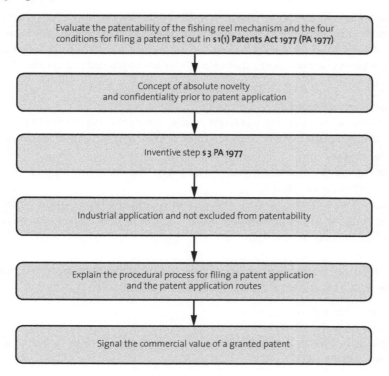

Evaluate the patentability of the fishing reel mechanism and the four conditions for filing a patent set out in **s1(1) Patents Act 1977 (PA 1977)**

Concept of absolute novelty and confidentiality prior to patent application

Inventive step **s3 PA 1977**

Industrial application and not excluded from patentability

Explain the procedural process for filing a patent application and the patent application routes

Signal the commercial value of a granted patent

ANSWER

Patent rights protect new, industrially applicable inventions and give the inventor or proprietor ('the patentee') a legally recognised monopoly to work the invention for a period of up to 20 years. A UK patent provides exclusive rights only in the UK, Isle of Man and some former British protectorates and does not protect an invention in any other country. Patents are legal instruments intended to encourage innovation by providing a limited monopoly to the inventor (or their assignee) in return for the disclosure of the invention. Publication of the invention is mandatory in order to be awarded a patent.

Frank Fysch can apply for a patent to protect his new reel-release mechanism (a mechanical device) if certain legal requirements for a UK patent to be granted are met, according to the **Patents Act 1977 (PA 1977)**. The requirements for obtaining a grant of a UK patent are now applicable in most of the important countries in the world due to the effects of various international conventions, especially the **Patent Co-operation Treaty 1970 (PCT)**.

As a patent is a territorial right, Frank should apply for protection in the UK, as a minimum. In order to determine *who* is entitled to a patent, it is necessary to institute a reference in time which will establish precedence by one inventor over another in case two or more inventors create the same invention. The traditional reference in time presently applicable is the date of filing, in the so-called 'first-to-file' system. The advantage of the 'first-to-file' system is that it provides certainty of ownership.

Frank's UK patent application must comply with certain administrative formalities as well as meeting the requirements for a patentable invention. There are four key legal, rather than administrative, requirements to be satisfied to conclude that a patentable invention exists in the new rod reel mechanism before Frank will be granted a UK patent. The invention must:

(1) be novel: **s 2 PA 1977**;
(2) involve an inventive step: **s 3 PA 1977**. In other words, the invention must be a technical advance over existing technological understanding ('the state of the art') which is not obvious;
(3) be capable of industrial application: **s 4 PA 1977**. This means that the invention can be carried out in an industry;
(4) not be excluded by law from being patented: **s 1(3) PA 1977** (e.g. not a method of treating the human and animal body; not a plant or animal variety; nor be contrary to public policy or morality).

These legal requirements cannot be understood without first being aware of three other fundamental concepts in patent law. These are the concepts of:

(1) the priority date of the patent;
(2) prior art; and
(3) the person skilled in the art, sometimes referred to as the 'man skilled in the art' or 'the skilled man'.

An understanding of these concepts is necessary to understand the process by which patents are granted and to appreciate how a patent might be attacked as being invalid. The classic defence to a patent infringement claim is to show that the patent is invalid.

The priority date of the patent application is the date on which it is tested against the 'state of the art': **s5(1) PA 1977**. This is normally the filing date of the application (unless an earlier date is claimed in the UK Patent Office, European Patent Office or Paris Convention country).

The prior art or state of the art is defined in **s2(2) PA 1977** as comprising all matter made available to the public before the priority date of the invention. This includes all knowledge anywhere in the world on the subject matter of the invention. Novelty-destroying prior art could include information that is part of common general knowledge, information disclosed by an earlier user of the invention, information disclosed in a single copy of a published document or by oral communication. Frank must ensure that he keeps the new reel mechanism absolutely confidential until he files a patent application. Only then will he be able to freely disclose his invention to the international companies and others (unless the companies agree to sign strongly drafted non-disclosure agreements).

Inventive step is a very different question to that of novelty and involves a qualitative assessment of the invention by reference to the 'skilled man'. The new reel mechanism should not be obvious to a person skilled in the art, having regard to all matters forming part of the state of the art at the priority date of the patent: **s3 PA 1977**. In deciding whether Frank's invention is obvious, the test in *Windsurfing International Inc v Tabur Marine* (1985) as modified by *PLG Research Ltd v Ardon International Ltd* (1995) can be applied:

(1) Identify the inventive step or concept.
(2) At the priority date, what was the state of the art relevant to that step?
(3) Identify the differences between the invention and the state of the art.
(4) Do the differences constitute steps which would have been obvious to the skilled man, or is there a degree of inventiveness?

In applying the *Windsurfing* test the scope of the state of the art is narrower for inventive step than it is for novelty (**s3 PA 1977**) because earlier patent applications do not form part of the state of the art.

Finally, Frank's application must be capable of industrial application: **s4(1) PA 1977**. This should not be a problem because the new reel mechanism clearly produces some tangible and physical consequence. In *Chiron v Murex Diagnostics* (1996) Morritt LJ at 178 stated that 'the section requires that the invention can be made or used "in any kind of industry" so as to be "capable" or "susceptible of industrial application" '. The connotation is that of trade or manufacture in its widest sense and whether or not for profit.

Assuming that Frank's invention meets the four legal requirements, he should feel confident about filing his application with the UK Patent Office. The procedural steps will involve the following:

(1)   Completing the Patent Form 1/77. The patent application must contain a specification containing a description of the invention, as well as a claim for the patent and any drawing referred to in the description or the claim as well as an abstract.

(2)   Filing (**s 5(1) PA 1977**).

(3)   Preliminary examination and limited search (**s 17 PA 1977**) within 12 months from filing date. The application is referred to a patent examiner for a preliminary examination and search to ensure that the application complies with the Act's requirements.

(4)   Publication (**s 16(1) PA 1977**) by the Patent Office in the *Official Journal (Patents)* allowing public inspection of the claims. Publication of the patent application can give rise to third-party objections to the grant of the patent.

(5)   Substantial examination and search within six months after publication, requested by applicant.

(6)   Grant – comptroller must publish notice in the *Official Journal (Patents)*; certificate issued to the applicant.

(7)   Monopoly lasting 20 years for patent proprietor.

THE NATIONAL, REGIONAL OR GLOBAL PATENT FILING ROUTE?

Frank's patent filing strategy should begin with his key markets for recreational or sport fishing and thus he should consider filing in the UK, with the European Patent Office (EPO). Frank may wish to focus on English-speaking countries such as the United States, Canada, Australia and South Africa and other countries where sport fishing is especially popular. As the UK is a signatory to the **Patent Cooperation Treaty 1970** (**PCT**) which is administered by the **World Intellectual Property Organization** (**WIPO**), Frank could opt for this patent filing route, which offers an international patent filing system to expedite the application process for registering patents in PCT member states around the world. This option is particularly attractive if Frank's invention is commercially successful and he later wishes to file in any countries beyond the UK.

In conclusion, a patent is an exclusive monopoly right granted to an inventor such as Frank for a fixed period. This is a commercially valuable right even though it can take around two years to obtain a granted patent. However, it does not make good business sense for Frank to obtain a patent for his invention unless he believes it will result in a worthwhile financial return. The process of applying to register a patent costs time and money; however, firms that apply for patents have undertaken a commercial analysis of the pros and cons of patenting an innovation and concluded that the benefits of obtaining a monopoly over their invention exceed the costs and that the patent rights will provide stronger protection than keeping the invention confidential and out of the public domain. For example, the cost associated with obtaining a patent usually includes legal fees, filing fees, prosecution fees, translation costs and maintenance fees. From a strategic point of view, Frank may wish to patent his rod reel mechanism invention to: (1) prevent others from copying or free-riding; (2) block other firms from competing with him; (3) use the patents in cross-licensing negotiations and raise licensing revenue; and (4) enhance his business reputation. Once Frank's patent(s) has been granted, he will have the legal authority to prohibit others from making or selling the invention in the country or countries where the patent was granted for the duration of the patent's life.

Common Pitfalls

Avoid simply reciting the law and be willing and able to apply it to the specific facts of the scenario. Make sure you keep your answer relevant and provide an appropriate balance between the various issues.

Aim Higher

Think through a patent filing strategy for Frank in line with the nature of his invention and potential markets.

QUESTION 23 -

Critically discuss the key advantages and disadvantages of patenting an invention under the **Patents Act 1977** from the point of view of the patentee.

How to Read this Question

This question encourages the student to carry out an objective evaluation of the advantages and disadvantages of patenting for a patentee (i.e. as opposed to, for example, the consumer), drawing on all aspects of the patent law system, but using only relevant material.

How to Answer this Question

Never start an essay with the phrase, 'In this essay I am going to…'. The marker knows what you need to do. The sooner your writing focuses on the question, the more marks you will attract. One of the most common and useful beginnings to a patent law essay is to start with an explanation of what a patent does.

Answer Structure

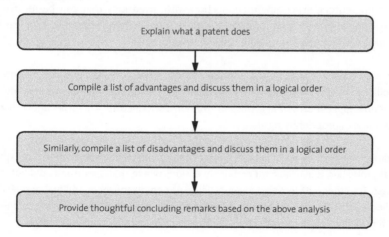

Explain what a patent does

↓

Compile a list of advantages and discuss them in a logical order

↓

Similarly, compile a list of disadvantages and discuss them in a logical order

↓

Provide thoughtful concluding remarks based on the above analysis

Up for Debate

The importance of patents has increased tremendously over last few decades. Companies, institutes and universities are creating strong patent portfolios. However, the patent system only covers some forms of innovation, but not others, due to exclusions from patentability on the grounds of public policy and morality. This is a disadvantage for patentees but thought to be in the best interests of the public.

ANSWER

Patents protect new, industrially applicable inventions and give the inventor or proprietor (the 'patentee') a legally recognised monopoly to work the invention for a period of up to 20 years. There are both advantages and disadvantages to patent protection, as the procedure for obtaining a granted patent is costly, lengthy and complex. How does an inventor or owner benefit from having a patent monopoly? It is important to consider the pros and cons before either publishing the invention or applying for the patent.

ADVANTAGES OF PATENT PROTECTION

The key advantage of filing a patent is that a patent monopoly is granted for a potential duration of 20 years and can prevent unauthorised third parties from using the invention during that period. While under monopoly protection, the **Patent Act 1977** (**PA 1977**) provides that only the patentee is lawfully allowed to commercially exploit the invention through manufacturing and licensing. In other words, the patentee has an exclusive legal property right. The scope of that right in any particular case is determined by the claims in the patent specification. This usually includes reverse-engineering, since a valid patent protects the ideas and information in the way described in the patent's claims and using such information obtained via reverse-engineering in the ways described in the patent claims will infringe the patent. Thus a patent is an effective tool against imitators as it deters competitors, especially in connection with inventions that can be reverse-engineered. The patentee is even protected against someone who subsequently creates the same invention entirely through his or her own efforts.

Other advantages of obtaining a granted patent include the fact that the patentee has the ability to file for protection in other jurisdictions using the original priority date. Once the patent application is filed, the information contained in it can be freely disclosed without loss of proprietary rights.

In addition, the boundaries of subject matter susceptible to patent protection has expanded so that protection is available for certain inventions where that opportunity did not exist in the past. Together with novelty, inventive step or non-obviousness, utility, the question of whether a particular subject matter is patentable is one of the fundamental requirements for patentability. This means that the system is flexible and capable of adapting.

Perhaps the most important advantage is that a patent is a form of property that can be licensed to generate royalties and future income. Once granted, the patent owner can sue for patent infringement dating back to the priority date. Nevertheless, there is no legal requirement to file for a patent and an inventor could decide to keep the invention secret so the system is not mandatory. The decision to file a patent application is not irrevocable; it may be withdrawn at any time before publication by the Patent Office.

Other advantages of applying for and being granted a valid patent under the **PA 1977** include the fact that patents avoid the need to maintain complete security for inventions to be kept as an internal trade secret – and still allow for relief even if others independently develop the same innovation and 'innocently' infringe.

If a patent is infringed, a variety of legal remedies are available, some unique to patents such as a 'declaration of validity'.

Finally, a patent has an economic value – the value patents furnish as assets potentially useful for cross-licensing technology in settlement of patent infringement (or other) litigation. Patent registrations are evidence of an intangible asset that can more easily valued for finance purposes than confidential information. In terms of revenue, as the patent creates a monopoly over the invention, the patent holder can sell the patented invention at any price they believe to be suitable for the duration of the patent. In contrast, because confidential information lacks exclusivity, trade secrets are generally considered to be not as valuable as patents. And finally, although patents are commercially advantageous for a number of reasons, two stand out: first, to set up a start-up firm patents are needed to attract venture capital; and second, without patents, large competitors could quickly adopt the technology and reduce the inventor's ability to enter the market.

However, with these numerous benefits come certain drawbacks. The disadvantages of patenting an invention are discussed below.

DISADVANTAGES OF PATENTING

On the other hand, the key disadvantage of filing a patent is that the invention must be disclosed in the application. In return for patent protection, the patentee must consent to publication of the details of the new invention. A patent's disclosure (after issuance or publication) can sometimes provide a 'roadmap' facilitating an unscrupulous competitor's copying of an invention in a way that changes the form, but not the substance, yet still suffices to avoid the legal scope of the patent. This means that third parties can 'invent around' or improve on the invention.

Patent protection is territorial and will only cover the UK, although patents may, if certain requirements are met, be filed in other countries for an additional cost via the **European Patent Convention** (**EPC**) and **Patent Cooperation Treaty** (**PCT**) routes. The patent application may need to be translated if filed in other jurisdictions, further adding to the costs involved. If the EPC or PCT route is used, the patent application will still need to undergo a national phase in each designated country. As yet there is no single global patent in existence, although the **World Intellectual Property Organization (WIPO)** is currently engaging in this debate. Many stakeholders in the patent system are calling for the creation of a global patent system to make it easier and faster for corporations to enforce their intellectual property rights around the world.

Another disadvantage is the cost of obtaining a patent. Given the importance of the claims determining the scope of the patent monopoly, it is generally recommended that a patent specification be prepared by a patent attorney or a person familiar with the state of the art of the invention and the patent process. This increases the cost of the patent application process. Furthermore, a significant disadvantage relates to the length of time it takes to secure a patent, which, on average, is over three years. After the lengthy, time-consuming process and expense, some are disappointed by the fact that a patent provides a mere 20-year monopoly, after which anyone may exploit the invention. Compare this with the duration of the monopoly afforded copyright holders whose work is protected for their lifetime plus 70 years under the **Copyright, Designs and Patents Act 1988**.

Again on the subject of costs, the patentee must pay ever higher fees to continue to renew the patent until the 20-year monopoly has expired.

Although not required for legal protection, the patented invention should be marked with the granted patent number as a deterrent for potential infringers.

Another important disadvantage of the patent system, from the point of view of the patentee, is that disclosures by others can ruin novelty. Nothing can be done if someone else engaged in similar research makes the invention public before a patentee applies for a patent. Even once the patent has been granted, opposition proceedings may be started. This means that the patent can be challenged and possibly revoked.

Finally, unless the patent owner reserves its rights, once a patent product has been sold, the purchaser has an implied right to sell that product to anyone in the world, who in turn has the same right. This can cause problems for patentees who want to control commercial export and import of their products.

In conclusion, while there are certainly several disadvantages to the patent law system, the **UK Intellectual Property Office** reports steadily increasing levels of patent application activity. Indeed, patent activity is mushrooming across virtually every sector of the UK economy as patentees seek to gain a proprietary market advantage, an exclusive hold over a new technology. Registered patent rights have also seen a boom in revenues derived from patent licensing and have served as a hidden motive behind a number of the biggest corporate mergers in the last decade. It is not just the UK economy that is affected by these trends, patent activity is on the rise worldwide, spurred in part by the World Trade Organization's **Agreement on Trade-Related Aspects of Intellectual Property Rights (TRIPS)**. Concerns have been raised about the recent trends in patent activity – the patenting of biotechnological inventions, business methods and databases – and that these may actually stifle academic freedom, scientific inquiry and technological innovation. However, there is little doubt, as evidenced by dozens of studies by economists and Gower's *Review of Intellectual Property*, published in December 2006, that the patent system is, on balance, an effective instrument for fostering innovation and technology diffusion. A patent is simply a reward for the inventor, providing the patent holder with a medium (a monopoly and property right) to benefit from the invention. If the path of filing a patent application is selected, it must be done with the knowledge that it is subject to the legal conditions set out by the **PA 1977**.

Common Pitfalls

This question calls for effective time management in order to cover both parts of the question, namely, the advantages and disadvantages of the patent law system. Ensure your answer provides a balanced discussion and offers a conclusion.

Aim Higher

A critical essay is a piece of writing, aimed at presenting objective analysis of the subject matter, narrowed down to a single topic, in this case patents. The main idea of the critical analysis is to provide an opinion either of positive or negative implication. As such, a critical essay requires strong discussion coupled with a sharp structure.

QUESTION 24

Critically discuss whether the granting of patent monopolies is necessary for incentivising the development of new inventions, for example, in relation to medical methods.

How to Read this Question

Writing a critical discussion requires two steps: critical reading and critical writing. A critical discussion is subjective writing because it expresses the writer's opinion or evaluation on the topic. The student should break down the question into its constituent parts which can be identified by reading the key words/concepts in the question: (1) patent monopolies; (2) how to incentivise inventions; especially in the case of (3) medical methods, which are currently excluded from patentability.

How to Answer this Question

In order to adequately deal with the question, students should:

- ❖ introduce the patent monopoly as a framework for rewarding inventors;
- ❖ discuss the requirements for patentability, and the medical method exclusion in **s 4A Patents Act 1977**.
- ❖ explain the methods of treatment, for example, surgery, therapy and diagnosis;
- ❖ consider the types of medical methods that are not excluded from patentability;
- ❖ first and second medical use;
- ❖ consider the 'reward for innovation' theory.

Up for Debate

For some medical inventions it is difficult to determine whether they encompass a medical method: for example, imaging methods used during surgery. Thus, whether a specific medical method is excluded from patentability under the **European Patent Convention** depends on the technical details and has to be decided on a case-by-case basis. It is a complex area. Developments in medical technology over the last decade have led to a high number of patent filings in this area and a number of important decisions from the European Patent Office's boards of appeal.

ANSWER

Patents are monopoly rights. However, there is a widely held view that patent monopolies or patent protection are inappropriate for the medical field and in particular for medical methods. Consequently, some areas of medical invention such as methods of treatment, surgery, therapy and diagnosis have been removed from patentability. Indeed, **Art 2(3)** of the **Agreement on Trade Related Aspects of Intellectual Property 1994** (**TRIPS**) allows members to exclude from patentability methods of medical treatment on humans and animals. The **European Patent Convention 2000** (**EPC**) incorporates the exclusion of medical methods in **Art 53** on public policy grounds. These medical methods are now excluded from patentability under **s 4A** of the **Patents Act 1977** (**PA 1977**) (recently amended by the **Patents Act 2004**), which states:

(1)   A patent shall not be granted for the invention of –
    (a)   a method of treatment of the human or animal body by surgery or therapy; or
    (b)   a method of diagnosis practised on the human or animal body.

The exclusion of methods of treatment and diagnosis reflects the concern to ensure that such methods can be freely disseminated by the medical profession in the public interest: *Schering and Wyeth's Application* (1985).

In *Shell/Blood Flow* (1993) 'treatment' was defined as any non-insignificant intentional physical or psychic intervention performed directly or indirectly by one human being on another using means of medical science. In the same case, 'surgery' was defined as medicine concerned with the healing of disease, accidental injury or bodily defects by operating on the living body. This includes both conservative (non-invasive) procedures and operative (invasive) procedures using instruments.

The decision in *Unilever (Davis's) Application* (1983) confirmed that both preventative and curative treatments fell within the meaning of 'therapy' and are therefore excluded.

However, a method of contraception, for example, was allowed in *Schering's Application* (1971), as contraception did not amount to the treatment of disease. A method of treatment for lice infestation was held to be patentable in *Stafford-Miller's Application* (1984), because it was regarded as a treatment for lice rather than a treatment for a disease. In contrast, a method of abortion was refused a patent in *Upjohn's Application* (1976).

The exclusion is only for methods of treatment; the **PA 1977** does not exclude:

❖ medical device claims for medical hardware provided they meet the usual criteria of novelty, inventive step and industrial applicability;
❖ substance claims, for example for pharmaceuticals; or
❖ claims for medical uses for known substances (this was a special concession with regard to novelty and was the result of lobbying by the drug industry).

This shows that although there are some restrictions on the patentability of medical methods in the public interest, the **PA 1977** nevertheless allows for a wide degree of patentability. In the recent past, where doubts arose as to the patentability of an invention involving a method of treatment, claims were made in the form of a 'Swiss' claim, developed in the Swiss Patent Office. The Swiss claim extends to second medical uses of known medical substances and covers the method for making a known substance for a new use. Swiss claims were controversial, because it was argued that novelty in the invention is lacking, but nevertheless they are applied in the UK.

Now, however, as a result of reforms contained in the **Patents Act 2004, s 4A PA 1977** is amended to provide:

(1) **Subs (1)** above does not apply to an invention consisting of a substance or composition for use in any such method.
(2) In the case of an invention consisting of a substance or composition for use in any such method, the fact that the substance or composition forms part of the state of the art shall not prevent the invention from being taken to be new if the use of the substance or composition in any such method does not form part of the state of the art.
(3) In the case of an invention consisting of a substance or composition for a specific use in any such method, the fact that the substance or composition forms part of the state of the art shall not prevent the invention from being taken to be new if that specific use does not form part of the state of the art.

Methods of medical treatment nonetheless involve substantial work, financial investment and time to develop and turn into something practical and successful. Without the incentive of a patent monopoly, people may not do that work or spend the time and money developing medical methods of treatment. One could argue that the courts' role is not to uphold any claim to a monopoly for an idea which requires investment and risk to bring to market, only for those ideas which are new, non-obvious and enabled as required by the **PA 1977**.

Indeed, in 2012 Professor Josef Bille of the University of Heidelburg won the European Inventor of the Year Award for inventing an ophthalmological device that revolutionised certain kinds of laser eye correction. He developed a method for mapping irregularities in the cornea with unprecedented precision and fine-tuning the lasers to repair them. This wavefront technology is a measurement technology which uses so-called aberrometers to scan the human eye in a very detailed manner for small errors. By having a very detailed map of these errors, it is possible to devise much more precise surgical procedures (wavefront-guided laser-eye surgery) or to produce tailor-made lenses. This ground-breaking invention, and its continuous improvement, has corrected near-sightedness, far-sightedness and astigmatism in millions of patients worldwide.

His invention received a patent from the European Patent Office, despite the fact that medical methods that can be directed to surgery, therapy or diagnosis are not patentable. Indeed, they are explicitly excluded from patentability under **Art 53** of the **EPC**. However, in this case the European Patent EP2481346 (A1) was drafted to cover the 'device' aspect of the invention, 'A device to compensate for asymmetrical aberrations in a beam of light includes at least one dual compensator positioned on the beam path.' The reason for excluding medical methods from patents is the notion that doctors and veterinarians need to be free to use their skills and knowledge of the best available medical treatments for their patients. They should not have to worry that what they are doing might be covered by a patent. On the other hand, do the monopolies provided by patents hinder research? The answer may vary in different technology areas, but in the medical field they seem to be important to attract investment money.

The medical industry is predicted to continue its impressive growth as the population enjoys greater longevity and innovation stimulates demand for new medical treatments. Patents are critical to investment in such innovation, especially where lead-times to market are long. The medical field of patents has its own set of exclusions from patentability for reasons of policy and ethics. But it is clear that the boundaries of patentability in relation to medical methods will continue to be tested and the extent of patentable subject matter is likely to continue to expand in order to fulfil the aim of incentivising medical research and providing a reward for expensive and time-consuming innovation.

Common Pitfalls

Although this question appears to focus on patents and the exclusion of medical methods from patentability (and novel new uses), the underlying theme the student will need to ensure is covered relates to the 'reward for innovation' theory.

Aim Higher

The ability to explain how the law might or might not operate in the context of a particular scenario such as Professor Bille's laser eye-correction invention is one of the hallmarks of a good legal mind. Think critically about the 'reward for innovation theory' and the different causes or consequences. A good analysis of the 'reward for innovation theory' will have a profound impact on the overall cogency of the student's essay and ability to impress the marker.

QUESTION 25

Do morality and public policy have a role to play in the patent system? Critically discuss with reference to biotechnological inventions and the relevant UK and EU jurisprudence and legislation.

How to Read this Question

It is difficult to be prescriptive as to how one might approach an analysis of the European Patent Office jurisprudence on the issues of morality and public policy, as so much depends on the individual's opinion. However, the main emphasis should be on analysis of the jurisprudence on morality and public policy.

How to Answer this Question

The most characteristic feature of a critical discussion is a clear and confident refusal to accept the conclusions of others without evaluating the arguments and evidence that they provide. Consider a thesis statement, arrange the parts, consider the language and decide on a conclusion. One example of a complete answer is to discuss aspects of the following:

- ❖ **section 1(3) Patents Act 1977**;
- ❖ biotechnological inventions and the development of patent law;
- ❖ *Harvard/OncoMouse* litigation and the utilitarian balancing exercise;
- ❖ **Article 53(a)** of the **European Patent Convention**;
- ❖ **Schedule A2 Patents Act 1977**.

Up for Debate

There are several controversial issues in relation to the patenting of biotechnology (e.g. patenting life, nature and parts of human beings). These include potentially broad patent claims that stifle research opportunities by non-patent holders; the increase in healthcare costs that could result from patent monopolies; bio-piracy; patent office backlogs and 'evergreening' (obtaining a further patent term for an invention by filing new patents which protect the original invention).

ANSWER

Section 1(3) of the **Patents Act 1977** (**PA 1977**) provides that where the commercial exploitation of an invention is contrary to public policy or morality, the invention is unpatentable, so morality clearly has *some* role to play in the patent system. There is little modern UK jurisprudence given that the circumstances in which the commercial exploitation of an invention would be contrary to public policy or morality are extremely rare. However, the decision of the European Patent Office (EPO) in *Harvard/OncoMouse* (1991) involved a consideration of a biotechnological genetic engineering invention and the issue of patentability. The science of biotechnology concerns living organisms, such as enzymes, proteins and plasmids. As scientists have developed new processes to modify the genetic composition of living organisms, the field has grown in importance because such inventions may directly affect humankind's future existence, particularly in relation to medicine, food, agriculture, energy and protection of the environment.

WHY PROTECT BIOTECHNOLOGICAL INVENTIONS?

As in other fields of technology, there is a need for legal protection in respect of biotechnological inventions because they are, nevertheless, the creations of the human mind just as much as are other inventions. Biotechnology inventions are generally the result of substantial research, inventive effort and investment in sophisticated laboratories. Typically, enterprises engaged in research only make investments if legal protection is available for the results of their research. As with other inventions and industries, the need for investment in research and development efforts creates an obvious need for the protection of biotech inventions. This need is not only in the interest of inventors and their employers, but also in the public interest of promoting technological progress.

The patenting of biotechnology innovations has been accompanied by controversy, as has the use of some of these new innovations. Policy-makers of all countries, however, have been careful to avoid extending patent rights to things as they exist in nature or to natural phenomena. A new plant species discovered in the wild, for instance, cannot be patented and neither can laws of nature.

The line between discovery and invention can be difficult to draw, but it is clear that a 'mere' discovery must be developed and applied in some way before it constitutes an invention. Therefore, finding a naturally occurring compound in the human body would be considered to be a discovery, but processes used to isolate or purify such a compound or a synthetic version of the naturally occurring compound would be inventions.

INVENTIONS CONTRARY TO PUBLIC POLICY OR MORALITY

Examples of subject matter contrary to public morality or policy in **s1(3) PA 1977** include obscene matter and possibly inventions which involve criminal acts. However, **s1(4) PA 1977** provides that just because an invention is illegal it is not sufficient cause to deem the invention to be contrary to public policy or morality.

The famous decision of the EPO in *Harvard/OncoMouse* (1991) developed the law and established that morality and public policy should be assessed using a 'utilitarian' balancing exercise. Harvard University had made an application for a genetically engineered live mouse (or other non-human mammal) which had an increased susceptibility to cancer for use in cancer research. A patent had been granted in the US; however, in the EPO it was first refused. After the university appealed, the European Board of Appeal sent the application back to the EPO Examining Division. They provided instructions on the application of the provisions at issue including **Art 53(a)** of the **European Patent Convention (EPC)** (the counterpart of **s1(3) PA 1977**) and the patent was eventually granted. The

Board of Appeal set out the 'approach' to be taken when conducting a 'utilitarian' balancing exercise. This involved the EPO weighing up the suffering of the 'OncoMouse' and the possible environmental risks posed by the genetically modified mouse against other factors, such as the usefulness of the invention as an aid to cancer research to humans. The EPO determined that the patenting of the OncoMouse was not immoral. However, the prohibition in **s1(3) PA 1977** on patenting inventions which are generally offensive still remains, and would be appropriate to control unwelcome animal experimentation.

PATENTS ACT 1977 SCHED A2 IMPLEMENTS EU BIOTECH DIRECTIVE 98/44/EC

Because of the specific legal and scientific concerns regarding public policy and morality relating to genetic engineering, **PA 1977 Sched A2** provides clear guidance on biotechnological inventions that are contrary to **PA 1977 s1(3)**. This Directive, in effect, harmonises EPO jurisprudence to the moral and public policy concerns in relation to biotechnological inventions.

(i) **PA 1977 Sched A2 para 3(b)** provides that human cloning processes are not patentable inventions. The formation and development of the human body and mere discoveries of elements of the human body (this includes gene sequences) are not patentable inventions. However, where a technical process is used to isolate or produce elements (including genes) from the human body, this may be patentable (**PA 1977 Sched A 3(a)**).

(ii) **PA 1977 Sched A2 para 3(c)** provides that processes for modifying human germ line genetic identity, that is genetic changes that can be passed to the next generation, are not patentable inventions.

(iii) **PA 1977 Sched A2 para 3(e)** specifically provides that genetic engineering of animals which is likely to cause the animal to suffer without a substantial medical benefit either to man or animals, does not constitute a patent invention.

(iv) Animal and plant varieties, or essentially macro-biological processes (**PA 1977 Sched A2 para 3(f)**).

PA 1977 Sched A provides that although biological products and processes are not, per se, un-patentable, certain biological subject matter cannot constitute patentable inventions.

In *Harvard College v Canada (Commissioner of Patents)* (2002) where the *OncoMouse* litigation saga continued, the Supreme Court of Canada ruled that the OncoMouse was not patentable, despite the many patents for it then held in the US, Japan, Australia and the European states. The majority, in a 5:4 split decision, held that patenting of higher life forms was a matter for Parliament and not the courts. Subsequently, the Technical Board of Appeal has further restricted the European patent to 'transgenic mice'.

In 2009 in the case of *WARF/Stem Cells (G2/06)* (2009) EPOR 15 (EPO EBA) it was held that a process that necessarily involved the destruction of human embryos was not patentable under the **Art 6(2)(c) EPC** and that the biotechnology-specific exclusions were examples of a general morality exclusion.

More recently, in *Brüstle v Greenpeace (C-34/10)* (2012) 1 CMLR 41 the patent claims covered the use of human embryos for scientific research purposes. It was held that this amounted to industrial or commercial use in the context of a patent and that only use for therapeutic or diagnostic purposes which are applied to a human embryo and are useful to it would be patentable.

As a result of the above case law, there is no doubt that morality and public policy have a role to play in the future development of the law relating to biotechnological invention. In each country, the laws on patentability of biotechnological inventions need to be consulted to learn the availability of patent protection and its scope.

In conclusion, genetically modified transgenic mice, human clones, part-human, part-animal creatures are just a few of the morally controversial biotech inventions that have garnered public attention in recent years. It is clear that morality-based controversies over the patenting of biotech inventions are not limited to the UK and the EU. The global moral controversies surrounding these and other biotech inventions stem from several concerns including those arising from the mixing of human and animal species, the perceived denigration of human dignity, the destruction of human life, the exploitation of women for their eggs, and the concept of ownership of humans. The convergence of this new technology with legal and regulatory systems makes biotechnology an evolving and complex component of intellectual property law. Because the patenting of morally controversial biotech research involves such serious, deeply felt issues, the patenting decision must not be left, as it currently is, to scientists pushing the frontiers of technology, motivated by factors beyond public comment and scrutiny. Nor should it be left to individual patent examiners to determine what is comprised in the word 'human'. In the contemporary patent landscape, the boundaries of patentability must be shaped by the legislature of the UK and the EU with respect to their territories.

Common Pitfalls

This is an essay question that could potentially be answered in a wide range of ways and the topic can generate very strong views. Nevertheless, students should be wary of writing an answer with 'too much opinion, and not enough law'.

Aim Higher

Credit will be given for critically examining in depth why the grant of certain patents invoke moral controversy. Why should anyone care whether human embryos, or foetuses, or clones, or human–animal chimera are patentable? Patentable inventions define property rights that create a social trajectory. Consider whether society is uncomfortable with the concept of nature or humans as personal property, commodities that can be bought or sold for commercial or even humanitarian benefit.

QUESTION 26

Dr Durant was the Director of Research of Selecta, a UK pharmaceutical company. The company applied for a patent for a new drug, taxachol, on 1 January 2014. The patent was published in January 2015. However, earlier, on 3 October 2013, Dr Durant had given a lecture at the Pharma Biotech 2013 Conference held at Trent University on use of the taxachol drug to treat ovarian cancer. Dr Durant's lecture was published in written form and circulated electronically to conference attendees. Dr Durant's lecture contained language that echoed the patent claims, although not precisely, nor in every respect.

Dr Frith, an employee of a competing pharmaceutical company, Pfitzer, later discussed Dr Durant's research with his company's legal advisers. Pfitzer issued revocation proceedings against Selecta on 15 January 2015 in relation to the taxachol patent.

▶ **Discuss the likelihood of Pfitzer successfully revoking Selecta's patent. Consider the application of relevant case law.**

How to Read this Question

This problem question deals with the issue of whether Selecta's taxachol patent application is at risk of being revoked on the basis that it has not met the criteria for patentability. Some students will recognise that the facts are similar to those in the case of *Bristol-Myers Squibb Co. v Baker Norton Pharmaceuticals* (2001) RPC 1.

How to Answer this Question

The student needs to cover three key issues: the nature of patent revocation proceedings, and the concepts of novelty and anticipation (which destroys novelty).

Applying the Law

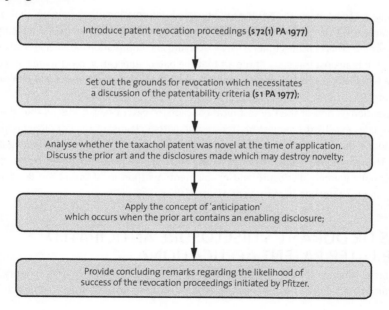

Introduce patent revocation proceedings (s 72(1) PA 1977)

Set out the grounds for revocation which necessitates a discussion of the patentability criteria (s1 PA 1977);

Analyse whether the taxachol patent was novel at the time of application. Discuss the prior art and the disclosures made which may destroy novelty;

Apply the concept of 'anticipation' which occurs when the prior art contains an enabling disclosure;

Provide concluding remarks regarding the likelihood of success of the revocation proceedings initiated by Pfitzer.

ANSWER

At the UK Intellectual Property Office (UKIPO) and at the European Patent Office (EPO) there is a general principle that it is in the public interest that invalid monopoly rights are not maintained. As such, revocation proceedings are seen as being prosecuted in the public interest and not merely as contentious proceedings between two parties. Nevertheless, a typical strategy employed by a commercial competitor is to attempt to revoke a granted patent on the grounds that it should never have been issued in the first place. This is the issue at hand. Revocation proceedings are usually filed in an attempt to gain access to a patented technology. Generally, the instigator of a revocation such as Pfitzer is concerned either that the patent covers an existing product or that the patent covers a planned future product. As well as providing the possibility of revoking the patent, filing revocation proceedings may also give a strengthened position for a negotiated settlement involving a licence agreement.

Section 72(1) of the **Patents Act 1977** (**PA 1977**) provides that

> Subject to the following provisions of this Act, the court or the comptroller may by order revoke a patent for an invention on the application of any person (including the proprietor of the patent) on (but only on) any of the following grounds, that is to say – (a) the invention is not a patentable invention.

The criteria for a patent to be granted are novelty, inventive step, susceptibility of industrial application and not falling within the list of exceptions and exclusions: **s1 PA 1977**. The key issue and patentability weakness arising on the facts relates to novelty. This involves considering the prior art as at the date on which the validity of an application for a patent is decided. With respect to the taxachol patent application, this date will be the actual filing date of the application in the UK, namely 1 January 2014.

The prior art to be assessed as at the priority date is information of any kind which has been made available to the public. **Section 2(2) PA 1977** contains the phrase 'in the United Kingdom or elsewhere'. This indicates that novelty is absolute and information worldwide is taken into account. It is against this state of the art that the patent application is compared in order to decide whether it meets the requirements of novelty and inventive step: **ss 2 and 3 PA 1977**.

'Anticipation' is one of the key technical concepts of patent law. It means that the prior art matches exactly the subject matter (i.e. the patent claims) of the later invention so as to render it not new. Anticipation occurs where the prior art contains an enabling disclosure. This composite phrase comprises two separate issues which must be dealt with sequentially, namely disclosure and enablement: *Synthon BV v Smithkline Beecham plc* (2005) per Lord Hoffmann at 19–33 and Lord Walker at 58.

HAS DR DURANT'S DISCLOSURE ANTICIPATED THE LATER PATENT APPLICATION?

The facts show that on 3 October 2013 (prior to the taxachol patent priority date) Dr Durant had given a lecture at the Pharma Biotech 2013 Conference held at Trent

University on use of the taxachol drug to treat ovarian cancer. Dr Durant's lecture was published in written form and circulated electronically to conference attendees. The lecture contained language that echoed the patent claims, although not precisely nor in every respect. This is very problematic and has the potential to destroy novelty as the disclosure may amount to an 'enabling disclosure' in which case the patent application will not meet the patentability criteria.

However, there is some hope for the validity of the patent given that Dr Durant's lecture contained language that merely echoed the patent claims, although not precisely nor in every respect. A case on point is *Bristol-Myers Squibb Co. v Baker Norton Pharmaceuticals* (2001) RPC 1. Here a lecture given by the patentee's Director of Research before the priority date on use of the taxol drug to treat ovarian cancer over a shorter infusion period amounted to 'enabling disclosure'. Aldous LJ (at page 46) said that using the information from the lecture, members of the public could carry out the procedure without the need for any further information from the patent. The lecture contained 'clear and unmistakable directions' to carry out what was being claimed in the patent. The court will apply the above test to Dr Durant's disclosure at the lecture.

THE TEST FOR AN ENABLING DISCLOSURE AND THE LINK WITH INVENTIVE STEP

The test of enabling disclosure is very precise, so that if an individual item of prior art does not contain *all* the elements (integers) of the later claimed invention, then the invention is valid for novelty. In doing so, the court will assess whether the prior art contains an enabling disclosure by carrying out a comparison through the eyes of the skilled addressee of each claim of the patent with each individual item of prior art. If the prior art contains a signpost, pointing in the general direction of the invention, that does not suffice for anticipation. It may well, however, give the skilled addressee sufficient information to make the invention obvious. Note that in *Actavis Ltd v Janssen Pharmaceuticals NV* (2008) EWHC 1422 one of the reasons why the patent was lost was the fact that one of the patent holder's employees had discussed the subject matter of the patent in a lecture given at a scientific conference before the patent had been registered.

The facts of this problem shows that this kind of issue arises fairly regularly within the scientific community as the researchers often have little understanding of the requirements of patentability and are keen to publicise their research to the wider community.

PROCEEDINGS TO REVOKE THE TAXACHOL PATENT UNDER S 72 PA 1977

The fact that the taxachol patent has been granted was published in the *Patents Journal*. There is no suggestion that Selecta wished to withdraw its patent beforehand or that the information it contains is prejudicial to the defence of the realm or the safety of the public (in which case the UKIPO would have prohibited its publication): **ss 16, 22 and 24 PA 1977**. The taxachol patent monopoly will exist for 20 years, calculated from the filing date (**s 25 PA 1977**) unless is it revoked or allowed to lapse.

Interestingly, there is no system of opposition under UK law (although there was under the **Patents Act 1949**) but a European Patent can be opposed at the EPO during the nine-month period after it has been granted. In the UK, third parties can make observations to the UKIPO under **s 21 PA 1977**. There are no facts to suggest that Pfitzer has made any such observations.

Rather, Pfitzer has presumably applied for total or partial removal of the taxachol patent from the register of patents, as from the filing date. In practice, revocation actions are often brought as a counter-claim by defendants in infringement actions. However, it is becoming increasingly common, particularly in the pharmaceutical sector, for companies to 'clear the way' by applying to revoke relevant competitors' patents prior to launch of a product on one or more of the following grounds:

(1)   it is not a patentable invention;
(2)   the invention has been granted to the wrong person;
(3)   the invention has insufficient description (to enable searching);
(4)   it has been the subject of an impermissible amendment to the patent claims: **ss 72–74 PA 1977**.

The first ground of revocation is the most likely to be relied on by Selecta citing a lack of novelty as at the filing date (1 January 2014). Selecta will allege prior disclosure of the taxachol invention and it must ensure that it sufficiently identifies the disclosure to allow Pfitzer to appreciate the scope of the allegation it is required to meet. In the case of information made available to the public by written description this will include the date on which and the means by which it was so made available. In the UK, the revocation proceedings may be brought in the UKIPO, the Patent Court or the Intellectual Property Enterprise Court.

The English courts use expert evidence to determine what was generally known to the hypothetical person skilled in the art at the priority date of the patent. Sometimes it may be necessary to hear evidence from more than one expert. In pharmaceutical cases, for example, it may be necessary to instruct both an organic chemist and someone else suitably qualified in analytical techniques. Typically, infringement/revocation actions in the UKIPO take around 6–9 months and may cost in the region of £10,000 to £50,000. There will be a hearing if experts are to be cross-examined. Selecta may wish to contest the revocation proceedings by way of a counterstatement and may offer to amend the patent. If Pfitzer's revocation proceedings are successful, revocation has effect *ex tunc* and the taxachol patent will therefore be deemed never to have been granted. If Pfitzer is unsuccessful, Selecta should apply for a Declaration of Validity to confirm the patent's future validity.

Common Pitfalls

Read each sentence of the fact scenario carefully. Discuss the issues in the order they arise in the facts. You need to be precise in your analysis of the facts and application of the relevant provisions of the **Patents Act 1977** and case law.

Aim Higher

Ensure you consider the point of view of the client you are advising. What do they want to know? Identify the corresponding legal issues. In other words, what sort of legal argument needs to be advanced in order for the client to get what they want? What sort of claim might they be facing if someone else wants something? Work your way through the various legal issues as they arise in the question, interchangeably stating the given legal requirement or legal principle and how this might apply to the facts. Note if there is a gap in the law or an ambiguity in the facts. It is important that you identify these and explain how this might affect your reasoning. State the possible outcome(s).

QUESTION 27

The newly promoted Research and Development Director of a scientific research company consults you regarding six projects currently afoot. He needs to allocate limited financial resources and wants to fund only those projects capable of being protected by and exploited by patents.

▶ **Advise on the patentability of each of the following projects:**

(a) A new type of non-invasive laser heart bypass surgery;
(b) The discovery of the technique of DNA cloning which allows genes to be transplanted between different biological species;
(c) The leukaemia-fighting drug 6-mercaptopurine;
(d) A stem cell line to treat autism which results in the test mice developing autism;
(e) An improved microphone for use in a foetal monitor to hear a foetal heartbeat;
(f) A new variety of rose plant called Princess Consort Camilla.

How to Read this Question

This is a practical problem question that requires the student to be familiar with the requirements for patentability and the exclusions from patentable subject matter under the **Patents Act 1977**.

How to Answer this Question

The purpose of this question is for the student to demonstrate that s/he can apply the laws. In terms of structure of the answer it is important to briefly introduce the task at hand and the law, followed by a detailed consideration of each project clearly logically discussed in alphabetical order (a)–(f), concluding with a thoughtfully reasoned ranking of the projects based on your earlier analysis.

Applying the Law

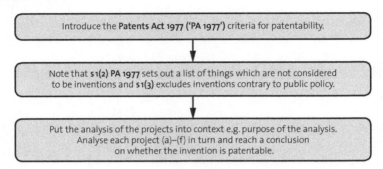

Introduce the **Patents Act 1977** (**'PA 1977'**) criteria for patentability.

Note that **s 1(2) PA 1977** sets out a list of things which are not considered to be inventions and **s 1(3)** excludes inventions contrary to public policy.

Put the analysis of the projects into context e.g. purpose of the analysis. Analyse each project (a)–(f) in turn and reach a conclusion on whether the invention is patentable.

ANSWER

A patent is a legal document that grants a potentially economically valuable limited 20-year monopoly to make, use and sell the patented invention. In return the patentee must publish the practically useful technical information concerning the invention to the public. The patent law system in the UK is governed by the **Patents Act 1977** (**PA 1977**) and **Patents Act 2004**. The system is justified on the basis that the monopoly granted provides incentive for new inventions. The basic requirements for a patent to be registered in the UK are set out in **s 1** of the **PA 1977**. In essence, for an invention to be patentable, it must:

(1)   be novel: **s 2**;
(2)   involve an inventive step: **s 3**;
(3)   be capable of industrial application: **s 4**; and
(4)   not be excluded by law from being patented: **s 1(3)**.

A range of factors need to be taken into account when evaluating whether to patent an invention. The issue of concern is the extent to which the various projects involve subject matter that is patentable. This is sometimes controversial because patent law must determine whether to grant property rights in a new technological invention which may raise complex cultural, political and social questions.

There are several ways that subject matter that is potentially patentable under the **PA 1977** is regulated. First, to be patentable an invention must be capable of 'industrial application': **s 1(1)(c)**. Second, **s 4A(1)** provides that a patent shall not be granted for methods of medical and veterinary treatment. Third, **s 1(2)** provides a non-exhaustive list of things which are not regarded by law to be inventions (e.g. a discovery, scientific theory or mathematical method). Fourth, **Sched A2 para 3(f)** states that a patent shall not be granted for 'any variety of animal or plant or any essentially biological process for the production of animals or plants, not being a microbiological process or the product of such a process'. Finally, accordingly to **s 1(3)** patents will not be granted for immoral invention or inventions contrary to public policy.

The patentability analysis that follows will assist the R&D Director to determine which projects are likely to result in granted patents that can subsequently be successfully exploited economically by the company.

PROJECT ANALYSIS

(a) A New Type of Non-Invasive Laser Heart Bypass Surgery

The issue is whether this non-invasive (non-scalpel) form of surgery is excluded under **s 4A(1)(a) PA 77**. This section provides that a patent shall not be granted for an invention of a method of treatment of the human body by surgery. In *Shell/Blood Flow* (1993) EPOR 320 the word 'surgery' was judicially considered and defined as medicine concerned with the healing of disease, accidental injury or bodily defects operating on the living body. 'Surgery' was held to include both conservative (non-invasive) and operative (invasive) procedures using instruments. The non-invasive laser heart bypass surgery fits within the definition and therefore is non-patentable subject matter. However, the R&D Director should be advised that the laser hardware may be patentable if it meets the requirements of **s 1(1) PA 77** as it is not excluded by **s 4A**. For example, the method by which the laser controls power and/or accuracy may be new and involve an inventive step.

(b) The Discovery of the Technique of DNA Cloning Which Allows Genes to Be Transplanted between Different Biological Species

Prima facie, a 'discovery' is not patentable 'as such' according to **s 1(2) PA 77**. However, if a mere discovery may be further developed and applied in some way it may constitute a patentable invention. In other words, the method of demonstrating the discovery or transforming it into a product may make the discovery patentable. In *Chiron* (1996) FSR 153 Morritt LJ held that biological material isolated from its natural environment or produced by means of a technical process may be the subject of an invention even it if previously occurred in nature. The use of the word 'technique' in the description of the project suggests a degree of development. However, biotechnological inventions are caught by the public policy and morality exception in **s 1(3) PA 77**. Nevertheless, **Sched A2 PA 77** provides additional guidance in **paras 3(b)–(c)** which state that the 'technique' must not be excluded on the grounds of public policy or morality. Human cloning per se is not patentable: **Rule 23d, Art 53 European Patent Convention**; however, the decision in *Leland Stanford Modified Animal* (2002) EP 2 confirms that controversial technology itself is not a bar to patenting. Accordingly, a carefully worded set of patent claims detailing the specific enabling technique may be patentable. Note also that the creation of inter-species embryos is foreseen in the new **Human Fertilisation and Embryology Act 2008**.

(c) The Leukaemia-Fighting Drug 6-Mercaptopurine

Administering a drug per se is not the same as a method of treatment: *John Wyeth & Bros Ltd's Application* (1985) RPC 545. Accordingly, a drug to treat leukaemia is potentially patentable and not excluded subject matter under **s 4A** which provides that the exclusion shall not extend to 'an invention consisting of a substance or composition used in any such method'. Indeed, there are strong arguments in favour of patenting drugs to reward pharmaceutical companies for their up-front research and development costs. However, a patent search would reveal that 6-mercaptopurine, first synthesised in 1951, was patented, is in the public domain, forms part of the state of the art and is therefore not patentable, unless the project has resulted in a *new use* for an existing drug which may be patentable. The patentability of a new use of an existing drug is covered by **s 1** in the **Patents Act 2004**.

(d) A Stem Cell Line to Treat Autism Which Results in the Test Mice Developing Autism

This project concerns a biotechnological invention. Advances in stem cell technology raise issues about the patentability of stem cells and processes involving these cells. Uncertainty about what can be patented in this field arises due to **s1(3) PA 77**, as amended to implement **EU Biotech Directive 98/44/EC**, which excludes inventions that are contrary to public policy or morality. However, **Sched A2(3)(e) PA 77** confirms that subject to a human medical benefit, inventions can be patentable even though animals may suffer. A case in point is the *Harvard/OncoMouse* series of case law beginning in 1990 in which a patent was granted to Harvard University by the EPO following a 'balancing exercise'. This determined that the usefulness of the method for genetically engineering mice, causing them to develop life-threatening cancer to further cancer research in humans, outweighed the mice's suffering. By analogy, it is likely a patent would be granted for this project as autism is a condition that is currently incurable in humans, subject to **s1(1) PA 77**.

(e) An Improved Microphone for Use in a Foetal Monitor to Hear a Foetal Heartbeat

The microphone is a medical mechanical device which is prima facie patentable provided it meets all the criteria: it is novel, has an inventive step (non-obvious to a person skilled in the art) and is industrially applicable (**s1 PA 77**). Even minor improvements to existing technology may be patentable. If the 'improvement' represents a development to the foetal heart monitoring process (e.g. by providing additional information relating to the foetus) not previously known then it is potentially patentable.

(f) A New Variety of Rose Plant Called Princess Consort Camilla

Plant varieties are not patentable under **PA 1977** as they are subject to a parallel *sui generis* regime which covers plant breeders' rights. Monopoly rights in new plant varieties are enshrined in the **Plant Varieties Act 1997** (**PVA 1997**) which grants monopoly protection in a plant variety that is distinct, uniform, stable and new for a period of 15 years: **ss 4–7** and **Sched 2 PVA 1997**. Monopoly rights for the rose variety should be pursued under this regime. Note, however, that under **s3(2)** of the **Plant Breeders' Rights (Naming and Fees) Regulations 2006**, a name will be rejected if it is 'misleading'. This extends to names containing the name of a natural person, so as to convey a false impression concerning the identity of the applicant, the person responsible for the maintenance of the variety. The R&D Director should be advised to seek the permission of Her Royal Highness before proceeding with this name.

Common Pitfalls

The problem question in this case requires you to analyse the research projects listed as (a)–(f). It would be a mistake not to mirror this (a)–(f) structure in writing your answer. This question comprises six parts, each involving issues of similar complexity, so make sure your answer is appropriately balanced between these parts.

QUESTION 28

Critically discuss the landmark UK case *Koninklijke Philips Electronics NV v Nintendo of Europe GmbH* (2014) HC12E04759 United Kingdom High Court of Justice, Chancery Division, in which Japanese company Nintendo, the world's largest videogame maker, was found to have infringed Philips' motion-gesture tracking technology by using it without permission in its popular Wii game console.

How to Read this Question

This essay-style question involves a straightforward analysis of a landmark patent infringement case. What makes the case of particular interest to the examiner is, first, the subject matter, namely, interactive videogame technology (the *Island Cycling* videogame and the Wii controller), and second, that the claim for patent infringement claim was successful.

Applying the Law

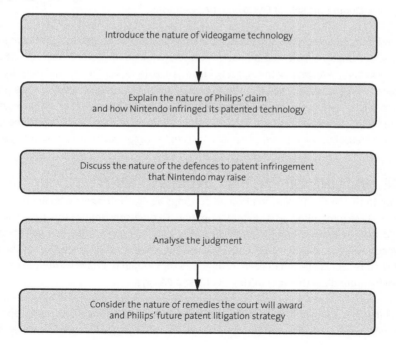

Introduce the nature of videogame technology

Explain the nature of Philips' claim
and how Nintendo infringed its patented technology

Discuss the nature of the defences to patent infringement
that Nintendo may raise

Analyse the judgment

Consider the nature of remedies the court will award
and Philips' future patent litigation strategy

ANSWER

Interactive media, where cutting-edge creativity meets the latest technology, is the fast-est-growing sector in the world. Since the first mainstream game console by Nintendo in 1985, videogames have become a global industry worth an estimated £40 billion. The industry is dominated by multinationals such as Sony, Nintendo, Microsoft, Apple and Samsung and publishers such as Activision, Electronic Arts (EA) and King (mobile). Intellectual property is at the heart of interactive media business involving videogame techno-logy. Interactive media means products including the well-known Wii controller, which uses digital computer-based systems to respond to the user's actions by presenting crea-tive content such as text, graphics, animation, video, audio, games, etc.

The videogame is incredibly popular and dynamic, arguably the most important develop-ment in entertainment since television. It's also a contemporary compendium of techno-logy, a piece of software and an engineering project. Videogame technology developers such as Dutch company Philips have taken steps to ensure that appropriate intellectual property (IP) protection is in place as this determines ownership enabling firms to share in the financial benefits from their work.

PATENTED TECHNOLOGY IN VIDEOGAMES

Patent protection in videogames typically covers the hardware technical solutions, inven-tive game or game elements, technical innovations such as software, network or data-base design. As the owner of patented technology in videogames and the economic rights in the interactive media, Philips is in a position to generate income from several revenue streams including the sale of DVDs and merchandising.

Patent infringement is not restricted to mere copying, it is also an infringement to manufac-ture, sell or import a patented product or process without the owners' consent: **s 60(1)(a) Patents Act 1977 (PA 1977)**. With respect to Philips' UK patents, Nintendo must have done one of these infringing acts in the UK. This can be a problem if the patented product is a gaming system and is being used on the Internet. In this situation, there will be no infringement where the host computer is located; rather the infringement takes place where the user is situated: *Menashe Business Mercantile Ltd v William Hill Organization Ltd* (2003) RPC 31A.

THE NATURE OF PATENT INFRINGEMENT

It is up to the owner, Philips, to bring proceedings against infringers who are performing any of these prohibited acts. Patent litigation is time-consuming and expensive and would only have been brought by Philips after carefully considering the validity of the claimed invention and that they could successfully prove to the satisfaction of the Court that their patent claim(s) had been infringed as they would not have wanted to make any unlawful groundless threat of infringement: **s 70 PA 1977**.

For Philips to successfully allege that their patent has been infringed, its patent specifica-tion will be closely scrutinised to confirm that the infringing act is indeed covered by the patent. Does Nintendo's 'infringing' product or process fall within the scope of the patent claims? In other words, patent claims define Philips' invention by describing a number of features of a product or process. To infringe a claim, Nintendo's product or process must contain every element. The precise technical scope of Philips' patent will be affected by how the words of the claim are interpreted by the Court. The **PA 1977** says nothing about claim interpretation; however, a UK court will adopt the 'protocol questions': *Improver Corp v Remington Consumer Products Ltd* (1990). Questions of fact relevant to a patent infringement matter require an understanding of the technology involved. The law makes use of the hypothetical skilled person to answer these questions. What would a reasonable person skilled in the art reading the patent claims think that Philips had claimed as its invention? (See *Pozzolli SpA v BDMO SpA* (2007) and the *Windsurfing* (1985)).

If Philips' patent has been copied exactly it will be reasonably straightforward to demonstrate that Nintendo has infringed, unless they have any defences to rely on. The best form of defence is attack and Nintendo argued that Philips' invention lacks novelty or is obvious (**s 4 PA 1977**) and that the patent should never have been granted in the first place. Where a defendant can show a patent is invalid, **s 74 (1)(a) PA 1977** confirms it is a complete defence to patent infringement: *Gillette v Anglo-American Trading* (1913) 30 RPC 465. On the other hand, it will be more difficult for Philips to prove patent infringement if the basic inventive concept has been used but Nintendo has made changes or variations to the way in which the technology works.

THE DECISION

In the UK Intellectual Property Enterprise Court, Chancery Division Judge Colin Birss held that the Nintendo console infringed two of Philips' patents. After having confirmed the scope of the patent claim, he compared each claim of the Philips patent(s) to the allegedly infringing Nintendo process and device. Only one claim of a patent needs to be infringed in order to have infringement of the entire patent. In analysing each claim, each element of the claim must be contained in the infringing device in order to show literal (direct) patent infringement. If even one element of the claim is missing from the allegedly infringing device, there is no literal infringement.

The first involved technology that controlled a virtual image, using software which stored a gamer's body-movement sequences. In particular, the judge said that Nintendo's *Island Cycling* game indirectly infringed Philips' patent as it used technology to convert a gamer's irregular variable motion into steady motion.

The second patent related to a pointing device which used hand-waving gestures to direct a fixed unit, such as a TV (as used in the *Wii Tennis* interactive videogame). The hand-held pointing device combined two main features, a physical motion sensor and a camera. Judge Birss determined that Nintendo's reasons for combining the two were not credible. Therefore Nintendo had infringed Philips' second patent as well.

The amount of damages (financial compensation) to Philips will be confirmed by the court soon, but is thought to be a very high figure given the commercial international success of the Wii. Philips is also bringing legal actions against Nintendo in the US, Germany and France. Nintendo says it will be appealing the case because it believes that Philips' patents for recognising hand gestures and motion are invalid.

It is helpful to evaluate whether the infringer, Nintendo, intentionally infringed Philips' patents or whether the infringement was done accidentally. This will be relevant when assessing any remedies the court may potentially award against them. Nintendo has a long history of developing innovative interactive media products while respecting the IP rights of others. However, on this occasion the company does not appear to have adequately considered the risk of patent infringement and the need for obtaining a licence from the patent owner. Philips' spokesman Bjorn Teuwsen reportedly told news agency Reuters that they had tried to persuade Nintendo to agree to license the use of their technology on fair terms since 2011 without success. Philips therefore decided to take legal action against Nintendo in the UK in 2012. This was a test case for Philips, who, clearly buoyed by their success, will seek further damages from Nintendo in other key international markets where they hold patents beyond the UK. This landmark videogame technology case demonstrates the commercial and reputational risks involved in not carefully clearing all IP rights that may be involved in an interactive media game such as the enormously successful Wii.

In conclusion, research commissioned by the National Endowment for Science, Technology and the Arts (NESTA) has found that 1,902 games companies were active in 2014, contributing an estimated £1.7 billion to the UK economy. The number of firms entering the videogame market every year is increasing at a rate of 22%, as consumer demand for interactive entertainment continues to grow. Interestingly, the average family spends more on videogames than on cinema tickets and recorded music combined. Games are also a major influence in other media such as television and film and offer some of the most popular apps on smartphones and social networking sites. As such there are likely to be more patent infringement cases involving videogame technology that are the subject of litigation in the future.

Common Pitfalls

After the scope of the patent claim is interpreted, each claim of the patent is compared to the allegedly infringing device. Do not forget that only one claim of the patent needs to be infringed in order to have a successful patent infringement action.

Aim Higher

There are several strategic issues that must be considered carefully as soon as a claim of patent infringement is made. Patent infringement questions will often include a discussion of the validity of the allegedly infringed patent.

QUESTION 29

Patent law confers employee inventors with a statutory right to claim compensation for an invention owned by the employer for which a patent has been granted. Critically analyse the effectiveness of the statutory employee inventor compensation scheme in light of the recent House of Lords decision in *James Duncan Kelly, Kwok Wai Chiu v GE Healthcare Ltd* (2009) EWHC 181 which concerned such a claim.

How to Read this Question

Inventor employee compensation law reform regularly arises in exams, so a student should ensure that they are familiar with the changes to the patent law system brought in by **s 10 Patents Act 2004**.

How to Answer this Question

❖ Introduce the statutory inventor employee compensation scheme in **ss 39–41 Patents Act 1977**.
❖ Briefly summarise the facts of *Kelly and Chiu v GE Healthcare Ltd* (2009).
❖ Explain the four-step approach for determining *whether a patent is of outstanding benefit to an employer*.
❖ Consider the rationale for the introduction of **s 10 Patents Act 2004**.

Up for Debate

The issue as to whether inventor employees should receive compensation for inventions made during employment has always been called into debate. From the employer's point of view, the employee's salary is sufficient financial reward, while inventor employees point to the sizeable profits produced from the invention for the employer. However, the UK Statutory Compensation Scheme is intended not to accommodate any loss, but rather to award successful inventor employees a share of the 'outstanding benefit' accumulated. There is no uniform international policy with respect to remuneration for inventor employees. For example, there are no statutory provisions in the law for remuneration of inventor employees in New Zealand and Australia, whereas in China and Japan there are.

ANSWER

The conventional justification for the existence of the patent law system is to give inventors and investors an incentive, namely a 20-year monopoly to make, use and sell an invention in return for disseminating technical information to the public. A statutory compensation scheme for employee inventors was introduced in the UK in 1978 via **ss 39–41 Patents Act 1977 (PA 1977)**. In essence, the general rule under **s 39 PA 1977** is that an employee's patent will belong to the employer provided it was made in the course of normal duties or was reasonably expected to result from the carrying out of his duties: **s 39(1)(a)**.

Section 40 PA 1977 allows the employee to claim compensation in certain limited circumstances if s/he is able to successfully argue that the patent in question provided an 'outstanding benefit' to the organisation (or in the second case that the benefit to the employee is inadequate in relation to benefit derived by the employer from the patent). Thus under the **PA 1977** compensation could not be awarded unless it was shown that the benefits in question result from the invention having been patented, rather than merely from the intrinsic merits of the invention itself: *Memco-Med Ltd's Patent* (1992). In practice **s 40 PA 1977** has been very difficult to rely on as it is generally felt that the bar is set too high. An employee inventor could secure compensation only if it was proved that the employer had derived 'outstanding benefit' from the patent (not the invention itself) having regard to the size and nature of the employer's undertaking: **s 40(1)(b)**. This was a very high hurdle to overcome. Only three cases were brought by employee inventors under this scheme and none of them were successful (*GEC Avionics Ltd's Patent* (1992) RPC 107; *British Steel Plc's Patent* (1992) RPC 117; *Memco-Med Ltd's Patent* (1992) RPC 403). There is no previously reported case of a successfully contested employee inventor compensation award under the Act.

KELLY AND CHIU V GE HEALTHCARE LTD (2009) EWHC 181 (PAT)

In early 2009, in a groundbreaking ruling in the Patent Court Mr Justice Floyd made the first ever court award of compensation under the **PA 1977** to employee co-inventors. Sizeable sums of £1 million and £500,000 were awarded to the co-inventor research scientists Drs Duncan Kelly and Kwok Wai Chiu, respectively, for their work in creating a diagnostic tool for detecting heart defects while employed by Amersham International Plc (now GE Healthcare Ltd). This was the first case in which it had been possible for claimants to prove that the patent to which they had contributed was of 'outstanding benefit' to the employer.

The case involves GE Healthcare (formerly Amersham International), a multinational corporation with expertise in medical imaging and information technologies. The company is a US$17 billion segment of the American General Electric Company and the first GE business to be headquartered outside the US. In the 1980s, GE Healthcare employed Dr Duncan Kelly and Dr Ray Chiu as research scientists, both of whom were crucial to the investigation and development of the first synthesis of the P53 compound. This compound was the basis for a radioactive imaging agent, registered trade mark MYOVIEW, patented in the 1980s which proved to be a great commercial success for GE Healthcare. Launched in the UK and Japan in 1994, followed by the US in 1996, the product was very profitable. With R&D costs of £2.4 million, first-year sales of MYOVIEW were £4.47 million and in the third year were in excess of £20 million. Total sales were in excess of £1.3 billion up to 2007. The precise profit figures were not published in the judgment, but were provided to the court as confidential information. In contrast, on retirement Dr Kelly was earning £71,500 per annum plus benefits with the company and Dr Chiu had left the company after two years' employment having earned not more than £15,000 per annum.

THE LAW

Drs Kelly and Chiu claimed under **ss 40 and 41** of the **PA 1977** for a share of the benefit derived by their employer from the MYOVIEW patent. **Section 41(4)** lists factors which determine the fair share to be awarded to the employee inventor. The court should take into account: (a) the nature of the employee's duties, his remuneration and the other advantages derived from the employment or derived from the invention; (b) the effort and skill which the employee has devoted to making the invention; (c) the effort and skill of any other person devoted to jointly making the invention as well as advice and other assistance contributed by any other employee who is not a joint inventor; and (d) the employer's contribution to the making, developing and working of the invention by his provision of advice, facilities or otherwise. **Section 41(5)** deals with the issue of awarding a fair share of compensation to joint employee inventors.

The difficulty is that while the statute lists the factors which determine the fair share to be awarded to the employee inventor, there had been no judicial guidance as to their interpretation. It is clear, however, that the UK inventor must be wholly or mainly employed in the UK or, if they have no main place of employment, be employed by an employer within its UK operations.

APPLYING THE LAW: WHAT AMOUNTS TO 'OUTSTANDING BENEFIT'?

In the instant case, two key issues then arose to be decided by the court: (1) how to determine the required scale of outstanding benefit to an employer that would merit an award of compensation to an inventor; and (2) the level of compensation the employee inventor should be awarded. The decision in *Kelly and Chiu* provides much-needed guidance as to how these key issues should be determined.

Proof of inventorship is an essential criterion for an employee to establish under **s 39 PA 1977**. An 'inventor' means the actual deviser of the invention and 'joint inventor' shall be construed accordingly: **s 7 PA 1977**. As a preliminary issue, Mr Justice Floyd confirmed Drs Kelly and Chiu were indeed co-inventors of the MYOVIEW patents potentially entitled to compensation under **s 40** and further that by virtue of **s 39(1) PA 1977** the invention had been assigned to their employer.

He then turned to consider the key contested question of whether the patents were of outstanding benefit for their employer. In doing so, he developed a four-step approach. This involved asking, first, whether the patent was a cause of some benefit. If yes, then, second, it was appropriate to consider how much of the total benefit could be attributed to the patent. This is a complex issue involving apportioning benefit from multiple causes. Third, one must determine whether the benefit was 'outstanding'. Floyd J remarked that the concept of 'outstanding benefit' means more than significant and 'out of the ordinary' or 'something special'. The benefit has to be greater than one would normally expect to arise from the employees' work. Finally, by reason of statute, it has to be just to make the award. On this question, Mr Justice Floyd stated that the court would be in a position to recognise situations in which it would be unjust to make an award, as and when they arose.

THE AMOUNT OF COMPENSATION

The judge then turned to the amount of the compensation. The Court was presented with evidence that the total sales of MYOVIEW between 2002 and 2007 amounted to some £1 billion. However, Mr Justice Floyd recognised the difficulties in quantifying the value of the benefit to the employer. He assessed what he considered to be the 'absolute rock bottom figure for the benefit from the patents' to the employer as £50 million. He then considered the nature of the employees' duties, remuneration and other advantages from the employment and concluded that Dr Kelly and Dr Chui were entitled to a 2 per cent (£1,000,000) and 1 per cent (£500,000) share, respectively, of the benefit derived by the employer from their invention. On this basis, the judge resolved that these figures represented a fair and just reward to the employees.

This is certainly a new development and it is unclear whether this decision could lead to a number of employees claiming compensation for their inventions from their employers. It is clear, however, that a high threshold of 'outstanding benefit' remains. However, the decision in *Shanks v Unilever* (2014) EWHC 1647 is a recent ruling which considered the size and nature of an employer's undertaking in connection with inventor employee compensation under **s 40 PA 1977**. The case was brought in 2006 before *Kelly v Chiu* was decided. The case was dismissed in 2013 and subsequently appealed in 2014 by Professor Shanks who argued that the total amount of Unilever's royalties on the invention constituted an 'outstanding benefit'. Unilever responded that its commercial success was not dependent on the patent. The court concluded that considering the size and nature of Unilever's commercial activities, the benefit the company derived from the patent was not outstanding. This later decision gives rise to certain inconsistency in approach given that the proportional contribution made by the employee inventors appears similar, but for the fact that Unilever did not put substantial resources at risk: *Shanks v Unilever* (2014) EWHC 1647 at para 120.

SECTION 10 PA 2004 COMPENSATION OF EMPLOYEES FOR CERTAIN INVENTIONS

In order to further the policy of rewarding employee inventors, the **Patents Act 2004 (PA 2004)** amends **PA 1977** in several respects, including compensation for employees of certain inventions.

Section 10 PA 2004 ('Compensation of employees for certain inventions') is an attempt to lower the high threshold by stating that the benefit to the employer should be assessed not only by reference to the patent itself, but also against the invention from which the patent arises. The commercial implications of **s 10** means employees will have a right to claim compensation if their employer gains a benefit from either the invention, the patent or both. In the event, **s 10 PA 2004** is a token gesture as far as employee inventors are concerned and some commentators have suggested that the outstanding benefit principle should have been repealed altogether.

Although, as before, compensation may be awarded only in respect of inventions which have been patented, it will no longer be necessary to show that the benefit in question flows from the patent itself (as opposed to the invention). Such benefits flowing from the patent will continue to be taken into account; however, if the invention has been beneficial for other reasons, those benefits may now also be taken into consideration. What constitutes an outstanding benefit will continue to depend on such factors as the size and nature of the relevant undertaking, which may be the whole or a division of the employer's business. **Sections 10(3) to (5) PA 2004** make consequential changes to **s 41**, which lays down how the amount of compensation awarded under **s 40** is to be assessed. **Subsection (6)** makes consequential changes to **s 43**.

Subsection (7) ensures that, for the purposes of assessing benefits under **s 40(1) or (2)**, and for the purpose of calculating the amount of compensation under **s 41**, those benefits which arise after the relevant patent has ceased to have effect (whether by expiry, surrender or revocation) cannot be taken into account. **Subsection (8)** is a transitional provision which ensures that the amended provisions do not apply to existing patents, nor to a patent for which an application is made before the amendments come into force.

Section 10(2) was introduced in order to further the policy objective of the employee compensation scheme, introducing the element of 'invention' as well as the patent.

CONCLUDING REMARKS

The legislative amendments introduced in the **PA 2004** were designed to make it easier to obtain such compensation by allowing for compensation whether either the patent or the invention, or both, are of outstanding benefit to the employer. This is thought to be a lower barrier that employee inventors need to overcome. Cases are now beginning to trickle in before the courts. Nevertheless, even though the threshold for outstanding benefit still remains high, the landmark decision in *Kelly and Chiu v GE Healthcare* (2009) HL will hearten employee inventors across the UK as it clarifies when inventors will be able to share in the benefits of a patent granted to their employers.

Common Pitfalls

This question should only be tackled by a student with a good knowledge of the relevant case. There is no scope for bluffing or waffle, as a precise analysis of the case is all that is required.

Aim Higher

While this essay question clearly demands a discussion of a House of Lords (now the Supreme Court) decision, it is important not to neglect the legislative provisions in **Patents Act 1977** and **Patents Act 2004** for a complete answer and the policy reasons for conferring employee inventors with a statutory right to claim compensation for certain inventions.

7

Passing Off

In the UK, the common law tort of passing off enables an enterprise to protect its business's goodwill. Goodwill is intangible and this is why the subject falls within the intellectual property law regime. Passing off may apply in situations where trade mark protection does not apply. If a registered trade mark exists, the proprietor can sue both for trade mark infringement as well as for passing off. The concept for passing off derives from the ancient case of *Perry v Truefitt* (1842), which ruled that a trader must not 'sell his own goods under the pretence that they are the goods of another man'.

For example, Trader A will commit a tort against Trader B if he passes off his goods or business as those of B. Trader B need not prove that Trader A acted intentionally or with intent to deceive. Nor does Trader B have to prove that anyone was actually deceived, if deception was likely. Further, this cause of action does not require Trader B to prove damage.

The tort of passing off is usually carried out by imitating the appearance of the claimant's goods, or by selling them under the same or a similar name. If the name used by the claimant merely describes the goods, then generally no action will lie. It is not necessary for the defendant's trade to be identical to that of the claimant if there is sufficient similarity to mislead the public.

False advertising is not generally considered to amount to passing off, but it may in exceptional circumstances. Reverse passing off may occur when the defendant holds out the claimant's goods as his own: *Bristol Conservatories Ltd v Conservatories Custom Built* (1989).

There is an international obligation to assure effective protection against unfair competition under **Art 10bis** of the **Paris Convention**. Finally, the remedies for a successful claim of passing off include an injunction and either damages or an account of profits. Damages will reflect the lost profit plus loss of goodwill and reputation. A delivery up order is also available.

QUESTION 30

Kensington Fashion Ltd has sold clothes under the 'Kensington Chick' label since the 1960s in their shops in Nottingham, Leeds and York but was refused trade mark registration. In 2007, another clothing manufacturing firm, Kensington Woman Ltd, proposed to extend their business from men's clothing to womenswear and brought out their own 'Kensington Chick' clothing line. The line sold successfully in Leicester, Coventry and Northampton. Kensington Fashion Ltd has plans to open a fourth store in Leicester in 2008.

▶ **Advise Kensington Fashion Ltd as to any cause of action they may have against Kensington Woman Ltd. If successful, would the appropriate remedy be an injunction covering all of the UK and Wales?**

How to Read this Question

Read each line of the question. Note that the facts disclose no registered trade marks. It is also important to note the specific cities where Kensington Fashion's shops are located and, similarly, those of Kensington Woman, as geography is relevant to the concept of goodwill.

The facts of the problem are based on the case of *Chelsea Man Menswear Ltd v Chelsea Girl Ltd* (1987) RPC 189. Lecturers often reconfigure the facts of an existing case, usually to reward those students who have done the recommended reading on the topic.

How to Answer this Question

This problem question focuses on the tort of 'passing off' as there are no registered trade mark rights. An action in passing off is a common law tort, whereas other forms of protection (i.e. copyright, trade marks, design rights and patents) are statute-based rights.

This problem question requires a straightforward analysis and application of the law of passing off to the facts. The law relating to passing off has developed via judge-made law, so it will be important to cite and apply the relevant case law. Students should:

❖ introduce and define the common law tort of passing off;

❖ outline the elements required for a successful action in passing off as established in *Reckitt and Coleman Products v Borden Inc.* (1990);

❖ apply each element to the facts in turn and reach a conclusion as to Kensington Fashion's likelihood of success;

❖ introduce the equitable remedy of injunction and how it will assist Kensington Fashion; and

❖ consider the terms on which the Court might injunct Kensington Woman from using the words 'Kensington Chick' in future.

Applying the Law

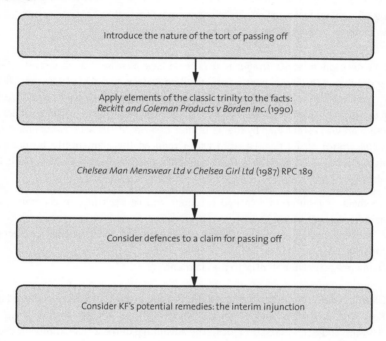

Introduce the nature of the tort of passing off

Apply elements of the classic trinity to the facts:
Reckitt and Coleman Products v Borden Inc. (1990)

Chelsea Man Menswear Ltd v Chelsea Girl Ltd (1987) RPC 189

Consider defences to a claim for passing off

Consider KF's potential remedies: the interim injunction

ANSWER

As Kensington Fashion Ltd (KF) has been refused trade mark registration they cannot rely on any registered rights under the **Trade Marks Act 1994** (**TMA 1994**). Further, the UK has no law of unfair competition as in the EU and other civil law countries. However, KF may have a cause of action against Kensington Woman Ltd (KW) based on the common law tort of passing off which has its origins in the tort of deception. The tort of passing off is sometimes referred to as protection of the goodwill in a business or a concept and makes it possible for a trader to protect a business's goodwill. Goodwill is an intangible concept but is nevertheless a property right. According to Lord MacNaughten in *Inland Revenue Cmrs v Muller & Co's Margarine Ltd* (1901) AC 217 the concept of goodwill means:

> Every positive advantage that has been acquired in carrying on the business which would give a reasonable expectancy of preference in the face of competition; the benefit and advantage of the good name, reputation, and connection of a business and the attractive force that brings in custom.

In other words, the positive benefits that attract a consumer to prefer one business's products (or in this case, clothing line) over another.

The underlying basis for an action for passing off is found in the case of *Perry v Truefitt* (1842) which held that 'A man is not to sell his own goods under the pretence that they are the goods of another man.' Passing off may therefore be defined as a misrepresentation in the course of trade by one trader which damages the goodwill of another. In the context of the problem at hand, this means that KF may be able to bring an action for passing off against KW for their use of the words 'Kensington Chick' in connection with the KW clothing sold in Leicester, Coventry and Northampton.

Since the decision in *Perry v Truefitt* in 1842 there have been several important cases that further developed the law of passing off including *Reddaway & Co Ltd v Banham & Co Ltd* (1896), *Spalding & Brov AW Gamage Ltd* (1915), *Bollinger v Costa Brava Wine Co Ltd* (1960) and *Warnink BV v Townend & Sons (Hull) Ltd* (1980). However, the classic legal definition of passing off was established by the 'Jif Lemon' case. In *Reckitt & Coleman Products Ltd v Borden Inc* (1990) All ER 1873 HL, Lord Oliver reduced the elements to be proved in a passing off action to three. These three elements are now known as the 'classic trinity' formulation:

❖ Goodwill or reputation attached to goods and services (e.g. in claimant's goods, name, mark, get-up etc.);
❖ A misrepresentation made to the public (leading to confusion or deception), causing…
❖ Damage – actual or potential to the claimant.

Lord Oliver's classic definition of an action for passing off has since been endorsed in *Consorzio del Prosciutto di Parma v Marks & Spencer Plc* (1991) RPC 351; *Harrods v Harrodian School* (1996); and *BBC v Talksport* (2001). The advantage of the 'classic trinity' formulation is that it is simpler and is preferred in practice. For KF to be successful in an action for passing off against KW, it must satisfy all three elements.

DOES GOODWILL EXIST IN KF'S CLOTHING LABEL NAME 'KENSINGTON CHICK'?

The words are descriptive in that 'Kensington' is a geographic word for the place known as Kensington in London and 'Chick' is slang for a young woman. In *County Sound plc v Ocean Sound Ltd* (1991) FSR 367 the court found that the purely descriptive words did not attract goodwill. However, one could argue here that this case can be distinguished as KF have been using the two-word combination for more than 40 years, whereas the use of descriptive words in *County Sound* was new use. Nevertheless, the length of time it takes to establish goodwill sufficient to bring an action for passing off is a question of fact in each case. However, in *Antec International Ltd v South Western Chicks (Warren) Ltd* (1998) EWHC Patents 330 goodwill was established through use of a name for a period of 10 years and in *Stennards Reay* (1967) FSR 140 goodwill existed after just five weeks' use. We will assume for the sake of further analysis that a Court would find that a period of 40-plus years' use by KF of the name 'Kensington Chick' would attract sufficient goodwill to found an action for passing off against KW. KF must be careful to ensure that goodwill exists (i.e. there are actual customers for its Kensington Chick clothing line) and not merely reputation as there is strong authority that the law of passing off only protects goodwill and not reputation. Indeed, in *Harrods Ltd v Harrodian School Ltd* (1996) Millet LJ stated that 'damage to reputation without damage to goodwill is not sufficient to support an action for passing off'.

Has KW made a material misrepresentation to the public (whether or not intentional), leading or likely to lead the public to believe that the clothing line sold by KW in Leicester, Coventry and Northampton are the clothing line of KF?

In other words, is KW's Kensington Chick clothing line associated in the minds of the public with that of KF? The fact that the public may be confused as to the origin of the clothing line may not necessarily amount to a material misrepresentation: *Phones 4u Ltd v Phone4u.co.uk Internet Ltd* (2007); *HFC Bank v HSBC Bank plc* (2000). An initial misrepresentation which is corrected before the actual point of sale or contract may not amount to a material misrepresentation and therefore no actionable misrepresentation in passing off: *BP Amoco plc v John Kelly Ltd* (2001). Further, customers will not be assumed to be 'morons in a hurry', to quote Foster J in *Morning Star Co-operative Society v Express Newspapers* (1979). On the other hand, KW will not have a defence by asserting that the public would not have been misled if they were more 'literate, careful, perspicacious or wary': *Reckitt & Coleman* (1990). As to whether KW has misrepresented a connection with the KF Kensington Chick clothing line, the court will assess the amount of attention a typical customer might be expected to exercise in purchasing the clothing, the type of shop in which the clothing is sold and generally the habits and characteristics of women's clothing consumers and how many customers have been misled. In relation to the number of customers deceived, KF will have to show that KW misled a substantial number of customers, but not all of the potential public: *Neutrogena Corp v Golden Ltd* (1996) per Morritt LJ. KF may wish to consider gathering survey evidence from customers and engaging an industry expert to give evidence to support its case.

IS THERE A REAL LIKELIHOOD OF DAMAGE TO KF'S GOODWILL?

The last element is damage (or the likelihood of damage) to KF's goodwill. KF must establish that there is a real likelihood of more than minimal damage to its goodwill: *Warnink BV Townend & Sons (Hull) Ltd* (1980); *Harrods Ltd v Harrodian School Ltd* (1996). Here, there is a strong likelihood of damage to KF's goodwill given: (1) the damage by association caused by KW's misrepresentation that there is some connection between the parties; and (2) the damage caused directly through lost sales to KW; or (3) the damage caused indirectly to the reputation of the Kensington Chick label.

ENFORCING GOODWILL

KF may bring an action for passing off in the county court and the High Court. KF will want to know what remedies it will have if it is successful in its action for passing off against KW and in particular how to stop KW from using the Kensington Chick name as quickly as possible. KF will seek an order for an interim injunction against KW which would result in KW being stopped from continuing to sell its Kensington Chick clothing line until the issues were resolved at trial.

DEFENCES TO PASSING OFF

The normal way in which a defendant such as KW will resist a passing off action is to challenge whether the claimant KF has actually established each of the three ingredients of the tort. Much will depend on the quality of evidence produced by KF to prove the 'classic trinity'. In this case KW may not be convinced that KF has the goodwill and reputation it claims.

THE SCOPE OF THE INTERIM INJUNCTION

In terms of an application for an interim injunction, only goodwill in the UK is relevant and while this does not present an issue for KF whose business is carried on in Nottingham, Leeds and York, one should consider the question of the geographical area over which KF's goodwill may be regarded as extending, as KF may have a reputation that is wider than Nottingham, Leeds and York. Further, KF have plans to open a fourth store in Leicester which would be in direct competition with KW's store. Here, it is likely that the defendants, KW, will argue that any injunction made against them should be confined to the areas of the claimants' (KF) pre-existing business, namely Nottingham, Leeds and York.

However, a similar argument was rejected by the Court of Appeal in *Chelsea Man Menswear Ltd v Chelsea Girl Ltd*, a case in point, which allowed an injunction covering all of England and Wales. The Court of Appeal had regard to the fact that both people and goods move around the country, and also to the claimants' desire to extend their business in the future (although no specific plans appeared to have been made). Furthermore, Nourse LJ noted that *A Levey v Henderson-Kenton (Holdings) Ltd* (1974) RPC 617 was the only reported case to have imposed a geographical limit and only at the pre-trial stage. In *Levey*, the claimant who had run a department store business in Newcastle-upon-Tyne was granted an injunction at trial to prevent the defendant from opening a furniture and furnishing shop under the name 'Kentons' in Newcastle or the Newcastle area. The defendant group already operated 'Kentons' shops in the south of England. The desire of businesses to expand legitimately in the future may well make the *Chelsea Man* case the model for the future. There may nevertheless still be circumstances in which local goodwill exists and in which a geographically limited injunction is appropriate. The *Daily Mail* newspaper relied successfully on its goodwill in London and the south-east of England to stop the publication of a London evening newspaper under the name *London Evening Mail*: *Associated Newspapers, Daily Mail & General Trust v Express Newspapers* (2003) FSR 51.

As we are told that KF may have a reputation that extends beyond the geographical areas of Nottingham, Leeds and York, if *Chelsea Man Menswear Ltd v Chelsea Girl Ltd* is followed, there is a strong inference on this basis that any injunction applied for at first instance to cover all of England and Wales will be granted.

Common Pitfalls

This question should only be tackled by a student with a good knowledge of the classic trinity as established in the 'Jif Lemon' case. Further, this is a typical problem question that might apply to many small to medium-size businesses. Ensure that your answer addresses the specific concerns tailored to those involved, rather than a general discussion of the law of passing off.

Aim Higher

This question calls for the effective deployment of the relevant case law to the facts. A detailed discussion of the concepts of goodwill, reputation and geographical origin will gain marks, while evaluation of their application to the fact scenario will demonstrate not only knowledge of the law but the ability to apply it.

QUESTION 31

'With the protection available to owners of intellectual property in the UK under the registered trade mark and registered design systems, it is difficult to see a significant role for the common law of passing off.'

▶ **Critically evaluate this statement.**

How to Read this Question

This is a general question, requiring an analysis of the common law tort of passing off and how it may (or may not) develop in the future, especially in light of the UK's membership of the EU and the concept of unfair competition.

How to Answer this Question

The essay question divides neatly into two main parts: (1) a discussion of the operation of the common law tort of passing off; and (2) how it may (or may not) develop in the future.

Answer Structure

- ❖ Introduce the nature of the common law action of passing off and concept of goodwill.
- ❖ Explain and give examples of 'orthodox' or 'traditional' passing off compared with more modern 'extended passing off' cause of actions in connection with character merchandising matters and celebrity image rights.

❖ Discuss the fact that English common law does not include a separate tort for unlawful misappropriation.
❖ Explain the international obligation to assure effective protection against unfair competition and the EU approach in this regard.
❖ Concluding remarks on the role of passing off.

Up for Debate

In 1875, the system for registering trade marks was introduced. More recently, the 1994 statutory reforms have further broadened the law in respect of registered marks. The increase in scope applies to both registrability and types of infringement and has been developed by the developing case law, particularly by the European Court of Justice's decision in *Arsenal Football Club v Mathew Reed* (2001) regarding the modern functions of trade marks. In other words, registered trade marks are no longer restricted by the origin function. This begs the question, what is the future role of the common law tort of passing off? The law of passing off has not been similarly developed or broadened in scope. It remains the case that in order to successfully prove passing off, a claimant must demonstrate that there has been a misrepresentation giving rise to a likelihood of confusion on the part of the consumer. On the other hand, there will always be marks that are ineligible for registration under the **Trade Marks Act 1994** based on **Directive 89/104/EEC** which leaves a role for passing off to 'fill the gaps' in protection for business reputation and goodwill.

ANSWER

In the UK, the common law tort of passing off enables an enterprise to protect the business's goodwill. Goodwill is intangible and this is why the subject falls within the intellectual property law regime. It should be made clear at the outset that passing off has always been available at common law for marks in use but not registered, ineligible for registration or refused registration.

Accordingly, passing off may apply in situations where trade mark protection does not apply so on that basis it is clear that there is still a significant role in modern times for the common law action of passing off. If a registered trade mark exists, the proprietor can sue both for trade mark infringement and for passing off. In other words, passing off has a further role as it is usually pleaded in the alternative when a claimant brings an action for trade mark infringement. Further, if a mark is invalid or revoked for non-use, then passing off will be relied upon to protect goodwill.

By way of background, the concept for passing off derives from the ancient case of *Perry v Truefitt* (1842) which ruled that a trader must not 'sell his own goods under the pretence that they are the goods of another man'. For example, Trader A will commit a tort against Trader B if he passes off his goods or business as those of B. Trader B need not prove that

Trader A acted intentionally or with intent to deceive. Nor does Trader B have to prove that anyone was actually deceived, if deception was likely. Further, this cause of action does not require Trader B to prove damage.

The tort of passing off is usually carried out by imitating the appearance of the claimant's goods, or by selling them under the same or a similar name. If the name used by the claimant merely describes the goods then generally no action will lie. It is not necessary for the defendant's trade to be identical to that of the claimant if there is sufficient similarity to mislead the public.

ORTHODOX, EXTENDED AND REVERSE PASSING OFF

Orthodox passing off includes protecting goodwill in a name, a mark, the get-up of a product (e.g. shape of packaging and of containers, the use of colour schemes, the layout of and typeface used on labels, indeed any aspect of the goods' appearance which helps the consumer to identify trade origin). Extended passing off involves a misrepresentation which does not cause origin confusion, rather it results in some other form of harm to the claimant's goodwill. The cases can be grouped together as follows: false suggestions of superior quality; geographical origin; advertising campaigns; comparative advertising and reverse passing off (where the defendant misleads by saying that the claimant's product is made by the defendant): *Bristol Conservatories Ltd v Conservatories Custom Built* (1989). These cases support the argument that there remains a significant role for the common law of passing off.

A WIDER VIEW OF PASSING OFF

Additionally, in a modern context, the common law action of passing off may also be a helpful cause of action in relation to character merchandising matters (*Mirage v Counter-Feat Clothing* (1991)) and celebrity image rights as there is no separate tort of misappropriation of personality in the UK. In the famous 'Jif Lemon' case of *Reckitt and Coleman Products v Borden Inc* (1990) the House of Lords (now known as the Supreme Court) began to recognise a wider view of goodwill which assists with the tort of passing off and character merchandising actions. Lord Oliver summarised the three elements to be proved in a passing off action, now known as the 'classic trinity' formulation:

(1) Goodwill or reputation attached to goods and services (e.g. in claimant's goods, name, mark, get-up etc.);
(2) A misrepresentation made to the public (leading to confusion or deception); causing…
(3) Damage – actual or potential to the claimant.

While false advertising is not generally considered to amount to passing off, it may amount to passing off in exceptional circumstances.

Is it appropriate for the tort of passing off to expand?

One should also note that there is an international obligation to assure effective protection against unfair competition under **Art 10bis** of the **Paris Convention**. The policy question facing the UK is whether it is appropriate for passing off to expand. If it is concluded that passing off should develop further into a form of protection against unfair competition, then the elements which at present have to be proved to succeed in a passing off action will need to be reconsidered. Alternatively, should passing off remain as a strictly defined, alternative means of protection to registered trade marks?

THE EU APPROACH TO UNFAIR COMPETITION

In the EU, unfair competition law is traditionally considered part of intellectual property law; however, it also has a role to play in the area of consumer protection law (since unfair competition law is partly oriented towards consumer protection). At the community level, there is a growing body of regulatory law dealing with unfair commercial practices. The **2004 Unfair Commercial Practices Directive** regulates unfair business-to-consumer practices. Within this framework, however, unfair competition law remains a matter for national law which depends on legal traditions, and cultural, linguistic and historical particularities. It is only the two combined – the European requirements including the judicial, and the practice of the European Court of Justice on the fundamental freedoms and national laws – which create European unfair competition law. This means that despite all their differences, all EU Member States have developed mechanisms based on the principle of fairness to control commercial activities. Nevertheless, is it correct to say that there is a European unfair competition law? Not in the sense of one uniform coherent set of regulations, which for a wide variety of reasons has not yet been achieved at Community level. What does exist, however, are selective regulations, regulations dealing with individual problem areas in the field of unfair competition. Thus, although the 'piecemeal approach' has predominated so far, there are a number of arguments that may justify the term 'European' unfair competition law.

THE UK 'PASSING OFF' APPROACH: IS A NEW TORT OF UNFAIR COMPETITION NEEDED?

Within the framework set by Community law, unfair competition law, however, is above all a matter for national law. In the UK the **Gowers Review (2006)** identified a need to protect brand owners against cheap imitations. This precise issue was the subject of the dispute in the matter of *L'Oréal v Bellure NV* (2008) RPC 196. To date the UK judiciary has resisted attempts to introduce a European-style law of unfair competition. The introduction of new legislation would involve a significant change in policy at a time when academic opinion is divided. Lord Justice Jacob (as he had become) stated at [141] that:

> the basic economic rule is that competition is not only lawful but a mainspring of the economy. The legislator has recognised that there should be exceptions. It has laid down the rules for these: the laws of patents, trade marks, copyrights, and designs have all been fashioned for the purpose. Each of them have rules for their

existence and (save for trade marks) set time periods for existence. Each has their own justification. It is not for judges to step in and legislate into existence new categories of intellectual property rights. And if they were to do so they would be entering wholly uncertain territory.

The argument against the UK having a new tort of unfair competition is that there is no specific justification for it – competition is lawful and in the public's interest.

In conclusion, only a detailed statutory law of unfair competition (as has developed in the European civil law countries) either alongside or in place of the common law of passing off will provide judges with sufficient detail to apply to the variety of fact situations it would cover. Until that time, there remains a significant role for the tort of passing off to play, particularly as an alternative means to protect registered, expired, non-registered marks and marks ineligible for registered trade mark protection.

Common Pitfalls

Avoid simply describing the elements of the common law action of passing off. Rather focus on the ways in which passing off can be used to protect against misappropriation of goodwill, the challenge of protecting brand owners from low-cost imitations and policy arguments for and against extending the law of passing off to encompass unfair competition.

Aim Higher

Extra credit can be expected for discussing the recommendations of the **Gowers Review** and the UK's international obligations in respect of unfair competition. In addition, students may wish to refer to refereed law journal articles on the topic such as Horton, A and Robertson, A, 'Does the UK or the EC Need an Unfair Competition Law?' (1995) EIPR 568.

QUESTION 32

Janet Torvin is a former Olympic gold medallist ice dancer who turned professional when she joined a company that toured across Britain and overseas in the 1980s. In late 2015, at 55 years old, Janet lives in the UK and is choreographing routines for her television ice-dancing show, *Ice Dancing Stars*, which she is also producing. Earlier in the year, another TV production company, Winter Sport Productions Ltd (WSP), produced a DVD entitled *Learn to Ice Dance Basics*, for sale in the UK market. To illustrate the cover of the DVD, WSP used a picture of Janet from a photograph taken by a member of their staff while Janet was performing a routine in a live show at the Nottingham Arena in 2014. Janet is now suing WSP for passing off.

▶ Advise Janet as to the prospects of success of her action against WSP.

How to Read this Question

This problem question relates to celebrity image rights and passing off (the extended form of passing off). Passing off is usually found within the world of business and relates specifically to a misrepresentation made by one party which damages the goodwill of another party.

How to Answer this Question

There is no statute concerning the law of passing off which has been developed in the UK solely by case law. The usual legal principles enshrined in the classic trinity test established in the 'Jif Lemon' case need to be applied to the facts. However, there are also issues as to Jane's image rights and the law related to false endorsement to discuss.

Answer Structure

❖ Introduce the notion of legal protection for personality and the legal recognition of image rights;

❖ Discuss the issues of false endorsement and merchandising: *Irvine v Talksport* (2002); *Fenty and others v Arcadia Group and another* (2013) EWHC 2310 (Ch) (*Rihanna v Topshop*);

❖ Consider whether the required elements of passing off are satisfied on the balance of probabilities; and

❖ Finally, assess whether Torvin has potential remedies against Winter Sport Productions Ltd.

Applying the Law

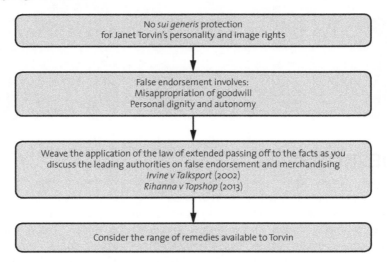

No *sui generis* protection
for Janet Torvin's personality and image rights

False endorsement involves:
Misappropriation of goodwill
Personal dignity and autonomy

Weave the application of the law of extended passing off to the facts as you
discuss the leading authorities on false endorsement and merchandising
Irvine v Talksport (2002)
Rihanna v Topshop (2013)

Consider the range of remedies available to Torvin

ANSWER

Some famous people, such as Janet Torvin, may be in a position to exploit their personality or reputation in a particular field by endorsing goods or services. A crucial first step is to distinguish 'endorsement' from the issue of 'merchandising'. In an endorsement, the celebrity informs the public that she approves of the product or service in question and is pleased to be associated with it. The celebrity adds her name to the product or service as further encouragement for the public to buy. The benefit to the endorsee is that with the addition of the goodwill of the famous personality, the product's attractiveness will be enhanced in the eyes of the target market. Where a real person is concerned, the legal issues arising not only relate to commerce, but also to personal dignity and autonomy.

The use of passing off in false endorsement claims is not new and dates back to the mid nineteenth century. In *Clark v Freeman* (1848) the court held a well-known doctor was unable to stop the defendant from selling pills under his name because he was not in the business of selling pills himself. This was followed by the decision in *Williams v Hodge & Co* (1887). The case of the *British Medical Association v Marsh* (1931) distinguished the previous cases when it barred the defendant from using the mark of the BMA as the name of his pharmacy chain. The injunction was granted because there was found to be a likelihood of damage in that the BMA's reputation would suffer, resulting in a loss of membership.

In Torvin's case, the public may infer from Winter Sport Productions Ltd's (WSP) representation that Janet Torvin is endorsing its ice-dancing instructional DVD entitled *Learn to Ice Dance Basics*. It is clear from the facts that Torvin did not authorise WSP to use her image on the DVD cover and that a cause of action may lie in passing off. Although not expressly stated, it would appear that Torvin would be more concerned with loss of commercial exploitation and profit than with damages for loss of dignity and autonomy, particularly as the market for the DVD is likely to be the same target market for her forthcoming *Ice Dancing Stars* TV show. As an internationally known ice dancer, Torvin is likely to have significant commercial potential for exploiting her identity. Passing off resulting from a false impression that Torvin has endorsed a product may be determined on the basis of what she would normally charge as a fee for such an endorsement.

IRVINE V TALKSPORT (2002)

The law of relating to celebrity endorsement and passing off has developed in particular as a result of the decision in *Irvine v Talksport* (2002) which accepted that falsely implying that a celebrity was endorsing a product is actionable under the common law tort of passing off. The court was very careful to distinguish *Talksport* as a false endorsement case and pointed out that 'nothing said [in the *Talksport* decision] touches on the quite separate issues which may arise in character merchandising cases'. For the first time, the UK courts acknowledged the right of celebrities to exploit their image and judicial notice was taken that celebrities do exploit their name and image through endorsements both inside and outside their own field. Justice Laddie indicated that the law of passing off had widened since the decision in *McCulloch v May (Produce Distributors) Ltd* (1947) to encompass celebrity endorsement.

The *Irvine* case involved the Formula One racing driver Eddie Irvine and concerned the manipulation of his photograph used in an advertising campaign for radio station Talksport. The mobile phone Irvine had been holding when the photograph was taken had been replaced by a superimposed picture of a radio and underneath was the caption 'Talk

Radio … We've got it covered'. In terms of Irvine's celebrity, he had since 1996 built up a worldwide reputation in the sport, which was accompanied by a growing business in endorsing products. Taking into account persuasive decisions from both Australia and New Zealand, Mr Justice Laddie found that the public can be misled if the likeness of a famous person is used to advertise a product without authorisation. It is necessary, however, that this person has built up sufficient goodwill and that the advertiser gives the impression that the person used really endorses the product. It would appear that although 'the man in the street' can still be used for advertising purposes without a licence, at least as far as the action of passing off is concerned, the same is not the case with a celebrity who may have image rights that need to be respected. Modern celebrities may have a reputation in their own field of endeavour which they may also use to endorse unrelated products for significant sums of money: for example, perfumes, clothing. Mr Justice Laddie found in favour of Irvine and held that a celebrity *did* have a monopoly over the use of his or her image. Laddie J stated, 'the endorsee is taking the benefit of the attractive force which is the reputation or goodwill of a famous person'.

Therefore, in order to be successful, Torvin will have to prove that:

❖ at the time the acts complained of occurred, she had a significant reputation or goodwill; and
❖ WSP's actions led to the false impression to a 'not insignificant section of her market' that Torvin had endorsed, recommended or approved WSP's actions.

The *Irvine* case clarified the law so that endorsement is definitely actionable where the celebrity in question has not consented to the use of his or her image. However, it could be argued that if a celebrity's image has been used without the implication of endorsement, the defendant may escape liability. This anomaly highlights the need for image rights per se to be legally protected. In some cases, it can also be defamatory to assert that a person has endorsed a product or service when this is not true. This is a matter of fact for the court.

Further, it is no longer the law that the parties must be in a common field of activity for passing off to occur, nor that damage will be confined simply to loss of sales. What is needed, however, is an association between the defendant's goods and the claimant. Clearly, where the parties do share a common field of activity it will be easier for the claimant to demonstrate that there has been a misrepresentation.

Accordingly, it would seem that Torvin's endorsement is indeed commercially valuable given her fame in the UK and internationally in the sphere of ice dancing. Although the endorsement on the *Learn to Ice Dance Basics* DVD is unauthorised, a significant number of members of the public is likely to infer endorsement from WSP's representation. As such, Torvin has every prospect of success in relation to her action for passing off. Torvin will suffer the loss of earnings both for this and for future endorsements, so the appropriate remedy is an award of damages. How should damages be assessed in this type of case? In *Irvine v Talksport*, Laddie J held that the principles used to assess damages for patent infringement should be applied to celebrity endorsement cases. Irvine gave evidence that he would not have 'bothered to get out of bed' for less than £25,000. Laddie J, however, assessed the damages as what would have been a 'reasonable' fee for Irvine's endorsement of the defendant's radio station. This was held to be the sum of £2,000. Irvine appealed and the Court of Appeal, which took into account his evidence, awarded him £25,000 in damages.

The decision in *Irvine v Talksport Ltd* represents a major step in the evolution of passing off as a viable cause of action in England and Wales. Now the courts will recognise damages in the form of lost royalties or licensing fees. More recently, in the case of *Fenty and others v Arcadia Group and another* (2013) EWHC 2310 (Ch) (*Rihanna v Topshop*), Justice Birss applied the principles set out in *Irvine v Talksport* and elaborated on the nature of false endorsement.

RIHANNA V TOPSHOP (2013)

The utility of passing off as a cause of action to be deployed by a celebrity whose image had been exploited without consent was once again brought to the fore in the *Rihanna v Topshop* (2013) case. The issue of whether merchandising can amount to passing off was revisited. Topshop is a well-known fashion retailer and Rihanna is a famous pop star. In March 2012 Topshop began selling a T-shirt with Rihanna's image on it. The photograph was taken by an independent photographer from whom Topshop had a licence. However, the company had not obtained a licence from Rihanna, who contended that the sale of the T-shirt without her permission infringed her rights.

Justice Birss found that in terms of goodwill, Rihanna is 'a world famous pop star with a cool and edgy image'. Further, through her companies, she runs a very large merchandising and endorsement operation and has endorsement agreements with Nike, Gillette, Clinique and LG Mobile. Importantly, the judge identified that for a false endorsement claim to succeed there must be a misrepresentation about *trade origin*. He stated that selling a garment with a recognisable image of a famous person is not, in and of itself, passing off. Instead, a false belief must be engendered in the product in order to constitute passing off. As for the image itself, the judge noted that it was a still from a video shoot which had become famous and widely reported in the UK because of the risqué clothing Rihanna had worn. As a result of the ensuing publicity, the image would be noticed by her fans. Therefore, the judge accepted that although a good number of purchasers would have bought the T-shirt without giving the question of authorisation any thought at all, a substantial portion of those considering the product would have been induced into thinking that the garment was authorised by Rihanna. Those persons would be Rihanna fans and they would have recognised, or thought they recognised, the particular image of Rihanna, not simply as her picture, but as a particular picture of her associated with a particular context, being the recent *Talk That Talk* album. For those persons, the idea that the product was authorised would have been part of what had motivated them to buy the T-shirt. Those purchasers would have been deceived. As for damage, since Justice Birss found a substantial number of purchasers were likely to have been deceived into buying the T-shirt under the false belief that it had been authorised, he held that it would obviously be damaging to the claimants' goodwill. It amounted to sales lost to Rihanna's merchandising business and also a loss of control over her reputation in the fashion sphere. This is the first reported English decision where the false endorsement principle has been extended to the unauthorised use of a celebrity's image in merchandising.

In the ice-dancing world, Torvin is an icon and the decision in the *Rihanna* case is directly on point. As Torvin is in the business of licensing the use of her name and image for merchandising purposes, Torvin's claim for damages will be assessed by considering the licence fee she would have charged for the lawful use of her image for such an endorsement. In light of the authority of *Irvine* and *Rihanna*, WSP may prefer to settle the matter with Torvin out of court by paying her a licence fee thereby avoiding the need to pay legal costs in addition to any damages award. However, some celebrities hold the view that meagre damage awards on the basis of lost royalties or licensing fees fail to account for the potential damage to the goodwill of a celebrity, nor does it account for the 'exclusivity' issue. For example, Torvin may not be able in the future to accept a large endorsement contract to promote another DVD. Torvin may wish to argue that the court take into account evidence of a 'minimum fee', where a 'reasonable fee' does not include a sum in respect of the exclusivity that comes with an endorsement.

In conclusion, although selling an item such as a DVD or garment bearing a recognisable image of a famous person is not, of itself, passing off, each case must be considered on its own facts. It is therefore important when considering whether there has been passing off to look at the nature of the relevant market and the perceptions of the relevant customers. The real issue in this case was therefore to understand why a person might buy the DVD, either because they wanted to buy a DVD adorned by the image of an ice dancer (and so there would be no misrepresentation), or because there was a misrepresentation that Janet Torvin had authorised the use of the image. High-profile individuals such as Torvin are often, unsurprisingly, highly protective of their image. In the absence of specific legal protection for personality or image rights in England and Wales, the extended use of the law of passing off through false endorsement continues to be used to prevent the misuse of a person's image in promoting third-party goods or services. Businesses such as WSP clearly take a risk if they choose to sell unauthorised products which could deceive the buying public.

Common Pitfalls

Even though it is tempting to do so, avoid treating this question as an invitation to write an essay on image rights. It is crucial to apply the relevant case law to the facts and provide solid commercial legal advice in terms of the likelihood of success of an action for passing off.

Aim Higher

Aim to provide a detailed discussion of the leading cases in this area: namely, *Irvine v Talksport* (2002) and *Rihanna v Topshop* (2013). Critically analyse the way in which the courts analyse the classic trinity and approach damages in false endorsement merchandising cases.

8 Registered Trade Marks

A trade mark is a sign used in relation to goods or services so as to indicate a connection in the course of trade between the goods or services and some person having a right to use the mark. In simple terms, a registered trade mark is intended to serve as a 'badge of origin'. It should give the consumer a guarantee that the product or services to which it applies emanate from a particular source.

A system for registered trade marks in the UK was developed in the nineteenth century and the legal regime is now enshrined in the **Trade Marks Act 1994** (**TMA 1994**). The **TMA 1994** regulates the registration of trade marks at the UK Intellectual Property Office (UKIPO) and the enforcement and commercial exploitation of registered marks.

However, trade mark law has now been harmonised throughout the EU. **Council Directive 89/104/EEC** made provision for the Community Trade Mark (**Council Regulation (EC) 40/94**) which created a single trade mark right extending throughout the EU and gives effect to the **Madrid Protocol for the Registration of Marks Internationally**. The original directive has now been replaced by **Directive (EC) 2008/95** ('**the Directive**') to take account of various amendments that had been made pursuant to the original. The Directive also forms the basis for a body of law regulating trade marks registered at the **Community Trade Mark Office** in Alicante, Spain (referred to as OHIM). A trade mark registered at OHIM has effect throughout the EU. The two regimes exist side by side, both based on the Directive and both capable of giving rise to case law emanating from the **Court of Justice of the EU** (CJEU; formerly the European Court of Justice). A judgment of the CJEU has effect on the interpretation by UK courts of the **TMA 1994** whether it results from an appeal from OHIM or from a reference by a UK court for guidance.

The key advantage of registering a trade mark is the mark is afforded greater legal protection and there is no need to prove elements of passing off and reputation in the mark. The trade mark registration system protects any sign that is capable of being represented graphically: **s 1(1) TMA 1994**. Currently there is a wide range of marks that are capable of registration, including conventional marks such as pictorial marks (letters, words, pictures or drawings) and unconventional trade marks including signs such as slogans; three-dimensional signs (shapes); colours; sensory signs, for example auditory (sound signs), gustatory (taste signs), olfactory (scent signs) and gestures; action signs; and, incredibly, holograms.

The legal purpose of a trade mark is to prevent others from using the mark and benefiting from the goodwill attached to the mark. A trade mark constitutes personal property and a monopoly over a registered trade mark can be renewed by the proprietor indefinitely. However, a trade mark can be removed from the register via revocation proceedings by reason of non-use or if the mark has become 'generic' or would mislead the public.

Checklist

Students should anticipate questions about the following:

- the nature and function of trade marks;
- the meaning of a 'mark';
- registrable trade marks (conventional and non-conventional);
- the impact of EU law;
- absolute and relative grounds for refusal of registration;
- trade mark infringement and defences;
- loss of registration, e.g. revocation.

QUESTION 33

Imagine you are a Trade Mark Examiner employed by the UK Intellectual Property Office Trade Marks Registry. You have received the following applications for registration. Examine the applications and set out the grounds of any objections you may have to the registration of the proposed marks.

(a) TM Application 1: 7 DAYS A WEEK, by a taxi service.
(b) TM Application 2: OLYMPIC, for shaving products for men.
(c) TM Application 3: The colour RED, for a telecommunications company.
(d) TM Application 4: The scent of a NUTMEG, by a furniture manufacturer, to be applied to furniture.
(e) TM Application 5: 'Catch a wrinkle in time', for a cosmetics preparation.
(f) TM Application 6: BACARDI, for a company that produces vodka.

How to Read this Question

This question requires the student to apply the law directly to six fact scenarios (a)–(f). In particular, the student should evaluate any absolute and relative grounds to refuse to register the applied-for mark.

How to Answer this Question

This question should be answered in order, that is, (a)–(f). The best approach to this type of question is to answer each part in turn, clearly identifying the separate parts of the answer. Unless you are told otherwise, it is reasonable for you to assume that each subsection carries equal marks. This means you may want to allocate equal time to each part.

Applying the Law

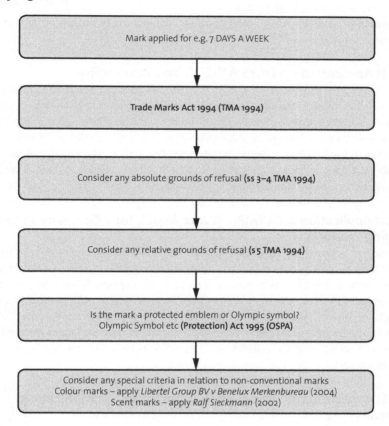

Mark applied for e.g. 7 DAYS A WEEK

↓

Trade Marks Act 1994 (TMA 1994)

↓

Consider any absolute grounds of refusal **(ss 3–4 TMA 1994)**

↓

Consider any relative grounds of refusal **(s 5 TMA 1994)**

↓

Is the mark a protected emblem or Olympic symbol?
Olympic Symbol etc **(Protection) Act 1995 (OSPA)**

↓

Consider any special criteria in relation to non-conventional marks
Colour marks – apply *Libertel Group BV v Benelux Merkenbureau* (2004)
Scent marks – apply *Ralf Sieckmann* (2002)

ANSWER

A trade mark is a sign used in the course of trade to indicate the source of goods or services and distinguishes them from the goods or services of other traders: **s 1 Trade Marks Act 1994**. Any sign that distinguishes will meet this requirement, according to the decision in *AD2000 Trade Mark* (1996). A trade mark is primarily a badge of origin, and it is used so that customers can recognise the product of a particular trader. As a result, trade marks are valuable commercial property and the choice of an appropriate mark requires care and effort. It is not compulsory to register a trade mark, but since registration provides considerable legal advantages it is highly desirable. However, not all marks are capable of being registered as trade marks. The substantive law of trade marks is contained in the **TMA 1994** which implements the **Trade Marks Directive (EC) 2008/95** ('**the Directive**'). A trade mark application is examined to determine if it complies with the Act and whether there are grounds for rejecting it. Objections to the registration of a mark may be raised either by the Trade Marks Registry during examination or by third parties during opposition proceedings. The grounds for refusing registration are divided into two categories:

❖ *absolute grounds* for refusal (**TMA 1994 ss 3** and **4**) which are concerned with objections based on the mark itself; and

❖ *relative grounds* for refusal (**TMA 1994 s 5**); these are concerned with conflict with third-party rights.

(a) *TM Application 1:* 7 DAYS A WEEK, by a Taxi Service

Many trades advertise that their goods or service are provided seven days a week. The mark breaches **s 3(1)(c) TMA 1994**, which prohibits the registration of a mark which consists exclusively of the 'time of rendering the services' and therefore is exclusively descriptive. However, a mark falling into this category could still be registrable if it has become distinctive in use, but this appears unlikely here. The mark is also possibly in breach of **s 3(1)(d) TMA 1994** because it could be considered to be customary in the current language. Both reasons are 'absolute grounds' for refusal.

(b) *TM Application 2:* OLYMPIC (Word Mark), for a Company's Men's Shaving Products

This mark is in breach of **s 4(5) TMA 1994** as a specially protected emblem. In the UK, special laws have been passed to give extra protection to some of the Olympic Games' marks. The proposed mark also breaches **s 3(1)(a)** of the **Olympic Symbol etc (Protection) Act 1995 (OSPA)** because the word 'Olympic' is a protected word under that Act. The **OSPA** protects the Olympic and Paralympic symbols, mottoes and various words. Added protection is provided by the new **London Olympic Games and Paralympic Games Act 2006**. This prevents the creation of an unauthorised association between people, goods or services and London 2012.

(c) *TM Application 3:* The Colour RED, for a Telecommunications Company

In the UK, the concept of a sign or trade mark is very wide and includes non-conventional trade marks such as a single shade of colour or a colour combination. The decision in *Philips v Remington* (1998) provides that anything that conveys information can be regarded as a sign. **Section 1(1) TMA 1994** states that the sign must be capable of being represented graphically. This can be done by citing the Pantone colour identification system number in the trade mark application: *Libertel Group BV v Benelux-Merkenbureau* (2004).

(d) *TM Application 4:* The Scent of a NUTMEG, by a Furniture Manufacturer, to Be Applied to Furniture

A 'scent mark' or 'olfactory mark' is regarded as a non-conventional mark which is more difficult to register because of the difficulty of representing the scent graphically, as required by **s 1(1) TMA 1994**. A sign must be represented in such a way that a third party is able to determine and understand what the sign is. In the case of *Ralf Sieckmann* (2002), the ECJ (now the CJEU) constructed a test which provides that the graphic representation must be:

(i)   clear
(ii) precise
(iii) self-contained

(iv) easily accessible and intelligible
 (v) durable, and
(vi) objective.

Before the decision in *Sieckmann* some scents had been registered as trade marks using written descriptions of scents, which had previously been regarded to meet the graphic representation requirements of **s1(1) TMA 1994**. Following the decision in *Sieckmann*, verbal descriptions, chemical formulae and a sample were all rejected as being insufficient to graphically represent a scent. As a result, it is highly unlikely that olfactory signs will be registrable as trade marks in the foreseeable future.

(e) *TM Application 5:* 'Catch a Wrinkle in Time', for a Cosmetics Preparation

Slogans are registrable as trade marks provided that they have the capacity to individualise the goods or services of one undertaking provided they are not composed of signs or indications which directly describe the goods or services or their essential characteristics, and are not devoid of distinctive character for any other reason.

In *Nestlé SA's Trade Mark Application (Have a Break)* (2003), the High Court ruled that registration of these words would not be granted as a trade mark because the phrase was not distinctive. However, the slogan 'Catch a wrinkle in time' probably is distinctive because it is fanciful and therefore is likely to be registrable. In *'Das Prinzip der Bequemlichkeit' ['The Principle of Comfort'] C–64/02 P*, the ECJ stated that slogans serving a promotional function which is not obviously secondary to any trade mark meaning will be objectionable because average consumers are not in the habit of making assumptions about the origin of products on the basis of such slogans. Further, it is clear that the slogan is not descriptive of the product and therefore is in breach of **s 3(1)(c) TMA 1994**.

(f) *TM Application 6:* BACARDI, for a Company That Produces Vodka

It is well known that the mark BACARDI is associated with the alcoholic rum drink. Here, there is likely to be an objection to registration of the mark in connection with spirit that is vodka-based on the relative ground of refusal contained in **s5(2)(a) TMA 1994**. **Section 5(2)(a)** provides that a trade mark shall not be registered if it is identical with an earlier trade mark and is to be registered for goods or services similar to those for which the earlier trade mark is protected. Vodka and rum are similar goods as they are both spirits (alcoholic drinks). Although the products have very different producers, it is common to find them being bought and sold by the same merchants and customers, and sold through the same outlets.

Common Pitfalls

The problem question in this case requires you to analyse the trade marks listed as (a)–(f). It would be a mistake not to mirror this (a)–(f) structure in writing your answer. This question comprises six parts, each involving issues of similar complexity, so make sure your answer is appropriately balanced between these parts.

QUESTION 34

Should colours or scents be protected by trade mark law? What problems may arise in protecting them? Support your answer with a critical analysis of the relevant legislation and case law.

How to Read this Question

This question requires the student to consider unconventional signs at the cutting edge of trade mark law. There are two parts to the question: (1) colour marks; and (2) scent marks. The discussion of the problems arising with non-conventional marks should feed into the analysis.

How to Answer this Question

Students should discuss the following in the body of their essay:

- ❖ Colour or scent marks as an unconventional sign or badge of origin;
- ❖ *Libertel Group BV v Benelux-Merkenbureau* (2004);
- ❖ **Section 1(1) TMA 1994** and the PANTONE colour identification system;
- ❖ Colour depletion theory and the shade confusion theory;
- ❖ *Ralf Sieckmann* (2002) ECJ (now the CJEU).

ANSWER

A trade mark is a 'sign' or 'badge of origin' that is used to identify certain goods and services as those produced or provided by a specific person or enterprise. A trade mark helps to distinguish those branded goods and services from similar ones provided by another trader. Trade marks fall into two categories, namely conventional and unconventional trade marks. Conventional trade marks include pictorial marks such as letters, words, pictures or drawings The range of non-conventional trade marks include signs such as slogans, three-dimensional signs (shapes), colours, sensory signs (e.g. auditory (sound) signs; gustatory (taste) signs, olfactory (scent) signs) and gestures, action signs and even holograms.

Certain types of non-conventional trade marks have become more widely accepted in recent times as a result of legislative changes expanding the definition of trade mark. Is a colour or a scent capable of acting as a sign or a badge of origin as required by **s 1(1)** of the **Trade Marks Act 1994** (**TMA 1994**)? There is no statutory definition as to what is meant by the term sign and there are very few restrictions placed on what may be registered as a trade mark. In *Wrigley/Light Green* (1999) the notion of a 'sign' was interpreted as being a very broad, open and general term encompassing all conceivable types of marks. Accordingly, the concept of a 'sign' in current UK trade mark law is very broad.

Section 1(1) TMA 1994 provides that to be registrable, a trade mark must be a sign capable of graphical representation. Additionally, the mark must be distinctive, not be descriptive, nor be excluded under the **TMA 1994**.

Does trade mark law currently protect colour or scent signs? The answer to this question depends on whether the unconventional marks are capable of graphical representation. In the past there have been difficulties with graphically representing unconventional marks such as colours and scents. However, while there is now a solution for graphically representing colour marks, the same cannot be said for scent marks.

COLOUR MARKS

While not specifically mentioned in **s 1(1) TMA 1994**, it is clear that colours are prima facie registrable where they are used as a trade mark. The main problem will be showing the mark is distinctive. In the leading case on colour marks, *Libertel Group BV v Benelux-Merkenbureau* (2004) Libertel was refused registration for the single colour orange (depicted without any reference to a colour code) by the Benelux Trade Mark office. The CJEU (formerly the ECJ) was asked whether a single colour could be distinctive. The CJEU held that it must decide as a preliminary matter whether a single colour could constitute a trade mark. The CJEU stated that that colour cannot be presumed per se to constitute a sign (without more), since it is normally merely a property of things. However, depending on the context, a colour may constitute a sign. A specific shade of colour can be registered, either as a single colour or as a colour combination. Some examples of colour marks include colours applied to:

❖ pharmaceuticals (*Smith Kline and French's Trade Mark* (1975));
❖ stripes on toothpaste (*Unilever's Application* (1984));
❖ single colours (such as orange for 'technical and business consultancy services in the area of plant cultivation, in particular the seed sector': *KWS Saat AG v OHIM* (2002)).

Applications usually include a colour specimen, but these are not sufficiently durable according to *Libertel* (2004), and the graphic representation of a colour now requires the designation of the colour using an internationally recognised colour identification system, for example PANTONE. In assessing the potential distinctiveness of a given colour as a trade mark, regard must be had to the general interest in not unduly restricting the availability of colours for other traders in the same field. However, this leads us to the policy arguments against the registration of single colours as trade marks. In this regard, there are two particularly interesting theories to explore: the colour depletion theory and the shade confusion theory.

COLOUR DEPLETION THEORY

This theory advocates that by registering one colour as a trade mark, the choice of colours left to other manufacturers will then be more limited. The more colours are trade marked in one area of trade, the fewer colours will be available for other manufacturers, and the list of available colours will therefore run out. Granting trade mark protection for colours is thought by some to be unfair and anti-competitive. While the virtually unlimited combination of letters ensures that word marks do not hinder competition, the same is not true in relation to colours. It is argued that the limited quantity of colours, and the need for one type of colour as opposed to another in a given area of trade, contributes to a state of unfair competition. This contention has been respected very strictly in the Netherlands, where the Benelux Trade Mark Office refused to register the single colour orange as a trade mark on the grounds that, *inter alia*, the colour orange played an important role as a national colour: *Libertel* (2004).

SHADE CONFUSION THEORY

This essence of this theory is that colours cannot function as trade marks because colours and their different shades can easily lead to confusion. This is a valid point not merely for infringement procedures but also when consumers are choosing goods prior to purchase. Using only slightly different shades of one colour as trade marks is likely to create confusion in the mind of consumers. Such potential for confusion allows us to infer that colours scarcely help consumers to identify the manufacturer of the goods on which the shade of the colour is applied, thereby failing to serve the prime purpose of trade marks as a sign capable of distinguishing enterprises or as a badge of origin.

TRADE MARK PROTECTION FOR COLOUR IN THE UK

In the UK, colours have been granted trade mark protection when used in specific, limited contexts such as packaging or marketing. For example, the particular shade of turquoise used on cans of Heinz Baked Beans can only be used by the HJ Heinz Company for that product. In another instance, BP plc (formerly British Petroleum), one of the world's six 'supermajor' oil and gas companies, claimed the right to use green on signs for petrol stations. The chocolate manufacturer Cadbury managed to secure a trade mark for its signature purple colour after a lengthy battle with rival Nestlé: *Société Des Produits Nestlé S.A. v Cadbury UK Ltd* (2013). Cadbury now has the exclusive right to use its own distinctive purple colour on its confectionery items. Nevertheless, people are sceptical about whether a particular colour should be monopolised by one company. However, in reality Cadbury does not 'own' the colour purple, rather it owns the particular purple associated with the Dairy Milk brand (Pantone 2685C) which only covers milk chocolate products and, within this category, chocolate bars and tablets, chocolate for eating, and drinking chocolate. Other uses of the purple colour in the remaining class of goods and services are potentially available for registration.

SCENT MARKS

Scent or olfactory marks also encounter practical difficulties carving out a monopoly and they are unlikely to be registrable in the foreseeable future. The leading case is *Dr. Ralf Sieckmann vs Deutsches Patent- und Markenamt (case C-273/00)*, a judgment of the CJEU issued in 2002. The case involved an application for a Community Trade Mark (CTM), described the structural formula of a pure chemical for a particular scent and stated that samples of the scent might be obtained from local laboratories. The scent was also described verbally as 'balsamically fruity with a slight hint of cinnamon'. The German Patent Office rejected the application. On appeal, the German Patents Court considered that scents could, from an abstract point of view, constitute an appropriate means of distinguishing the products of one enterprise from that of another, but it expressed doubts as to whether an olfactory mark was capable of being graphically represented. It referred the question to the CJEU. The CJEU was asked to decide whether the requirement for graphical representation could be satisfied by a chemical formula, a description, a deposit, or a combination of these elements.

The CJEU rejected 'verbal description', 'chemical formulae' or a sample as being insufficient to graphically represent a scent. It held that none of these methods of representation would suffice and a combination of these options would be even less likely to do so. According to the Court, for a sign to be registrable under **Art 2** of the Directive, it must have a distinctive character and be capable of being represented graphically in a clear and precise form that is understandable to the majority of manufacturers and consumers. The Court did not consider it possible to represent a scent with sufficient clarity and precision so that it was understandable to all.

Before the decision in *Sieckmann*, scent marks were registrable but the current position is that registration of scent marks seems unlikely until an agreed system of graphic representation exists. This will be difficult because although a scent is unique, the molecules of a scent must have actual contact with the potential consumer. The further away the consumer is from the scented product, the more difficult this will be. This problem is even more complex when factoring in any environmental conditions affecting the scent. Temperature, the level of humidity and wind conditions can change the strength of a scent. These factors can make the scent more difficult for the nose to detect as well as potentially altering the chemical composition of the scent, making it a different one than originally existed. A scent will also be altered when other scents interact with it. Due to its gaseous nature, a scent is very easily modified by the existence of nearby smells. That said, virtually every single individual's perception of a scent is different depending on the surrounding environment, the distance between the human body and the scent, whether the person experiences sinusitis, etc.

In summary, 'non-conventional' marks comprise a number of different types of trade marks which do not belong to the conventional categories of words, numerals, pictorial and logo marks, or a combination of these marks, and yet still serve the essential purpose of a trade mark by uniquely identifying products or services as being from a particular undertaking. In the UK, colours have been granted trade mark protection when used in specific, limited contexts such as packaging or marketing. Nor are scent marks currently able to meet the requirements of graphic representability. A chemical formula for the scent, description of the scent in written words or deposit of an odour sample, or a combination of those elements, remains insufficient.

In conclusion, the primary function of a trade mark is to distinguish the goods and services of one undertaking from those of other undertakings, whether the mark is visually perceptible or not. However, the moot question is whether a non-conventional mark can perform the primary function of a trade mark despite lacking the capability of graphical representation. Graphical representation of the mark must be such that it can be defined in order to determine the precise subject of monopoly protection afforded by the registered mark to the owner. The entry of the non-conventional mark in the register has the aim of making it accessible to the public. Consequently, the means of graphical representation must be unequivocal and objective. In summary, the core legal requirements of distinctive character and the ability to graphically represent the mark to create transparency continue to dominate the registration of trade marks. When seeking registration of non-conventional trade marks such as colours and scents it is important to remember that such identifiers are registrable and enforceable so long as they are capable of identifying the origin of the source of the goods and services.

Common Pitfalls

Avoid devoting too much of the essay to trade mark law relating to conventional marks, e.g. word marks, logos etc. The focus should be on non-conventional marks, which are often difficult or impossible to register, but which may nevertheless fulfil the essential trade mark function of uniquely identifying the commercial origin of products or services. Focus your legal analysis equally on colour marks and scent marks and the key case law in order to attract the maximum award of marks.

Aim Higher

Think critically about different causes or consequences of granting trade marks over colours and scents. Support your thinking with examples and case law. With a question like this, you could expand on the policy reasons for underpinning the reluctance to expand trade mark law to protect certain non-conventional trade marks.

QUESTION 35

L'Oceane plc is a producer and marketer of luxury perfumes. The company was established in the mid nineteenth century and had traded in the UK for over a century. It is the proprietor of well-known UK registered trade marks, some in the form of word marks alone, and others being word and figurative marks including a representation of a wave-shaped bottle and packaging for its best-selling 'Vagues de Desire' (waves of desire) perfume. L'Oceane invested in expensive advertising for its 'Vagues de Desire' perfume across several media, employing a famous and beautiful actress as the 'spokesmodel' for its campaign.

Another firm, Bella Ltd, had produced and marketed imitations of fine fragrances since 1990. Bella Ltd offered for sale a range of fragrance products at one-third the price, some of whose bottles and packaging were generally similar to those of products of L'Oceane plc. However, the similarity was unlikely to mislead professionals. Even the public could clearly identify that Bella's products were 'knocked off' and were inferior products to those of L'Oceane plc. Bella Ltd provided their retailers with lists which compared the scent of their 'knock-off' product with that of the L'Oceane product which was being imitated, in each case identified by reference to the word mark by which the L'Oceane product was known.

L'Oceane plc is vigilant in protecting its brand and wishes to bring trade mark infringement proceedings against Bella Ltd. What is the likelihood of success of such an action?

▶ **Advise L'Oceane.**

How to Read this Question

Note that this fact scenario is based on the common situation where one firm 'knocks off' or imitates the brand of another, as was the case in *L'Oréal SA and others v Bellure NV and others* (2009) WLR (D) 203.

How to Answer this Question

The answer to this problem question therefore requires a detailed knowledge of trade mark infringement law, comparative advertising law and the facts and judgment of the *L'Oréal SA v Bellure* case which concerns **s 10(6) Trade Marks Act 1994**.

Applying the Law

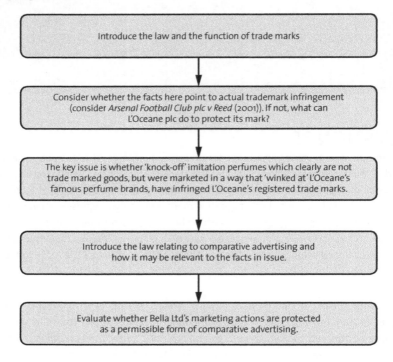

Introduce the law and the function of trade marks

Consider whether the facts here point to actual trademark infringement (consider *Arsenal Football Club plc v Reed* (2001)). If not, what can L'Oceane plc do to protect its mark?

The key issue is whether 'knock-off' imitation perfumes which clearly are not trade marked goods, but were marketed in a way that 'winked at' L'Oceane's famous perfume brands, have infringed L'Oceane's registered trade marks.

Introduce the law relating to comparative advertising and how it may be relevant to the facts in issue.

Evaluate whether Bella Ltd's marketing actions are protected as a permissible form of comparative advertising.

ANSWER

In the UK, trade mark law is governed by the **Trade Marks Act 1994** (**TMA 1994**) and is essentially territorial, meaning that a UK registered trade mark is only protected in the UK. **Section 1(1)** of the **TMA 1994** defines a trade mark as 'any sign capable of being represented graphically which is capable of distinguishing goods or services of one undertaking from those of other undertakings'. We are told that L'Oceane has registered trade marks so we can assume that these marks meet the criteria of the Act.

Trade marks can be very valuable in that they have a number of functions to play in modern business. The traditional view is that a registered trade mark, such as L'Oceane's word marks and pictorial marks, functions as an indicator of origin of the goods so that consumers reliably recognise the 'Vagues de Desire' branded perfume as originating from L'Oceane and not from some other enterprise such as Bella. This trade mark protection benefits the public as a guarantee of quality and also benefits L'Oceane in the marketplace by distinguishing its products from those of its competitors. This 'indicator of origin' function was confirmed by the European Court of Justice (ECJ) in several cases including *Arsenal Football Club plc v Reed (No. 2)* (2003). However, registered trade marks also play another important function in terms of their publicity value in that they create brand attractiveness and reputation. For example, a distinctive mark may not identify only origin, but also quality, reputation and renown of the producer particularly through the investment.

The **TMA 1994** implements the **Trade Marks Directive 89/204** so the final word on interpreting the terms of the Act lies with the ECJ to ensure a uniform approach across the EU. There has been significant debate in trade mark law circles over the extent to which the **TM Directive**, implemented into the UK **TMA 1994**, intended to give protection to the publicity value of registered trade marks, independently from their function as indicators of origin. Indeed, some European countries, such as the Benelux countries, already recognise this second function of registered trade marks. The language of the **TM Directive** is ambiguous. On the one hand, some argue that interpreting the **TMA 1994** to grant protection over this secondary function is simply common sense given modern advertising and brand attractiveness. On the other hand, would granting such protection give too much power to wealthy established brand owners such as L'Oceane to dominate aspects of language and shape to the detriment of healthy competition?

IS THIS A CASE OF BELLA INFRINGING L'OCEANE'S TRADE MARKS?

The owner of a registered trade mark has exclusive rights in the trade mark which are infringed by its use in the UK without consent: **s 9 TMA 1994**. The four main grounds for infringement are set out in **s 10(1)–(3)**. They are the same as the relative grounds for refusal of registration (**s 5(1)–(3)**). To infringe, the sign must be used in the course of trade: **s 103**. Bella Ltd provided their retailers with lists which compared the scent of their 'knock-off' product with that of the L'Oceane product which was being imitated, in each case identified by reference to the word mark by which the L'Oceane product was known. Bella used L'Oceane's marks on identifical products. Is this an infringement under **s 10(1)(a) TMA 1994** (**s 5(1)(a) TM Directive**)? We know that both professionals and the public can identify that Bella's products were 'knocked off' and were inferior products to those of L'Oceane plc; in other words, that the products did not originate from L'Oceane. Does providing such a list amount to infringing trade mark use? Bella will argue that providing a comparison list is non-trade mark use as the word marks referred to in the list are not used in a 'trade mark sense', that is, as an indicator of origin. There is a trilogy of cases that deal with these issues.

First, the question as to whether trade mark use is required to find infringement was referred to the ECJ (now the CJEU) by the High Court in *Arsenal Football Club plc v Reed* (2001). The ECJ held that the rights of a trade mark owner to prevent a third party from using his mark extended to any situation where such use was liable to affect its essential function as a guarantor of origin. Use in the course of trade is use which 'takes place in the context of commercial activity with a view to economic advantage and not as a private matter'.

The next case to consider the meaning of 'infringing use' was the ECJ's decision in *Adam Opel AG v Autec AG* (2007). Opel manufactured the Opel Astra car and was the registered owner of the OPEL mark for motor vehicles and toys. The defendant, Autec, manufactured scale model cars and used the OPEL mark on the radiator grille of a scale model of the Opel Astra. Opel brought an action for trade mark infringement. In its defence, Autec argued that its use of the OPEL mark was not 'trade mark use' as the public would know that Autec's scale model car products which carried the registered trade mark did not come from Opel, the car maker. The ECJ again confirmed the principle established in *Arsenal v Reed* (2003), namely that infringing use of a registered trade mark is use which affects the essential functions of a mark, in particular its use as a badge of origin. It concluded that as the average toy car consumer would not assume that the OPEL mark on the Autec scale model car was a badge of origin, but rather an indication that this was indeed a scale model of an Opel car, then the origin function of the OPEL mark as registered for toys would not be affected and was therefore not infringing use.

Any use of a registered trade mark that damages the origin function of the mark will be infringing whether or not it is trade mark use. On the facts here, there is no damage to the origin function of the mark. Neither professionals nor consumers believe that Bella's products originate from L'Oceane. Everyone is aware that Bella's products are inferior 'knock offs'. There is nevertheless a market for less expensive 'knock-off' perfumes. The key issue here is whether Bella takes unfair advantage of the reputation in L'Oceane's marks when producing its 'knock-off' imitation perfumes and whether this amounts to infringing use.

Most recently, in the third of the 'trade mark trilogy' of cases on important trade mark questions which were referred to the ECJ by the Court of Appeal, the question of what constitutes infringing use of a trade mark was considered in *L'Oréal v Bellure* (2007). This is clearly a case on point and has distinct similarities to the facts and legal issues arising involving L'Oceane plc and Bella Ltd. In *L'Oréal v Bellure*, the claimant, L'Oréal, argued that the use of its trade marks in Bellure's comparison list was infringing trade mark use. Bellure argued that their use of L'Oréal's marks was purely descriptive and not infringing trade mark use. L'Oréal responded that Bellure's use of their marks went beyond purely 'descriptive' use and took unfair advantage of L'Oréal's reputation, reputation or brand attractiveness being a second function of a trade mark distinct from an indicator of origin function. However, Lord Justice Jacob noted that while Bellure's use of the L'Oréal's marks did in fact assist the sales of their 'knock-off' perfumes, such use did not affect L'Oréal's image or the essential indicator of origin function of L'Oréal's registered trade marks, nor did it adversely impact on L'Oréal's sales. He stated, 'No one is deceived. No one thinks any less of the original brands.'

Jacob LJ referred the following question to the ECJ to determine:

> Where a trader, in an advertisement for his own goods and services, uses a registered trade mark owned by a competitor for the purpose of comparing the characteristics (and in particular smell) of the goods marketed by him with the characteristics (and in particular the smell) of the goods marketed by the competitor under the mark in such a way that it does not cause confusion or otherwise jeopardise the essential function of the trade mark as an indicator or origin, is that infringing?

IS THERE UNFAIR ADVANTAGE WITHOUT (A) CONFUSION OR (B) DETRIMENT TO THE EARLIER MARK?

In its judgment issued on 18 June 2009, the ECJ found in favour of L'Oréal and responded that **Art 5(2)** of **TM Directive 89/104** must be interpreted as meaning that the taking of unfair advantage of the distinctive character or the repute of a mark, within the meaning of that provision, does not require that there be a likelihood of confusion or a likelihood of detriment to the distinctive character or the repute of the mark or, more generally, to its proprietor. The advantage arising from the use by a third party of a sign similar to a mark with a reputation is an advantage taken unfairly by that third party of the distinctive character or the repute of that mark where that party seeks by that use to ride on the coat-tails of the mark with a reputation in order to benefit from the power of attraction, the reputation and the prestige of that mark and to exploit, without paying any financial compensation, the marketing effort expended by the proprietor of the mark in order to create and maintain the mark's image.

How can unfair advantage be proved? The ECJ stated that in order to determine whether the use of a sign takes unfair advantage of the distinctive character or the repute of the mark, it is necessary to undertake a global assessment, taking into account all factors relevant to the circumstances of the case, which include:

❖   the strength of the mark's reputation and the degree of distinctive character of the mark;

❖   the degree of similarity between the marks at issue and the nature and degree of proximity of the goods or services concerned.

As regards the strength of the reputation and the degree of distinctive character of the mark, the Court has already held that the stronger that mark's distinctive character and reputation are, the easier it will be to accept that detriment has been caused to it. It is also clear from the case law that the more immediately and strongly the mark is brought to mind by the sign, the greater the likelihood that the current or future use of the sign is taking, or will take, unfair advantage of the distinctive character or the repute of the mark or is, or will be, detrimental to them.

On the facts, Bellure had created a link, they had done so for commercial advantage and with the intention of creating an association with L'Oréal. This amounted to taking unfair advantage of L'Oréal marks. This means that the extent of exclusivity offered by a registered trade mark goes beyond a mark's essential function as an indicator of origin and is broader than how the English courts have traditionally interpreted trade mark use. The ECJ has confirmed that the indicator of origin function is not the only relevant function for infringement purposes. Trade mark owners can prevent 'free riding' even when there is no loss of any sort suffered by the brand, if it can be shown that there is no due cause for the mark to be used. For example, use of a slogan such as 'the De Beers of mineral water' would be prohibited and actionable by De Beers, the diamond firm, even if there is no loss or damage. Therefore, presenting a product as a replica or imitation will be a trade mark infringement.

Applying the principles in the *L'Oréal* decision, one may conclude that L'Oceane is now likely to be successful should it bring an action for trade mark infringement against Bella for using its marks without authority or payment of compensation. L'Oceane should insist Bella pay a licence fee for use of its marks to compensate L'Oceane for its marketing efforts expended in order to create and maintain the mark's image.

Common Pitfalls

Avoid reciting the law then failing to apply it to the facts. It is crucial to apply your knowledge of the legislation and case law to the factual scenario. The ability to construct an argument as to how the law might or might not operate in the context of a particular scenario is one of the hallmarks of a good legal mind.

Aim Higher

Aim to discuss the 'trade mark trilogy' of cases on important trade mark questions which were referred to the ECJ by the Court of Appeal. In particular, emphasise the decision in *L'Oréal v Bellure* (2007) as it is clearly a case on point and has distinct similarities to the facts and legal issues arising involving L'Oceane plc and Bella Ltd and deals directly with the question of what constitutes infringing use of a trade mark.

QUESTION 36

Waltham is an upmarket national food retailer. Its new marketing director consults you for trade mark advice as he advises that he has little knowledge of trade mark law. The marketing director tells you that for the past 20 years, Waltham have been sourcing organic chickens from four farms in the beautiful county of Rutland, which it sells in its stores. Waltham now wishes to register the mark OAKHAM for retail trade services in connection with its organic chicken range. Oakham is the main market town situated in Rutland, England's smallest county. In addition, he wishes to confirm whether it possible to protect the clear plastic chicken-shaped lid of the packaging that is used to display the chickens for sale .

▶ Advise Waltham.

How to Read this Question

This problem question requires a knowledge of the law relating to registered trade marks and involves the application of the requirements of **s1** of the **Trade Marks Act 1994** in connection with the possible registration of two signs as trade marks – a traditional mark and a non-traditional mark.

How to Answer this Question

This straightforward problem question divides neatly into two main parts and involves applying the relevant law to the application to register (1) a word mark; and (2) a shape mark. In relation to the latter, a key question is whether a shape consisting of three essential features that result from the nature of the goods themselves (the chickens) can be registered as a trade mark.

Applying the Law

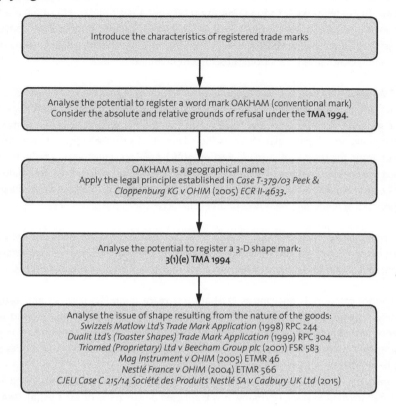

Introduce the characteristics of registered trade marks

Analyse the potential to register a word mark OAKHAM (conventional mark)
Consider the absolute and relative grounds of refusal under the **TMA 1994**.

OAKHAM is a geographical name
Apply the legal principle established in *Case T-379/03 Peek & Cloppenburg KG v OHIM* (2005) *ECR II-4633*.

Analyse the potential to register a 3-D shape mark:
3(1)(e) TMA 1994

Analyse the issue of shape resulting from the nature of the goods:
Swizzels Matlow Ltd's Trade Mark Application (1998) RPC 244
Dualit Ltd's (Toaster Shapes) Trade Mark Application (1999) RPC 304
Triomed (Proprietary) Ltd v Beecham Group plc (2001) FSR 583
Mag Instrument v OHIM (2005) ETMR 46
Nestlé France v OHIM (2004) ETMR 566
CJEU Case C 215/14 Société des Produits Nestlé SA v Cadbury UK Ltd (2015)

ANSWER

Trade marks operate as a sign which can distinguish Waltham's goods and services from those of its competitors. They serve to inform customers that the goods and services on which they are used emanate from a particular source, such as the Waltham enterprise in this case. Trade marks serve to protect, differentiate and add value to an enterprise's commercial activities. They come in many forms: for example, they can be words, logos, or a combination of both, or even shapes. Registered trade mark rights provide legal protection for some of the most important aspects of a brand. If Waltham is successful in registering the marks constituting its brand it will give them the exclusive right to use the marks for the classes of goods and/or services covered by the UK trade mark registration. Once a mark is registered, Waltham will be able to use the ® symbol next to it to warn others, particularly competitors, against using their proprietary marks.

The facts suggest that two marks are potentially registrable: (1) a traditional word mark OAKHAM; and (2) a non-traditional three-dimensional shape mark relating to the packaging of the chicken products.

THE OAKHAM WORD MARK

Section 1(1) Trade Marks Act 1994 (TMA 1994) sets out a basic statement of what a trade mark is. It is clear that a word mark such as OAKHAM is capable of graphical representation so that hurdle is cleared. However, is the OAKHAM word mark a sign capable of distinguishing Waltham's goods from those of another undertaking?

The **TMA 1994** then sets out various grounds for refusal of registration. The grounds are set out in two categories, the first being what are known as the 'absolute grounds' for refusal. These grounds focus on signs and trade marks that are not distinctive or fail to meet the basic requirement. In particular, students should note that **s3(1) TMA 1994** sets out the absolute grounds for refusal of a mark. **Section 3(1)(c)** prevents registration of marks which consist exclusively of signs or indications which may serve, in trade, to designate kind, quality, quantity, intended purpose, value, *geographical origin*, or the time of production of the goods or of rendering the service or other characteristic of the goods or services.

The second category involves what are known as 'relative grounds of refusal' which are based on conflict or potential conflict between the trade mark for which registration is sought and earlier trade marks (whether or not registered) and other earlier rights.

The former category is relevant as Oakham is a place name. Usually, an application to register a geographical name as a trade mark will be refused on this ground in the absence of distinctiveness acquired through use. However, for this ground to apply to a geographical name, it must be perceived as indicating geographical origin. If it does not, it may be registrable. In *Case T-379/03 Peek & Cloppenburg KG v OHIM a* (2005) ECR II-4633 an application was made to register CLOPPENBURG for retail trade services. Cloppenburg is a small town in Saxony, Germany. It was refused on the basis of **Art s3(1)(a) TMA 1994** but the applicant's appeal to the Court of First Instance was successful.

In contrast, the mark YORKSHIRE was also a geographical name that was successfully registered for tea. The mark proceeded to registration on the basis of distinctiveness acquired through use: UK Registration No 1570522. As Waltham has already been marketing the range as Oakham Chickens for the past 20 years this may get them over the hurdle of 'acquired distinctiveness' to enable registration.

The OAKHAM mark may achieve registration more easily if it is embellished to make it more distinctive. For example, Waltham may wish to consider the mark RED OAKHAM.

SECTION 3(1)(E) TMA 1994 AND THE 3-D CHICKEN SHAPE MARK

The courts have made it clear that shape marks are to be treated no differently from other types of signs for the purposes of fulfilling the requirements of the **TMA 1994**, with one important exception. Indeed, the distinctive Coca-Cola bottle was allowed registration. However, there are three specific grounds for refusal of registration (or invalidity). **Section 3(1)(e)** prevents the registration of signs which consist exclusively of:

(i)   the shape which results from the nature of the goods themselves; or

(ii)   the shape of goods which is necessary to obtain a technical result; or

(iii)   the shape which gives substantial value to the goods.

Shapes excluded can thus be described loosely as natural, functional or ornamental. It should be noted that 'acquired' distinctiveness does not apply to **s 3(1)(e)**.

There should be no difficulty in providing a graphical representation of a shape mark by means of a drawing or set of drawings from different angles, perhaps accompanied by a description which may also include some reference to dimensions. A written description alone is unlikely to suffice unless the shape is very well known, such as a sphere or a pyramid, but then other objections based on, for example, lack of distinctive character may be raised: *Swizzels Matlow Ltd's Trade Mark Application* (1998) RPC 244.

SHAPE RESULTING FROM THE NATURE OF THE GOODS

This ground for refusal prevents the registration of a shape which results from the nature of the goods themselves, examples being the shape of an apple, potato crisp, banana or tyre for a car. However, the inclusion of some additional stylised feature might overcome the ground for refusal. In *Dualit Ltd's (Toaster Shapes) Trade Mark Application* (1999) RPC 304, it was accepted that the shape of toasters, which registration was applied for, possess certain styling features which prevented them from consisting exclusively of shapes resulting from the nature of goods themselves (registration was refused on other grounds). Here the chickens have intrinsic form, as opposed to a liquid or powder which take the shape of their container.

Another disadvantage some shape marks may have to overcome to be registrable is that the public does not necessarily regard them as trade marks: see, for example, Jacob LJ in *Bongrain SA's Trade Mark Application* (2005) RPC 306 at para 25. The trade mark in question was for a shape applied to cheese. In other words, they are not necessarily distinctive.

Also, the shape mark must be capable of distinguishing foods of one undertaking from those of others. If the shape is not generally appreciated by the public as being a trade mark, it will not be registrable, even if the public recognises or is familiar with the shape. It has to operate as a trade mark – a badge of origin: *Triomed (Proprietary) Ltd v Beecham Group plc* (2001) FSR 583. For example, a competitor's turkey-shaped packaging may be problematic in that it could be confusingly similar, except for size as turkeys are generally larger than chickens.

The 3-D packaging, in order to be registrable, should not solely result from the chicken shape. In *Mag Instrument v OHIM* (2005) ETMR 46 it was held that the more a shape for which registration is being sought resembles the product itself, the less likely that shape would be granted registration. Waltham should be advised to consider designing the 3-D packaging to include some kind of additional stylised feature, for example raised lettering or logo, to distinguish the shape as well as distinguishing it from the competitor's 3-D tur-key-shaped packaging. All elements combined will be considered by the Registrar when assessing distinctiveness: *Nestlé France v OHIM* (2004) ETMR 566.

CLASSIFICATION OF GOODS AND SERVICES

The class of goods for the OAKHAM mark will likely include Class 29 (poultry) and possibly Class 31 (live animals). Some students will have searched the UK register and noted that the mark OAKHAM is already registered in class 29. Further investigation will be required to determine whether Waltham's OAKHAM mark is likely to be able to co-exist on the register.

In conclusion, if the marks are not able to be successfully registered then Waltham may have no option but to rely on the tort of passing off to protect its brand and 'get-up' or 'trade dress'. By 'get-up', this will include the shape of the packaging, the use of colour schemes, the layout of the typeface used on labels; indeed, any aspect of the goods' appearance which helps the consumer to identify origin. Passing off has always been traditionally used to protect a claimant's unregistered trade marks, provided factual distinctiveness is established.

Fortunately, the issue of protection for 'get-up' and 'trade dress' in the context of how to provide brand owners with protection against supermarket 'own-brand' lookalikes remains problematic.

Common Pitfalls

Don't spend all your time on discussing the OAKHAM word mark. Be sure to balance the time spent relatively equally between the OAKHAM word mark and the more problematic 3-D chicken shape mark. A balanced answer dealing with both marks will score the maximum marks for the question.

Aim Higher

The second mark is problematic. A 3-D shape trade mark is not registrable if the shape is typical of the goods (or part of them), has a function or adds value to the goods. Students should ensure they discuss the case law relevant to shape marks and apply these principles to the facts in their analysis. As this is a developing area of trade mark law, try to provide an in-depth discussion of the key shape mark case law in this area, in particular: *Mag Instrument v OHIM* (2005) ETMR 46 and *Nestlé France v OHIM* (2004) ETMR 566.

QUESTION 37

Safehold Secure Ltd owns the registered trade mark SAFEHOLD in Class 39 (packaging and storage of goods). In practice, the company's products are sold by reference to the brand 'SAFEHOLD SECURE', which encompasses its storage business and also its locks and packing requisites business which it provides from its own lock-up-style premises as well as through a chain of DIY stores. A competitor, Century Ltd, believes that using the composite phrase 'SAFEHOLD SECURE' does not constitute use of the trade mark, even though it includes the word 'SAFEHOLD'. Century Ltd has made an application to the UK Intellectual Property Office (UKIPO) to have the registration revoked for non-use. Safehold Secure Ltd disagrees and contends that its use of the phrase 'SAFEHOLD SECURE' is genuine use of the mark. Further, Safehold Secure Ltd confirms it has in any event made some use, albeit limited, of the single word mark in relation to its packing materials and removals services when it gave away 500 luxury water bottles bearing the mark SAFEHOLD at the Wimbledon Tennis Tournament in 2015. This was aimed at supporting the marketing of the company's storage services. The water bottles were given away as 'freebies' to encourage customers to purchase additional time at storage units.

▶ Advise Safehold Secure Ltd as to the likelihood it will succeed in resisting Century's application to revoke the registered mark SAFEHOLD for non-use.

How to Read this Question

In the case of trade marks, entry on the register is only prima facie evidence of its validity: **s 72 Trade Marks Act 1994 (TMA 1994)**. This is a practical problem question which requires a critical analysis of the rationale for loss of registration by way of revocation of a registered trade mark.

How to Answer this Question

A number of issues arise for consideration in order to advise as to the success of Century's application to revoke the registration of the mark SAFEHOLD. In particular focus on **s 46(1) (b) TMA 1994** on the grounds that Safehold Secure Ltd has mismanaged the mark. Consider any defences available to Safehold Secure Ltd. It will be important to cite the relevant case law and distinguish it if necessary in order to build the case on behalf of the trade mark proprietor.

Applying the Law

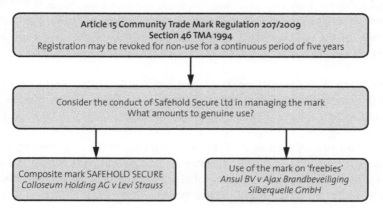

ANSWER

A registered trade mark is intended to serve as a 'badge of origin'. It should give the consumer a guarantee that the product or services to which it is applied emanate from a particular source. Therefore, an applicant for registration must declare an intention to use the mark applied for on specific goods and services. If the application is successful, the mark will be granted a monopoly in respect of those goods and services. While a registration remains on the register it may prevent competitors from using or registering an identical or similar mark. But if the owner is not in fact using the registered mark as an indication of source s/he should not be permitted to perpetually block other traders in that way. Accordingly, **s 46** of the **Trade Marks Act 1994** (**TMA 1994**) and **Art 15** of the **Community Trade Mark Regulation 207/2009** provide that a registration may be revoked if it is not put to use within five years of being registered, or if its use is discontinued for a continuous period of five years.

Revocation relates to the conduct of the trade mark owner (Safehold Secure Ltd) which has, since registration, somehow 'tainted' the mark by not using it. The effect of a successful application to revoke a mark is that SAFEHOLD would be removed from the register for the future (from the date of the application to revoke). Loss of registration is precisely what Safehold Secure seeks to avoid as the company would forfeit significant intellectual property rights in a valuable brand name which in turn would adversely affect the company's balance sheet and competitive edge in the storage facilities market.

SECTION 46 TMA 1994

As Safehold Secure Ltd has registered the mark SAFEHOLD in the UK, **s 46 TMA 1994** applies as the relevant law on the issue of revocation. An application to revoke a registered trade mark can be brought by any person. There is no requirement of *locus standi*. **Section 46(1)** contains two separate objections to a mark on the basis of non-use. They consist of five years of non-use of the mark since it was first entered on the register and any continuous five-year period of non-use: **s 46(1)(a) and (b)**. Both of these subsections require the trade mark owner to make 'genuine' use of the mark.

In effect, Century Ltd has based its case on **s 46(1)(b) TMA 1994** so it does not have to establish that Safehold Secured Ltd never used the mark, only that it has not used it in the five years immediately preceding the date of application to revoke. However, the burden of proof to show what use has been made of the mark falls initially on the proprietor, Safehold Security Ltd: **s 100 TMA 1994**. This will be assessed on the balance of probabilities.

Faced with this challenge to its registered mark, Safehold Secure Ltd should argue that its use of the composite phrase 'SAFEHOLD SECURE' does in fact constitute genuine use of the mark SAFEHOLD and further that it has made some use of the single word mark.

The facts raise two key legal issues. First, whether the use of the registered mark as part of a composite mark (SAFEHOLD incorporated into the phrase 'SAFEHOLD SECURE') qualifies as 'use' of 'the registration' or use of the registered mark 'in a form differing in elements which do not alter the distinctive character of the mark in the form in which it was registered': **ss 46(1) and (2) TMA 1994**. Second, whether the application of the mark as registered (SAFEHOLD on its own) to a small quantity of products (water bottles), which are not themselves covered by the registration, and which were not sold but were given away as a marketing incentive to customers to purchase additional time at storage units, constituted 'genuine use' under **s 46(1)**.

COMPOSITE MARKS AND GENUINE USE

In *Colloseum Holding AG v Levi Strauss Case C-12/12*, a CJEU decision of 18 April 2013, the court decided that a registered trade mark can be put to genuine use through its use within a composite mark, provided that the use of the registered mark continued to be perceived as indicative of origin. The case arose from a dispute in the German courts under **Art 15** of the **Trade Mark Regulation** but the judgment nevertheless has effect on **s 46 TMA 1994**, the equivalent UK provision. The CJEU concluded that the use of a composite mark may be sufficient to constitute genuine use of one of its elements, appearing on its own, if consumers would identify a product's source just from the appearance and location of the individual element, even though it had only ever been used as part of the composite mark. On that basis, the requirement for genuine use under **Art 15** (**s 46 TMA 1994**) may be satisfied by the use of the composite 'SAFEHOLD SECURE' if, on the facts of the case, the word SAFEHOLD has become distinctive in its own right even if it is only used through that composite mark. It will be necessary for Safehold Secure Ltd to provide satisfactory evidence that the word mark SAFEHOLD has in fact become distinctive and has a high recognition factor in the public's mind. In other words, it may be possible for Safehold Secure Ltd to demonstrate that the average consumer would perceive that the 'SAFEHOLD' component of the composite mark 'SAFEHOLD SECURE' retained a separate and distinctive identity such that, when seen on its own, the consumer would identify it as an indication that the storage services on which it appeared emanated from Safehold Secure Ltd.

IS USE OF THE MARK ON FREEBIES GENUINE USE?

The general principle is that, to qualify as 'genuine use', a mark must have been used in a way that enabled it to perform the essential function of identifying the origin of the goods or services for which it is registered. Thus, token use (e.g. a few sales made every five years just to maintain a registration) would not qualify. But if the use served a real commercial purpose, the fact that the number of products or services sold was quite small would not disqualify it.

Case C-40/01Ansul BV v Ajax Brandbeveiliging BV (2003) ECR-I-2439 is a CJEU decision that reaffirms the principle that the use relied on must serve the purpose of maintaining or creating a share in the market for the goods or services in question. This authority supports the proposition that the number of luxury water bottles distributed by Safehold Secure Ltd were not so low as to warrant them being ignored *de minimis*. However, this leaves open the question as to whether, regardless of the number of water bottles involved, the nature of the transaction was such as to qualify as genuine use.

In *Case C-495/07 Silberquelle GmbH* (2009) ECR-I-137 the CJEU ruled that there had not been genuine use of the trade mark (WELLNESS for drinks) where the owner had bottles of alcohol-free drinks which it then gave away free to customers who bought items of clothing sold under the same mark. The drinks mark (as opposed to the clothing mark) had been correctly revoked for non-use. The CJEU held that the concept of genuine use was not satisfied where promotional items were handed out solely as a reward for, and to encourage, the purchase of other goods. The Court's reason for not treating this as genuine use of the WELLNESS mark was that the free items were not distributed with the aim of creating or maintaining the market for drinks, but only to assist sales of goods in the separate clothing class. This decision can be distinguished by Safehold Secure Ltd on the basis that the specification of goods for which the SAFEHOLD mark is registered (Class 39) does not include water bottles. Water bottles are not within the scope of the registered mark. However, the freebie water bottles are given away to support storage services in Class 39.

A successful outcome in this scenario will rest on what amounts to genuine use sufficient to maintain the purpose of the trade mark registration. The nature of use of the registered mark SAFEHOLD that Safehold Secure Ltd is able to prove on the facts will be crucial.

Safehold Secure Ltd has presented two compelling arguments that have merit and will likely result in the application to revoke the mark being dismissed with costs. The maintenance of archive materials with dated samples showing actual commercial use in the relevant marketplace of the mark, as registered, for the services of registration will provide the best basis for evidence to be used in defence against a revocation action. This is, of course, not always easy to achieve, but is a good practice measure for at least Safehold Secure Ltd's major trade mark. Once a mark has been on the Register for more than five years anyone may apply to revoke the registration for non-use and trade mark owners may find themselves in the unfortunate position of having to defend their registrations against such actions on a number of occasions.

Common Pitfalls

Do not confuse revocation with invalidity. Revocation relates to the conduct of the registered trade mark proprietor since the registration, conduct which in some cases has 'tainted' a previously valid mark. In contrast, invalidity relates to the fact that the trade mark should never have been registered in the first place because at the time it was registered, it did not comply with the requirements of the **TMA 1994**.

Aim Higher

A detailed analysis of the relevant case law demonstrates the need for both sides to be careful and precise in addressing the issues in a revocation action. This is particularly important if revocation is being sought to clear the way for registration of the Applicant's own mark.

9 Confidential Information

Business depends on a range of innovations that are only capable of protection by confidential information (trade secrets or know-how). The confidential information confers significant advantages to the holder and significant benefits to society as a whole. In this chapter, our principal focus is on the way in which the action for breach of confidence operates in the commercial world (traditional breach of confidence). The law of confidential information, in a business context (as opposed to personal privacy), is essentially a legal methodology for stopping some types of economically valuable information being used by others without permission. It is an entirely abstract concept; there is no registered right to evaluate or assess. It is not like patents, copyright or design where a particular 'thing' is afforded protection. Rather, certain information or know-how is valuable precisely because it is confidential and not in the public domain. The extent of the confidential information or know-how is usually difficult to establish with certainty. The confidential information monopoly is very broad as it may involve protection of the whole of a commercially significant idea, potentially forever. Indeed, it is a requirement of the doctrine of breach of confidence that the confidential information must not become publicly known.

An action for breach of confidence may lie in equity, at common law or in contract. The equitable doctrine of breach of confidence is a set of principles developed over centuries by the courts. In other words, it is judge-made law. It is the application of those principles to particular fact situations which determines whether the information is confidential. To achieve fairness, broad legal principles have been developed to permit considerable flexibility. The fundamental legal principle that forms the underlying basis of the law of confidence is that a person who has received information known to be confidential from another will not take unfair advantage of it, nor profit from its wrongful use or publication.

Checklist

Students should anticipate questions about the following:

- knowledge of the key elements that must be proved in order to succeed in an action for breach of confidence;
- an understanding of the defences that can be raised;
- the role of confidential information in intellectual property law as an alternative to patents, copyright and design and to protect know-how.

Problem questions typically involve a discussion of the elements of the action for breach of confidence and the defences. Essay questions may require the student to evaluate the effectiveness of keeping information or know-how confidential and the consequences of disclosure.

QUESTION 38

For the past two years, Tim, a consultant aviation engineer and former airline pilot, has been independently developing an innovative highly geared bypass fan (HGBF). Tim has been careful to keep his innovation confidential and has not disclosed the details to any other third party. However, in January 2014, he attends a preliminary meeting at the London head office of Orion Aerospace and meets with the Research and Development director, Dr Sharp. At the beginning of the meeting Tim states that the subject matter of the meeting is confidential as between the two men. Dr Sharp nods in agreement and Tim proceeds to tell him about the details of his invention. Tim also shows Dr Sharp a technical drawing of the fan but retains this when he departs the meeting. Dr Sharp confirms Tim's innovation is of interest to Orion and that they should meet again to discuss proposals for the manufacture of a new aircraft HGBF. Two further meetings are held in February. However, after some disagreements between Tim and Orion Aerospace regarding the terms of a potential licence agreement and in particular the royalty rate, negotiations break down. In June 2014 Orion proceed to manufacture their own new aircraft bypass fan, the Orion X2014. In July 2014 Tim becomes aware of Orion's new development when he reads an article in an aeronautical engineering trade magazine which features a photo of Dr Sharp and two other members of his team standing beside the X2014 fan. Tim is livid and suspects that Orion has used at least some of the information he disclosed to Dr Sharp earlier in the year. Tim seeks your advice as to whether he has a case for breach of confidence. In particular, he is concerned that he did not insist that Dr Sharp sign a written non-disclosure agreement and enquires whether this will affect his legal rights.

How to Read this Question

When reading the fact scenario, put yourself in the judge's shoes. If Tim is able to establish the information was confidential and was communicated in circumstances importing an obligation of confidence, the court will ask whether the defendant in fact misappropriated the claimant's confidential information. It is on this question that confidential information cases are usually won or lost. The most significant predictor here is the judge's view of the actions of the defendant.

How to Answer this Question

This is a straightforward problem question concerning breach of confidence set in a commercial context which will require the student to support each stage of their answer with reference to relevant case law.

Answer Structure

The issues to be considered are:

- ❖ the implication of oral agreement and lack of a formal contract between the parties and the impact this may have on bringing an action for breach of confidence;
- ❖ whether the facts establish the elements of the action for a breach of confidence as set out in *Coco v AN Clark (Engineers) Ltd* (1969), namely that the information:
  - must have a necessary quality of confidence;
  - was communicated in circumstances importing an obligation of confidence; and
  - is used in an unauthorised way [possibly] to the detriment of the party communicating it.
- ❖ Are there any relevant defences that Dr Sharp and Orion Aerospace can rely on?
- ❖ What remedies available to Tim?

Applying the Law

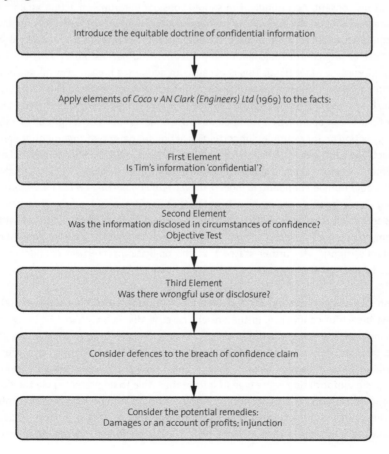

Introduce the equitable doctrine of confidential information

Apply elements of *Coco v AN Clark (Engineers) Ltd* (1969) to the facts:

First Element
Is Tim's information 'confidential'?

Second Element
Was the information disclosed in circumstances of confidence?
Objective Test

Third Element
Was there wrongful use or disclosure?

Consider defences to the breach of confidence claim

Consider the potential remedies:
Damages or an account of profits; injunction

ANSWER

Business people are always concerned about sharing their confidential information with others, but it is often necessary to do so in order to commercialise an innovation. As a consultant, Tim has used his expertise to solve a long-standing problem in the aviation industry and he approached Orion Aerospace, which he believed might be interested in his solution, with a view to collaborating to commercialise it. While Tim has taken the prudent step of verbally stating to Dr Sharp that the information he will disclose regarding his new highly geared bypass fan (HGBF) is confidential, he has not required either Dr Sharp or Orion Aerospace to sign a written agreement including terms to protect his confidential information, namely, the 'know-how' or 'trade secret' related to his HGBF, nor have the parties entered into a formal licence agreement. The difficulty for Tim will be to prove that an oral agreement exists, and while not impossible, this could be problematic. Fortunately, the law of confidence is often used to protect economically valuable commercial information such as Tim's HGBF design and his industrial 'know-how' (although it may apply equally to any information that has the necessary quality of confidence). Orion Aerospace and its employee Dr Sharp have possibly breached the law of confidence by designing their own HGBF if they have used any of Tim's information without his consent. Accordingly, Tim should consider initiating an action against Orion Aerospace relying on the doctrine of confidential information. To clarify, this means that the equitable doctrine of breach of confidence will operate as a stand-alone action regardless of any contractual relationship between the parties: *Prince Albert v Strange* (1849); *Morrison v Moat* (1851). This is because an action for breach of confidence has its roots in equity on the basis that it involves a breach of trust between the parties: *Coco v AN Clark (Engineering)* (1969); *Naomi Campbell v Mirror Group Newspapers* (2004). The law of confidence can operate as a stand-alone cause of action in its own right or as a supplementary action or, for example, supporting an action for patent infringement or breach of contract. The court can act independently in equity even in the absence of proof of an oral agreement between Tim and Dr Sharp that the information disclosed by Tim directly to Dr Sharp would remain confidential. Indeed, in *Saltman Engineering Co Ltd v Campbell Engineering Co Ltd* (1948) Lord Greene MR stated that 'If a defendant is proved to have used confidential information directly or indirectly obtained from the [claimant] with the consent, express or implied, of the [claimant], he will be guilty of an infringement of the [claimant's] rights'. He further stated that the obligation to respect confidence is not limited to cases where the parties are in a contractual relationship.

English law does not distinguish between types of information that may be protected against breach of confidence. In the ancient case of *Morrison v Moat* (1851) a recipe for medicine was protected via the doctrine of confidential information. There is a wide range of protected information which may include trade or technological secrets and know-how and commercial records: *Robb v Green* (1895). It is clear therefore that Tim's HGBF design information is the type of information able to be protected via the doctrine of confidential information. In *Seager v Copydex Ltd* (1967) the Court of Appeal confirmed that the court would act independently of the law of contract. The facts of *Seager v Copydex Ltd* (1967) are a case in point here. During preliminary negotiations with the defendants, the claimant revealed secret information to them about a carpet grip he had invented. After the negotiations had broken down, the defendants produced a carpet grip of their own which apparently made use of the claimant's information. There was no contract between the parties. In his judgment, Lord Denning MR stated:

> The law on this subject does not depend on any implied contract. It depends upon the broad principle of equity that he who receives information in confidence shall not take unfair advantage of it. He must not make use of it to the prejudice of him who gave it without obtaining his consent.

Prima facie Tim has an action against Orion Aerospace for breach of confidence. The three elements of an action were established by Megarry VC in the seminal case of *Coco v AN Clark (Engineers) Ltd* (1969) as follows: (1) the information must have a necessary element of confidentiality; (2) the information was communicated in circumstances of an obligation of confidentiality; and (3) the information is used in an unauthorised way (possibly) to the detriment of the party communicating it. Note, however, that Tim's action for breach of confidence against Orion Aerospace will fail unless all the essential elements for a successful action are shown. Each element of the test for breach of confidence will be considered in turn below.

First, for Tim's HGBF design information to be 'confidential' it must not be public property or knowledge. Specifically, in *Saltman Engineering v Campbell Engineering* (1948) Lord Greene MR stated that information must have 'the necessary quality of confidence about it, namely it must not be something which is public property and public knowledge'. It is clear that Tim's information is valuable technical information and is not mere 'trivial tattle'. The facts do not suggest that Tim's information has entered the public domain. However, Tim's design information and know-how must be shown to be clearly identifiable and sufficiently well-developed so as to be capable of realisation: *De Maudsley v Palumbo and Others* (1996); *Lock International plc v Beswick* (1987). This could be done by referring to specific documentation such as Tim's technical design drawing and his research notes which clearly confirm the HGBF technical information and suggest it was not merely an idea, but rather was sufficiently developed. It would be very helpful if such documentation was marked with the words 'confidential information' or the like and dated. If Orion Aerospace has reproduced the documentation, in particular if they have reproduced a technical design drawing incorporating Tim's information, an action may also lie for breach of copyright.

Second, the next question is whether Tim's HGBF information was communicated in a way that obliged Dr Sharp and Orion Aerospace to keep the information confidential. At their preliminary meeting in January 2014, Dr Sharp, employed as the Research and Development director for Orion Aerospace, expressly agreed to keep Tim's HGBF information confidential. The objective test formulated by Megarry J in *Coco v Clark* is clearly satisfied:

> If the circumstances are such that any reasonable man standing in the shoes of the recipient of the information would have realised that upon reasonable grounds the information was being given to him in confidence, then this should suffice to impose upon him the equitable obligation of confidence.

Dr Sharp will have the expertise and experience in the field to realise that Tim is disclosing the information on a confidential basis. Dr Sharp (and therefore his employer Orion Aerospace, which is vicariously liable for Dr Sharp's conduct) has a clear obligation to keep the information confidential and not to use it without Tim's permission. The second element of the action for breach of confidence is made out.

Third, has Orion Aerospace used the information in an unauthorised way to Tim's detriment? This is not clear on the facts. We are told that Dr Sharp and his team at Orion Aerospace have developed their own HGBF known as the Orion X2014. It may be that the company has used Tim's confidential HGBF technical information to its advantage as a 'springboard'. Tim will require further evidence as to the nature of the Orion X2014 and its development process in order to establish this third element of the action for breach of confidence. In his favour, Tim has not placed his HGBF in the public domain such that the information is accessible by the public, so Orion Aerospace will have to explain how it developed its Orion X2014. As Roxburgh J stated at 392 in *Terrapin v Builders Supply*:

> A person who has obtained information in confidence is not allowed to use it as a *springboard* for activities detrimental to the person who made the confidential communication, and springboard it remains even when all the features have been published or can be ascertained by actual inspection by any member of the public … The possessor of the confidential information still has a long start over any member of the public.

If Tim is able to prove that Orion Aerospace has used his confidential information to assist it to develop its Orion X2014 then an inference of breach of confidential information could certainly be drawn on this point. There are many examples of cases where suppliers or manufacturing companies take the original inventor's ideas and manufacture their own products. For example, the new carpet grip invented by Mr Seager, which Copydex 'unconsciously' used after licensing negotiations with Mr Seager broke down: *Seager v Copydex Ltd* (1967), as mentioned earlier. See also *EPI Environmental Technologies plc v Symphony Plastic Technologies plc* (2004).

Orion Aerospace does not appear to have any relevant defence. Tim's technical HGBF information is not in the public domain, nor has there been any undue lapse of time, nor does a 'public interest' argument arise on the facts.

In *Coco v Clark*, Megarry J questioned whether the claimant must show that he has suffered or will suffer detriment by the breach of confidence. In *A-G v Guardian Newspapers Ltd* (1989), the 'Spycatcher' case, Lord Keith made the point that detriment is usually present in commercial cases. Here, it would be a very straightforward matter for Tim to show financial detriment by Orion Aerospace's unauthorised use, especially given the negotiations between the parties as to a licence agreement and royalty rate in February 2014. He could also rely on the time he spent and expenses incurred in developing the fan.

In conclusion, Tim has a strong case against Orion Aerospace for breach of confidential information. Tim should immediately apply for an interim injunction to restrain any further publication of the detailed technical HGBF design information and know-how pending a full hearing of an action for breach of confidence, in order to preserve the status quo for as long as possible. In reality, judges in confidential information cases are heavily influenced by their moral views concerning the behaviour displayed by each party which is appropriate given that the law evolved as an equitable doctrine.

However, Tim's action must be for damages (*Seager v Copydex Ltd (No. 2)* (1969)) and not simply for restraint. In *Dowson v Mason Potter* (1986), the Court of Appeal set out that damages should be based on the market value between a willing seller and buyer. In a case where the claimant would wish to have retained the information, a loss of profits calculation would be entertained: *AG v Blake* (1990). Further, an award of an account of profits may be available where, although the information has passed into the public domain, the defendant is set to gain financially by breaching his obligation of confidence. In future, Tim should be advised to seek a confidentiality agreement in writing before he discloses commercially valuable confidential information to another party.

Common Pitfalls

Avoid reflecting on the patentability of Tim's innovation which is not in the public domain as this is not the focus of the question. This question should only be tackled by a student with a good knowledge of the equitable doctrine of confidential information. There is no need to cite any legislation to answer this problem. Instead, explain how the action for breach of confidence is judge-made law. Apply the principles established by key case law to the facts of the problem to determine the legal outcome.

Aim Higher

Analyse any potential defences to an action for breach of confidence. Provide advice regarding appropriate remedies that should be sought in the circumstances. This will assist the student to gain marks for providing a full answer to the problem question.

QUESTION 39

Critically analyse the pros and cons of relying on the doctrine of confidential information to protect an invention as opposed to applying for a patent.

How to Read this Question

A pros and cons essay encourages you to develop critical thinking skills by examining an issue from different perspectives. Analyse in detail the legal protection afforded by the two regimes in order to demonstrate an understanding and/or explain it.

How to Answer this Question

This essay question requires a high level of critical analysis and the development of a strategy for good decision-making when choosing between the legal protection afforded by the doctrine of confidential information and patent protection. The body of your answer should clearly outline the pros and cons of a particular issue. Devote at least one paragraph to each argument. Be even-handed, fairly summarising the strongest points. One should not forget, however, to refer to relevant legislation and case law where appropriate.

Answer Structure

❖   Nature of patent protection under the **Patents Act 1977** (**PA 1977**) as amended;

❖   Nature of confidential information protection as an alternative to copyright, design and patent protection;

❖   How to choose between confidential information and patent protection.

Up for Debate

Tension frequently exists between the options of keeping an invention confidential or filing a patent application which discloses the invention. Relying on the equitable doctrine of confidential information may eliminate any possibility of ever being able to patent an invention if the secret is later disclosed and enters into the public domain. That said, the publication of a patent destroys any confidential information which it discloses. Sometimes, the choice to patent an invention or to maintain it as confidential information is clear. Usually, however, the decision involves a balancing exercise between the various commercial and legal factors.

ANSWER

All innovation begins with ideas, information and know-how. While the proprietors generally wish to let others know that the new technology is effective, they also want to keep other information confidential in order to secure a patent or other intellectual property right, or because there is no other form of intellectual property right available for that information. For example, certain know-how may not be protected by the claims of a patent specification.

How businesses and inventors protect their confidential information or innovations generally begins with the decision either to apply for a patent application or keep it confidential. As patent protection and the doctrine of confidential information work in diametrically opposite ways (i.e. patents protect through disclosure and confidential information protects through concealment), the best route to take may be obvious. However, the choice may not always be so simple. Balancing a number of commercial and legal factors with the facts and circumstances of each particular case is required to arrive at the optimum decision.

A patent is a legally recognised 20-year monopoly which the Government grants in exchange for a complete disclosure of how to make and use an invention: **Patents Act 1977**. Confidential information, on the other hand, covers a wide variety of categories of information such as personal secrets (*Argyll v Argyll* (1967)); commercial records (*Anton Piller KG v Manufacturing Processes Ltd* (1976)); trade secrets (*Seager v Copydex* (1967)); and government secrets (*A-G v Guardian Newspapers* (1990)). To be protected, the information must have 'the necessary quality of confidence about it, namely, it must not be something which is public property and public knowledge' per Lord Greene MR in *Saltman Engineering Co Ltd v Campbell Engineering Co Ltd* (1948).

Commercial confidential information is essentially of two kinds. On the one hand, confidential information may concern innovations or manufacturing processes that do not meet the patentability criteria and therefore can only be protected as trade secrets. On the other hand, confidential information may concern inventions that would fulfil the patentability criteria and could therefore be protected by patents. In the latter case, a business or inventor will face a choice: to patent the invention or to keep it as confidential information.

Because of the disclosure requirements of patents and the secrecy requirements of confidential information, these two forms of intellectual property cannot usually co-exist for any one particular technology. A choice must be made either to apply for a patent or to keep the invention confidential. Confidential information can take place with immediate effect, and further, there is no need to comply with formalities such as the disclosure of the information to a Government authority.

HOW TO CHOOSE BETWEEN CONFIDENTIAL INFORMATION AND PATENT PROTECTION

In deciding whether to proceed with a patent, many factors must be considered. Several factors weigh strongly in favour of patenting. Other factors weigh strongly in favour of maintaining the invention confidential. Other considerations are less clear in favour of one alternative or the other and require a balancing of several factors.

The critical factor is to assess how realistic it is to keep the information confidential and for how long.

❖ If the information can be kept confidential for approximately as long as the commercial life of the products made using it, patent protection may not be required.

❖ Equally, if the information can be kept confidential for even longer than the 20-year patent term, then the information might be best protected as confidential information.

However, the duration of confidential information is uncertain. The protection for the confidential information can be lost overnight if the secret is publicly disclosed, even if the disclosure was not intentional.

THE NEED-TO-KNOW FACTOR AND EX-EMPLOYEES

In relation to a typical business, if only a few people need to know about the invention, secrecy may be a viable option. The difficulty arises when employees leave. The ex-employee may be subject to a contractual restraint of trade obligation, but this is limited in duration and scope. In other words, an ex-employee cannot be restrained from using every 'secret', especially if it is their stock-in-trade.

REVERSE-ENGINEERING

Another consideration is whether the information can be kept secret after the product has been made available to the public – can the product be easily reverse-engineered? Confidential information does not protect against reverse-engineering which is lawful unless patent-protected. Accordingly, it is of no use to protect a product which can be reverse-engineered. In this situation, a patent is the only option.

A classic example is the formula for Coca-Cola, which to date has not been reverse-engineered. If the formula had been patented when it was first used in 1886, it would have been in the public domain a century ago and would now be free for anyone to use. However, by maintaining the formula as a trade secret, Coca-Cola has continued to dominate the worldwide soft drink industry. Note, however, that the 'secret' ingredient is almost certainly nutmeg sourced from the Banda Islands, a fact well known to all Coke's competitors, although perhaps not the precise mix.

INDEPENDENT INVENTION

Similarly, the equitable doctrine of confidential information is of little use when dealing with an invention that is likely to be independently invented by another. In fact, this situation presents the dangerous possibility that the second inventor may file for and obtain a patent on the invention. The second inventor may then prevent the proprietor of the confidential information from practising the invention. Therefore, filing a patent application is the clear choice in this situation, especially where the proprietor is in a race with competitors to invent.

MARKET LIFE OF THE PRODUCT

It is important to consider the nature of the invention; a product with a short market life, such as an electronic children's game design to be updated annually may be adequately protected by confidential information giving the proprietor a good 'head start' in the market. However, compare this with an invention for an X-ray airport security system that may become a worldwide standard for many years.

If the major competitive advantage is by being 'first to market' or if the technology will be obsolete in less time than it would take for a patent to issue then a patent is of little or no use.

THE NEED TO GRANT LICENCES

For the invention to be licensed out, a licensee may be more willing to pay for an invention that is patented. Licensees may worry that their rights are less clearly defined by the doctrine of confidential information and that the value of a licensed invention may be abruptly lost if the licensor fails to maintain the secret.

PATENTS

The decision to file a patent application is not irrevocable. The act of filing a patent application does not result in loss of confidential information rights. In the UK, patent applications are kept confidential and are generally published 18 months after the initial filing date. Therefore, if a patent is not granted on an application, or if the application is abandoned, the confidential information disclosed in the application will not be published and secrecy can be maintained.

Therefore, one effective strategy may be to file a patent application and also to continue to maintain confidential information during the application process. This will provide a substantial delay for the need to decide whether to abandon confidential information status in favour of a patent.

A granted patent is a sword, not a shield. It gives the right to attack a competitor who makes commercial use of ('infringes') the patented technology. Contrary to common belief, it does grant the right to practise your technology free of interference. Patents are often quite narrow and can be circumvented. For example, they might apply to a specific design element or combination of characteristics. Further, they have effect only in the jurisdiction of the patent-granting authority: effective world coverage requires a family of patents in different countries. The patented technology on its own is usually insufficient to deliver the product. Finally, enforcing a patent is very expensive; however, a judgment in favour of the patent holder will substantially increase the value of the patent and reduce the likelihood of future infringement occurring.

COST

An advantage of confidential information over patents is that there are no official prosecution costs or maintenance fees in order to establish confidential information or to keep it in force. Patenting costs may amount to several thousand pounds or more. These costs are not incurred if an invention is maintained as confidential information.

However, this does not mean that there are no costs involved in maintaining confidential information. Quite the opposite: in some circumstances, confidential information can be expensive to maintain. For instance, there may be costs associated with physically preventing the public from learning the confidential information. These costs may include: physical plant construction to restrict access to the grounds and buildings; checking on repair and service people; restricting information to individuals in the company who need to know; fragmenting information so that no single individual has access to complete confidential information; labelling containers so that process variables and ingredients are not shown; marking documents confidential; using encryption technology. There may also be legal costs for the preparation of contracts which clarify the existence of confidential information and the duty not to disclose. These contracts may have to be signed by suppliers, licensees, customers, consultants and others with whom the proprietor does business, such as those considering engaging in a joint venture or to include restraint-of-trade terms for employees leaving the organisation.

For example, the well-known fast-food chain Kentucky Fried Chicken (KFC) has zealously protected its famous recipe of 11 herbs and spices for more than half-a-century. In 2011, KFC relocated the original copy of the recipe written by Colonel Sanders to a high-level security complex which included numerous motion detectors, cameras and guards who ceaselessly monitored the vault. To some, this may look like an exaggerated marketing ploy to garner the public's attention; however, KFC executives probably had other underlying motivations.

The costs and difficulties encountered in maintaining confidential information can be significant to the extent that this consideration is enough to tip the balance in favour of patenting (if the innovation meets the patentability requirements), despite the fact that other considerations might favour relying on the doctrine of confidential information.

FREEDOM OF INFORMATION AND THE PUBLIC INTEREST

Another difficulty with maintaining an invention confidential may occur whenever documents are submitted to the Government. Due to the UK's **Freedom of Information Act 2000**, it can be problematic to prevent information contained in these documents from being discovered by competitors or litigants who make freedom of information requests under the Act. This is because the Government can argue that a public interest excuses its use or disclosure of the information.

ENFORCEMENT

Arguably an action for breach of confidence is more difficult to enforce than a patent. The level of protection granted to confidential information varies significantly from country to country, but is generally considered weak, particularly when compared with the protection granted by a patent.

On the other hand, enforcing patent rights is notoriously expensive.

CONCLUSION

Whether to seek patent protection or rely on the doctrine of confidential information is a complex matter that needs to be considered on an individual case basis by examining the specific factors in issue.

In at least two situations, patents are a clear choice over maintaining an invention confidential. If an invention can be reverse-engineered or independently developed, if there is a need to disseminate information about the invention, or if the invention is a technology for which a licensee will only pay if it is patented, then the choice is clearly in favour of patents. On the other hand, if the information or know-how is not patentable, if it provides an advantage which is of a shorter duration than the time it would take to obtain a patent, or if the information will be valuable for a very long time and secrecy can be maintained during that time, then the choice is clearly in favour of confidential information. For the most part, the choice is not black and white, so the various commercial and legal considerations must be carefully weighed up in order to arrive at a reasoned and practical decision.

Common Pitfalls

The most common mistake is to write too generally around the topic of the question, without paying attention to the specific instructions and parameters of the question. For example, avoid stating everything you know about how patents are granted followed by a lengthy discussion of the legal principles of the equitable doctrine of confidential information. Stick closely to the instructions you are given; other aspects of the topic may well be very interesting, but if part, or all, of what you write lacks relevance to the objective of the question, you will definitely lose marks. Keep asking yourself if what you are writing is relevant. If it isn't, don't write it.

Aim Higher

Your essay could be a simple summary of the pros and cons of an issue, or better, you could synthesise the pros and cons into concrete recommendations. As with all essays, a clear thesis guides the direction of your answer. Use headings to add structure to your essay by highlighting the specific issues you are critically analysing. The key here is to carefully analyse the issues that should be taken into account when determining which regime to rely on in order to protect innovation.

10 Enforcement of Intellectual Property Rights

A strong intellectual property (IP) system is key to encouraging innovation and delivering continued economic growth. The methods of enforcing IP rights (whether copyright, designs, patents or trade marks) are of great practical importance as rights that cannot be enforced are ultimately worthless. The importance of litigation in the IP field should not be underestimated. There is a range of court orders, statutory, common law and equitable remedies that are available to an IP rights owner to enforce their rights. These have developed over time on a piecemeal basis; however, the **Enforcement Directive** (**Directive 2004/48/EC**) has produced a degree of standardisation. A solid knowledge of these legal remedies is important for answering problem questions that require the student to advise a party as to their 'rights and remedies'.

Essentially, IP infringement can be described as tortious in nature and as a wrong committed against property. Under the **Senior Courts Act 1981** all civil actions for IP infringement are allocated to the Patents Court, part of the Chancery Division of the High Court of England and Wales. The Patents Court in fact deals with all types of intellectual property and has specialist IP judges. IP actions involving smaller monetary sums can now be brought in the Intellectual Property Enterprise Court (IPEC) (formerly the Patents County Court) based in the Royal Court of Justice in London. IPEC was established to provide a less costly and quicker way for small business to proceed to litigation on IP matters using either the small claims or a multi-track procedure. The small claims track was introduced in 2012 in response to the **Hargreaves Report** and has helped improved access to justice by small business in IP matters. The most important civil remedies for successful claimants in IP actions are: (1) injunctions (an equitable discretionary remedy which needs to be considered in almost every situation); and (2) damages or an account of profits. The purpose of awarding damages is to compensate the IP owner for the loss caused by the defendant's infringement. In claiming damages, the IP owner will need to establish:

❖   that the claimed method for assessing damages is appropriate (measure); and
❖   that the damages are not too remote (remoteness).

Sometimes, the remedy of damages will be inadequate. Equity therefore developed a number of remedies, discretionary in nature, directed towards ensuring that a claimant was not unjustly treated by being confined to a remedy in damages. An injunction is an example of a remedy that seeks to restrain the defendant from committing infringement(s). Another example is an account of profits, which seeks to take back from the defendant profits made through the unauthorised use of the claimant's intellectual property. An account of profits is usually accompanied by an injunction and it is granted at the discretion of the court. In addition to civil remedies, UK law provides criminal sanctions for a variety of infringing acts. Moreover, IP rights are increasingly exploited internationally, giving rise to transnational litigation.

Checklist
Students should anticipate questions about the following:
■ IP infringement, piracy and counterfeiting;
■ the way in which IP rights are enforced;
■ pre-trial remedies;
■ post-trial remedies;
■ the role of the court, when granting relief, in protecting IP owners' rights counterbalanced with free competition.

QUESTION 40

According to the UK Intellectual Property Office (UKIPO), there is evidence that intellectual property (IP) piracy and counterfeiting crime is increasingly well organised. Are the current remedies available to IP owners to enforce their IP rights adequate or is there a need for further measures? Critically discuss.

How to Read this Question

The examiner has made a statement and is looking for an answer that either agrees or disagrees with it. The main issue is whether current legal remedies are adequate to combat piracy and counterfeiting crime.

How to Answer this Question

The question expects the student to demonstrate a knowledge of the range of civil remedies and criminal sanctions available for IP infringement and whether or not they are fit for the purpose.

❖ Clarify and distinguish between piracy and counterfeiting.
❖ Evaluate the range of civil remedies.

Up for Debate

The US Chamber of Commerce's Global Intellectual Property Center released the third edition of its **International IP Index** on 4 February 2015 which rated the UK as number one in the world for IP enforcement.

The report, which is a tool for governments across the globe to understand key IP factors, listed the UK second out of 30 countries – a mix of developed economies and emerging markets – for its IP environment and number one for its IP enforcement. Germany came third and France fourth, while Thailand, India, Vietnam and Indonesia received the lowest overall scores. The report welcomed the UK's 'high' enforcement levels and commended the country's 'highly advanced and sophisticated national IP environment.' Other key strengths of the UK that were highlighted in the report were:

❖ highly advanced and sophisticated national IP environment;
❖ protection for confidential information;
❖ framework in place to promote action against online piracy;
❖ commitment to and implementation of international treaties;
❖ consistent, effective and innovative border protection against counterfeited and pirated goods.

While the UK is a leader in this area compared with other nations, do the current IP enforcement systems provide effective protection against organised crime or serial IP infringers? One starting point is reading the *IP Crime Report 2013/2014* published by the UKIPO on behalf of the IP Crime Group.

ANSWER

While it is important to ensure that the various intellectual property (IP) regimes offer appropriate and adequate protection for the results of creative effort, the other side of the coin is the availability of measures to enforce those rights.

Piracy and counterfeiting are a real threat to IP owners, domestically and internationally, as well as for consumers and the government. Counterfeiting refers to wilful trade mark infringement: for example, fake replica rock band or football shirts; shoes and clothing branded with fake marks. Piracy refers to wilful copyright infringement such as fake digital versatile discs (DVDs) and compact discs (CDs), or unauthorised downloading of music or computer software from the Internet, and so on. Counterfeiting and piracy are facilitated by modern digital technology which enables copying much more quickly and accurately than ever before.

A frequent criticism of the operation of the system of IP laws in practice is the difficulties encountered when IP owners seek to enforce those rights. Such arguments have particular force in relation to combating organised crime, given that IP litigation is both expensive and time-consuming. Enforcement has become an increasingly challenging area in the fight against the importation of fake goods as well as due to the rise of the digital environment. Historically, crime has always followed the economy and as the knowledge-based economy provides more opportunities, that is where the criminal element has moved.

EUROPEAN IP ENFORCEMENT DEVELOPMENTS

In July 2014, the European Commission adopted the **Communication 'Towards a renewed consensus on the enforcement of Intellectual Property Rights: An EU Action Plan'**. In the

Action Plan, the Commission seeks to reorient its policy for IP enforcement towards better compliance with IP rights by all economic actors. Rather than penalising the citizen for infringing IP rights (often unknowingly), these measures pave the way towards a 'follow the money approach' that seeks to deprive commercial-scale infringers of the revenue flows that draw them into such activities. As announced in the **Communication on a Digital Single Market Strategy for Europe**, the European Commission will make proposals in 2016 to modernise the enforcement of IP rights, focusing on commercial-scale infringements (the 'follow the money' approach) as well as cross-border applicability.

TYPES OF IP ENFORCEMENT ACTIONS

Usually, an IP owner will focus on obtaining civil remedies, but some criminal sanctions are also available. However, not all cases that fall within the criminal law provisions will be dealt with as criminal offences and in many cases business-to-business type disputes are tackled by the civil law. In the UK there are a range of civil remedies and criminal sanctions available in order to enforce IP rights. These are interim and final injunctions, damages, an account of profits, search orders, orders for delivery up and destruction, and declarations of infringement. Four types of IP enforcement action are possible:

❖ civil proceedings;
❖ criminal proceedings;
❖ administrative action by giving notice to UK HM Revenue & Customs, or the UK Advertising Standards Authority; and
❖ self-help by IP owners.

PRE- AND POST-TRIAL ORDERS AND REMEDIES

When an IP owner brings a claim for IP infringement, a successful action will be of little practical use if the defendant has continued to trade, destroyed evidence or moved assets out of the UK. So, in order to preserve the status quo a wide range of pre-trial orders is available:

(1) interim injunctions (see *American Cyanamid v Ethicon* (1975) AC 396);
(2) freezing injunctions;
(3) *ex parte* orders;
(4) discovery orders – court order for a party to reveal relevant information (**CPR 31**/ *Norwich Pharmacal* order);
(5) search orders (see *Universal Thermosensors v Hibben* (1992) 3 All ER 257).

Post-trial non-pecuniary (i.e. non-monetary) orders include:

(1) declaration of infringement or non-infringement;
(2) delivery up and destruction;
(3) final injunctions.

Final pecuniary (monetary) remedies such as damages or an account of profits provide financial compensation for losses caused by infringement. However, an IP rights owner cannot enjoy both damages and an account of profits. They have to make an informed choice to elect one or the other. The most common award is for damages and these are calculated on the basis of compensating for lost profits or on a royalty basis: *General Tire v Firestone Tyre* (1975). See **Patents Act 1977, s 61(1)(c)**; **Trade Marks Act 1994, s 14(2)**); **Copyright, Designs and Patents Act 1988, s 9(2)**; **Registered Design Act 1949, s 9(1)**. Aggravated damages may be available, for example, to include a restitutionary element: *Nottinghamshire Healthcare NHS Trust v News Group Newspapers Ltd* (2002). Account of profits is an equitable remedy (**PA 1977, s 61(1)(d)**; **TMA 1994, s 14(2)**; **CDPA 1988, ss 96(2)** and **229(2)**)) for infringement of registered designs. The case of *Celanese International Corporation v BP Chemicals* (1999) provides guidance as to how to calculate an award under account of profits.

CRIMINAL LIABILITY

Criminal sanctions are sometimes available, for example:

❖ patents (**PA 1977, ss 109 and 110**);
❖ trade marks (**TMA 1994, ss 59, 60, 92**);
❖ copyright (**CDPA 1988, ss 107–110, 198, 297, 297A, 196ZB and 201**); and
❖ registered designs (**RDA 1949, ss 35 and 35A**).

STATE ASSISTANCE FOR THE IP OWNER

IP owners may invoke state assistance to help protect their private IP rights. In relation to administrative proceedings, customs officers, trading standards authorities and the Advertising Standards Authority (ASA) play an ancillary role in the enforcement of IP rights. The most important role belongs to the customs officers who, at the request of the rights holder, may arrest infringing imports at their point of entry in the UK. These measures operate together with an EU Regulation (**Council Regulation 3295/94**) to stop the release of counterfeit goods into free circulation. The EU Regulation gives the rightholder 10 days from notification of seizure to start full-scale infringement proceedings and counterfeit goods are normally destroyed.

SELF-HELP FOR IP RIGHTS OWNERS

In relation to 'self-help', **s 100** of the **CDPA 1988** gives the copyright owner an additional right. This is the only example of self-help in the IP field. **Section 100** enables the copyright owner or his agent to seize and detain infringing copies. However, a series of restraints applies to this far-reaching right. First, the infringing copy must be exposed or otherwise immediately available for sale or hire. Second, no force may be used, and advance notice of the time and place of the proposed seizure must be given to a local police station. Third, nothing may be seized from what appears to be a normal place of business. Finally, only premises to which the public has access may be entered in the exercise of this right: for example, a market stall, a car boot sale. Self-help is increasingly popular and several IP owner organisations have been established to assist in enforcing IP rights. These include the Federation Against Software Theft (FAST); the Federation Against Copyright Theft

(FACT); the IFPI, which represents the recording industry; and Anti-Copying in Design (ACID).These organisations are active in enforcing their members' interests by providing advice on interim measures and initiating civil proceedings to deter and ultimately prevent infringement.

COOPERATION IN INTELLIGENCE AND EVIDENCE GATHERING

Efforts to tackle IP crime involve the continuing cooperation between government, industry and enforcement agencies. In the UK, the Department of Business, Innovation and Skills (BIS) and the UKIPO are responsible for government policy on IP rights enforcement. The UKIPO's *IP Crime Report 2013/2014* published on behalf of the **IP Crime Group**, whose members include private industry, law enforcement and government representatives, reports that social media platforms are now a lead location for investigating IP crime, particularly for Trading Standards. The group collects the intelligence gathered by industry and enforcement agencies in order to track illegal infringement activities and the criminals involved. The report claims that greater collaboration between the group's members has helped to boost the fight against IP crime and further that industry has responded well, noting for example that the British Phonographic Industry removed 72 million instances of infringing digital material in one year.

To further encourage greater collaboration in the enforcement of IP rights, the European Observatory on Infringements of Intellectual Property Rights, based in the Office for Harmonization in the Internal Market (OHIM), is tasked with encouraging greater collaboration between public and private stakeholders. At the international level, the World Intellectual Property Organization (WIPO) has created an Advisory Committee on Enforcement.

In conclusion, legal instruments such as the **Enforcement Directive** already exist in the EU to prevent the infringement of IP rights. But to make them more effective, stronger cooperation between authorities at all levels in the fight against IP infringement is still needed. The UK's traditional remedies for infringement normally granted to successful claimants at trial have their place in the IP system. IP infringement often requires immediate action or a pre-emptive strike (pre-trial measures). This is where the interim injunctions and self-help play an important role. Finally, however, gathering evidence which is vital for the full trial is not easy but it is hoped that increasing the cooperation between government, industry and enforcement agencies will ensure that that IP rights owners now have better access to justice and more and more counterfeiters and pirates do not escape justice.

Common Pitfalls

Avoid writing a composition with a narrow focus on only one or two remedies. More marks will be gained by discussing remedies in the wider context of IP enforcement policy and developments.

QUESTION 41

When granting an interim injunction in connection with intellectual property infringement, what issues and principles must a court consider? Critically discuss with reference to relevant case law.

How to Read this Question

The question is asking students to demonstrate a good critical knowledge of why and on what basis a court will grant an interim injunction in practice in intellectual property cases.

How to Answer this Question

This question focuses specifically on the pre-trial interim equitable remedy of an injunction and requires a thorough discussion of the relevant case law and legislation:

- ❖ *American Cyanamid* (1975);
- ❖ *Series 5 Software v Clarke* (1996);
- ❖ impact of the **Human Rights Act 1998**;
- ❖ *A v B and C plc* (2002).

ANSWER

The modern law on the practice of granting an interim injunction is the result, in some measure, of the role intellectual property (IP) litigation has played over the last 40 years. The claimant's first concern in cases of IP infringement is that the infringing act stops. Even today, it is rare for an IP case to go all the way to trial. This is largely because wilful disobedience of an interim injunction will amount to contempt of court, and contempt is punishable by fine, imprisonment or sequestration of assets. Typically, an interim injunction is the only order that a claimant needs to prevent further infringement by the defendant. The sooner this happens, the easier it will be to limit the damage to his business, rights and reputation. The remedy is also known as an 'interlocutory' or 'temporary' injunction.

Accordingly, an interim injunction is designed to give preliminary relief in circumstances where allowing ongoing infringement, while the substantive merits of the case are determined, would cause irreparable damage to the IP rights owner. Interim injunctions are governed by the **Senior Courts Act 1981 s 37** together with the **Civil Procedure Rules Part 25**.

An interim injunction is a court order directing that certain acts do or do not take place or should not continue, pending the final determination of the parties' rights by the court. Therefore an interim injunction may be used to prevent imminent infringement, preserve evidence (where there is sufficient evidence that key evidence relating to the infringement would be destroyed or otherwise concealed) or to preserve the assets of the infringer. The order to award an interim injunction is made at the court's discretion; therefore it is an equitable remedy.

The principles governing the grant of an interim injunction were first laid down by the House of Lords in *American Cyanamid v Ethicon* (1975). This case sets out the standard principles on which interim injunctions will be granted:

❖ the claimant should have a prima facie (arguable) case;
❖ damages would not provide an adequate remedy in the circumstances; and
❖ the court will consider the balance of commercial convenience. If this is equal, then the courts should act to preserve the status quo.

Justice Laddie reviewed the principles in the *American Cyanamid* decision in the case *Series 5 Software v Clarke* (1996). The *American Cyanamid* principles were criticised because it was felt that interim injunctions were being awarded too easily. Laddie J held that when considering whether to grant interim relief, the court should bear in mind the following:

(1) the grant of an interim injunction is a matter of discretion and depends on all the facts of each case;
(2) there are no fixed rules; and
(3) the court should rarely attempt to resolve difficult questions of fact and law.

Nevertheless, *American Cyanmid* is still good law and the preferred judicial approach. Improved court efficiency in hearing cases at trial more quickly than in the past appears to have resulted in fewer interim injunctions being awarded in recent years.

An example of an appropriate case for interim relief was that of the *BBC v Precord Ltd* (1992). In this case, the defendants proposed to make a rap record featuring illicitly obtained extracts from an unbroadcast interview in which the then Opposition leader had famously lost his temper.

In contrast, in *Mothercare UK Ltd v Penguin Books Ltd* (1988), a complete lack of confusion meant that no interim relief was permitted in the passing-off claim. The defendants were allowed to continue publishing a serious sociological study entitled *Mother Care/Other Care*.

Overall, the post-*Cyanamid* approach to the award of interim injunctions shows the courts are generally able to react in a sensible way.

However, the **Human Rights Act 1998 (HRA 1998)** has made an impact on the award of interim injunctions. The **HRA 1998** has reduced the availability of interim injunctions in respect of breach of confidence cases and issues relating to freedom of expression. In light of the **HRA 1998**, the *American Cyanamid* principles have been restated. First, the claimant should have a prima facie (arguable) case, as per *A v B and C plc* (2002), except in breach of confidence cases where issues of freedom of expression are raised – here a higher standard should apply. More recently, in *Cream Holdings and others v Banerjee and others* (2004) the House of Lords held that the court should consider whether the applicant's prospects of success at trial are sufficiently favourable to justify the order. Second, whether damages would provide an adequate remedy in the circumstances and the ability of the parties to pay (*Series 5 Software v Clarke* (1996)); and finally, the court will consider the balance of commercial convenience. If this is equal, then the courts should act to preserve the status quo.

In breach of confidence cases, where an issue of freedom of expression arises, the court should weigh up the claim based on freedom of expression as against the claimant's position. If the claimant invokes a claim of privacy, the court should weigh the claim to privacy as against that of the claim of freedom of expression. An injunction should be granted only when justified.

Generally in the UK, the applicant for an injunction must provide several things for the court to consider. This will include documentation to prove validity of the IP right it seeks to enforce, for example a patent or trade mark certificate and certificates of payment of renewal or annuity fees. Evidence relating to the alleged infringement needs to be presented – for patents, this shall include the alleged infringing product, a description of the technical features of the patented process/product and a comparison thereof; for trade marks, a sample of the product bearing the alleged infringing trade mark should be produced. Where a licensee is applying for relief, evidence of the licence – copy of the licence, certificate of recordal of licence with appropriate authorities (a non-recorded licensee may never enforce licensed IP rights against a third party). Where a sole licensee is applying for relief, in addition to the evidence above, evidence that the patentee or trade mark registrant itself has abandoned its right to apply for relief is necessary. Where a legal heir is applying for relief, evidence that the legal heir has inherited or is in the process of inheriting the patent or trade mark right. Finally, the applicant may be ordered to pay a monetary bond against possible damage caused to the injuncted party if the injunction is subsequently found to be unwarranted. However, the injuncted party cannot seek to have the injunction lifted by pledging a counter-bond.

In conclusion, in order to obtain an interim injunction, it is important to remember that an injunction is an equitable remedy and is thus subject to equity's ever-present requirement of conscionability (acceptable to one's conscience or contrary to good conscience). The court will consider a variety of factors such as the public interest, the size of the parties and the nature of any competition between them and whether there has been any delay by claimant. A final injunction can be granted after the conclusion of the trial in which the infringement of the claimant's right is established.

Common Pitfalls

Avoid dwelling on the specific facts of the case law cited; rather it is preferable to discuss the relevant legal principles established by the case law and their application in the field of IP law enforcement.

Aim Higher

In the concluding remarks section of your composition, revisit the issue of interim injunctions as a key pre-emptive measure for enforcing IP rights.

Appendix I

INTELLECTUAL PROPERTY LAW EXAM TECHNIQUE

Prior preparation and practice prevent piss-poor performance.

The 'Seven Ps' – an old Royal Navy saying

(1) Well before your exam, read your syllabus or module handbook and confirm precisely what is examinable.

(2) Ensure you have all the materials you need to study (e.g. textbook, lecture notes, tutorial questions, marked assignments, up-to-date unmarked copy of the relevant statutes, etc.).

(3) Draw up a study timetable and stick to it.

(4) Prepare and revise the examinable material. Re-read and condense your notes, don't write more notes. Use visual aids such as colour-coding, diagrams, flowcharts or mind maps to condense the information into one-page summaries of each topic.

(5) Practise answering past exam questions set by the module leader in previous years.
   - Do not endlessly revise, only to apply your hard-won knowledge for the first time in the exam. You wouldn't run a race without training.
   - Law questions assess your ability to critically analyse and discuss issues within a limited time frame, so it is sensible to practise this skill before the exam.
   - Students are still required to write law exams in longhand. If you are used to using a computer keyboard to type assignments and notes, don't forget to practise writing out your answers. You will be surprised how much harder it is to write a good answer without being able to cut and paste, delete, format, etc.

(6) Ensure you are familiar with the format, style and duration of the exam.

(7) Avoid 'question spotting' or adopting the risky study strategy of selecting a minimum number of topics to concentrate on. The odds will be against you.

(8) Confirm which materials will be permitted to be brought into the exam, if any: for example, unmarked statute books or the like.

(9) Plan your answer before you start to write. Use the 'How to Read this Question' and 'How to Answer this Question' in this text as a guide.

(10) Answer every part of the question.

(11) Do not ramble on; keep your answer to the point.

ESSAY QUESTIONS

Allow for flexibility to include the knowledge you have acquired and to adapt it to the question. After completing an answer plan, include a brief introduction to contextualise the IP law topic at hand, use headings to signpost the issues to be discussed to the examiner, and end with insightful concluding remarks. Underline or highlight relevant cases to assist the marker to award marks to your exam script.

A good approach is to:

❖ define and explains the key terms included in the essay question itself;

❖ compare and contrast;

❖ critically analyse the social, economic and political circumstances that impact on the development of the relevant law;

❖ identify any areas ripe for reform;

❖ suggest possible reforms;

❖ summarise the key points you have covered in a couple of sentences, followed by your concluding remarks.

Students should avoid adopting an overly 'journalistic' style or writing an answer with 'too much opinion and not enough law'.

Throughout the essay, students should ensure that they refer to relevant statutory provisions and leading cases, and highlight any controversial issues they are aware of from their wider reading.

PROBLEM QUESTIONS

Problem questions largely determine the structure of answers. An appropriate answer can be structured by legal issue or by party, as required.

It is good advice to question the significance of all the information provided in the question. Dates, acts, events are usually all relevant, although occasionally an examiner will plant a red herring.

The facts of leading cases are regularly adapted for use in problem questions. If this happens, ensure you mention the similarity in the factual situations and analyse the decision in the relevant case – will it be followed or can it be distinguished?

IN THE EXAM

❖ Bring all required materials with you: for example, your student ID, sufficient pens, pencils, erasers, highlighters, rulers, tissues and a bottle of water to hydrate (if permitted).

❖ Use the reading time to work out which questions you will answer, in what order.

❖ Keep an eye on the clock – work out a strategy for writing your exam answers based on the length of time and the number of questions to be answered. If you give yourself one hour per question, stick ruthlessly to your plan. You will achieve a better mark for completing all questions, rather than not having enough time to attempt one.

Appendix II

INTELLECTUAL PROPERTY LAW EXAM METHODOLOGY

Law exams commonly contain three types of questions: essay, problem and mixed topic.

ESSAY QUESTIONS

An essay question is often a short statement of law contained in a quotation from a court judgment or an academic article, which requires the student to answer the query or proposition within it. Essay questions are designed to test the student's depth of understanding of IP law and issues as well as their ability to critically analyse the law. The best approach is to adopt a succinct style, following an answer plan that covers the basic principles. Set out below are three examples of typical essay question terminology.

'Critically Analyse'

You may be asked to 'critically analyse…'. In this case, a useful approach is to provide an objective assessment of the positive and negative points of the subject. Ensure that your answer is clearly structured to signpost the progression of your argument(s).

'Critically Discuss'

Another commonly used instructing phrase are the words 'critically discuss'. This is an instruction to discuss the keywords identified in the essay question and form a view as to whether the law is developing in the most appropriate way.

'Subdivided' Questions

Some essay questions are broken down into subsections: for example, (i), (ii) … or (a), (b) … The best approach to this type of question is to answer each subquestion in turn, clearly identifying the separate parts of the essay. Unless you are told otherwise, it is reasonable for you to assume that each subdivision carries equal marks. This means you may want to allocate equal time to each subsection.

In general, when dealing with an essay question, the following approach is suggested:

Step one

What is the widest possible classification of the specific topic? For instance, copyright law, design law, etc.

Step two

Identify the focus within that topic – for example, whether the fair dealing provisions in the **Copyright, Designs and Patents Act 1988** provide the public with sufficient access to copyright works.

TABLE A

Subject	Copyright Law
Topic	Defences
Focus	Whether the fair dealing defences provide the public with sufficient access to copyright works.

Step three

Identify the key words in the title and explain and define them in the course of your essay. The key words here are: (1) fair dealing; (2) public; (3) access; and (4) copyright. Make sure aspects of each key word are addressed. Refer to relevant statutes and case law that support your thesis. There is no excuse for not citing cases accurately. Use the correct name for an Act (the short title).

From your experience of exams so far, you know that beginning to write is difficult, so do not start writing until you have an idea of what you want to say. Creating a brief answer outline will help you to plan the beginning, middle and end of your answer. Each example in this text contains a short 'How to Answer this Question' section for you to emulate.

Step four

Attempt to weave analysis, constructive criticism and evaluation of the law into your essay. There are always two sides to an issue and it is important to engage in a balanced discussion. Use the 'Up for Debate' section in each question in this text to assist you.

Step five

Review and proofread your essay to ensure that everything mentioned in it is relevant to the title. This is how to attract marks. End your essay with a brief summary and reach a sensible and reasoned conclusion.

PROBLEM QUESTIONS

Problem-solving questions contain a set of hypothetical facts and read like a short story. The facts may be based on or similar to a decided case or may be completely made up. The difficulty lies in recognising the areas of law from the factual circumstances. In answering the problem question, in essence, you put yourself in the position of the judge. Judges try to evaluate the strength of each party's position and arrive at a logically reasoned decision through the application of the relevant law. A problem question is NOT an invitation to write an essay. The facts of the case are important and should be specifically referred to in your answer. Most intellectual property law problem questions can be dealt with by adopting the following methodology:

IP Law Problem Question Checklist

❖   Classify the key facts (e.g. items of property, relevant dates, significant events, etc.).
❖   Identify the area(s) of intellectual property law concerned.
❖   Identify the author, inventor and/or owner of the right concerned.
❖   Note all the elements that need to be proved for the right to subsist, be registered, be granted, etc. In other words, explain the applicable law and conclude as you progress.
❖   Assess whether the alleged infringer has infringed by setting out all the elements that need to be proved. Deal with the facts as you progress.
❖   Consider whether the alleged infringer is able to rely on any defences.
❖   If the cause of action is established, consider what remedies are available.
❖   Advise the party(s) as to the strength of their case.

Examiners differ in their preferred practice for answering problem questions. The above checklist is general guidance.

There are also two acronyms that may help when dealing with problem questions:

TABLE B

IRAC	**I**ssues	**IDEA**	**I**dentify the legal issue
	Rules		**D**efine the legal rule
	Apply		**E**xplain how the rule works
	Conclude		**A**pply the rule to the facts

Each question in this text contains a helpful 'How to Apply the Law' section for you to structure your advice.

MIXED TOPIC QUESTIONS

A mixed topic question includes two or more topics on the syllabus in the same question. This type of question is often used both to increase the level of difficulty and to ensure that students cannot study topics in an overly selective manner. Typical combinations of intellectual property topics involve:

Copyright + Moral Rights
Copyright + Design
Trade Marks + Passing Off
Trade Marks + Image Rights
Patents + Design
Patents + Confidential Information/Know-How

Note, however, that any form of intellectual property right that arises in the syllabus can be combined with:

❖ 'traditional justifications for intellectual property';
❖ 'international themes in intellectual property';
❖ enforcement;
❖ remedies; or
❖ law reform.

The key answering a mixed topic question is to engage in a balanced discussion of each of the main issues.

GRAMMAR, SYNTAX AND SPELLING

Developing a good writing style is crucial for law students because the law is all about communicating through words. Keep sentences relatively short to avoid grammar and syntax errors. Do not adopt an overly journalistic or casual style of writing. On the other hand, avoid grandiose and flowery language. Use plain English where possible and write succinctly. Well-written answers have more authority and will attract better marks.

Appendix III

INTELLECTUAL PROPERTY EXAM CRAM GUIDE

Type of IP Right	Key Attribute	Subject Matter	Procedure	Right Created	Duration
Copyright	Originality	Literary, dramatic, musical and artistic works ('LDMA' works), sound recordings, films and broadcasts, etc	Statutory right arising automatically under the **CDPA 1988** No registration	Exclusive rights of reproduction, distribution, public performance, broadcasting, including in a cable program, adaptations (except fair dealing)	Variable Maximum of the life of the author plus 70 years
Moral Rights	Rights of author-creator vs those of the entrepreneur who exploits the work Originates from **Art 6 Berne Convention** See also **Art 27** of the **Universal Declaration of Human Rights**	Literary, dramatic, musical and artistic works Moral rights do not apply to: • computer programs • where ownership of a work originally vested in an author's employer • where material is used in newspapers or magazines • reference works such as encyclopaedias or dictionaries	Statutory right under the **CDPA 1988** which are personal to the author No registration, but must be asserted	There are five: (1) Right to Paternity (2) Right of Integrity (3) Right to object to false attribution (4) Right to privacy for photographs and films (5) Artist's Resale Right	Right of integrity and paternity last for the same period as the relevant copyright The right to false attribution exists for 20 years from the death of the person subject to the false attribution
Patent	New invention	Requirements: • Novelty • Inventive step • Capable of industrial application • Not excluded	Statutory right under the **Patents Act 1977** obtained by being granted a patent by the Patent Office. See also the **Patent Act 2004** and the **Intellectual Property Act 2014**	To exclude all others from making or using the subject matter	A maximum of 20 years

Type of IP Right	Key Attribute	Subject Matter	Procedure	Right Created	Duration
Registered trade mark	Trade Mark means a sign capable of graphic representation which can distinguish the goods of one undertaking from those of other undertakings: **s1 TMA 1994**		Statutory right under the **Trade Marks Act 1994** obtained by being granted a patent by the UK IPO Trade Marks Registry	Trade mark proprietor is given the right to stop third parties from using the mark or a similar one: **s10 TMA 1994**	Indefinite as long (as renewal fees paid)

Appendix IV

USEFUL RESOURCES

Actors' Guild of Great Britain www.actorsguild.co.uk

ACID Anti Copying in Design www.acid.uk.com

Alliance Against IP Theft www.ipaware.net/node/26

Authors' Licensing and Collecting Society www.alcs.co.uk

Brand Enforcement www.brandenforcement.co.uk

British and Irish Legal Information Institute: UK cases and legislative materials www.bailii.org

British Library Business and IP Centre www.bl.uk/bipc/index.html

British Literary and Artistic Copyright Association www.blaca.org

Chartered Institute of Patent Attorneys www.cipa.org.uk

China IPR SME Help Desk www.china-iprhelpdesk.eu

Community Trade Mark/Design Office https://oami.europa.eu

Community Plant Variety Office www.cpvo.europa.eu

Copyright Licensing Agency www.cla.co.uk

Department of Business, Innovation and Skills www.gov.uk/government/organisations/ department-for-business-innovation-skills

European Commission http://ec.europa.eu/index_en.htm

European Court of Justice http://europa.eu/about-eu/institutions-bodies/court-justice/ index_en.htm

European Free Trade Association www.efta.int

European Patent Office www.epo.org

Esp@cenet www.epo.org/searching/free/espacenet.html

European Union http://europa.eu/index_en.htm

Federation against Copyright Theft www.fact-uk.org.uk

Federation against Software Theft www.fast.org.uk

Her Majesty's Customs and Excise www.hmrc.gov.uk

Her Majesty's Stationery Office www.hmso.gov.uk

Judicial Protection for IP in China www.chinaiprlaw.com

ICANN www.icann.org

IFPI (Recording Industry) www.ifpi.org

Intellectual Property Enterprise Court www.justice.gov.uk/courts/rcj-rolls-building/ intellectual-property-enterprise-court

Intellectual Property Owners Association www.ipo.org

Intellectual Property Regulation Board www.ipreg.org.uk

IP Bar Association www.ipba.org.uk

IP Europe www.ip-europe.org

IP and Media ADR Group www.ipandmedia.co.uk

IP Law Firms Database www.intellectualpropertylawfirms.com

ITMA (Institute of Trade Mark Attorneys) www.itma.org.uk

Law Society of England and Wales www.lawsociety.org.uk

Music Publishers' Association www.mpaonline.org.uk

Office for Harmonization in the Internal Market: EU Trade Mark and Design Office https://oami.europa.eu/ohimportal/en

Performers' Rights Society www.prsformusic.com

UK Courts www.courtservice.gov.uk

UK Intellectual Property Office www.gov.uk/government/organisations/intellectual-property-office

UK Music www.ukmusic.org

UK Trade & Investment www.gov.uk/government/organisations/uk-trade-investment

World Intellectual Property Organization www.wipo.int

World Trade Organization www.wto.org

FURTHER READING

Arnold, R. *Performers' Rights* (4th edn, 2008) Sweet & Maxwell

Davies, G. *Copyright Law for Artists, Photographers and Designers (Essential Guides)* (2010) A & C Black Publishers Ltd

Davies, G. *Copyright Law for Writers, Editors and Publishers (Essential Guides)* (2011) A & C Black Publishers Ltd

Drucker, P. *Innovation and Entrepreneurship* (2006) HarperBusiness

Howell, C. and Bainbridge, D. *Intellectual Property Asset Management: How to Identify, Protect, Manage and Exploit Intellectual Property within the Business Environment* (2013) Routledge

Jacob, R., Alexander, D. and Fisher, M. *Guidebook to Intellectual Property* (2013) Hart Publishing, Oxford

Kamina, P. *Film Copyright in the European Union* (1st edn) 2002) Cambridge University Press

Smith, S. *Legally Branded: Logos, Trade Marks, Designs, Copyright & Intellectual Property, Internet Law & Social Media Marketing* (2012) Rethink Press Limited

BLOGS

Duetsblog www.duetsblog.com (US)

AwesomelyTechie http://awesomelytechie.com

Fashion & Apparel Law Blog www.fashionapparellawblog.com (US)

Protecting Designs Blog www.protectingdesigns.com (US)

The Fashion Law www.thefashionlaw.com (US)

The IPkat http://ipkitten.blogspot.co.uk (UK)

Index

account of profits *see* remedies

acknowledgement, in fair dealing **24**

Agreement on Trade-Related Aspects of Intellectual Property Rights *see* TRIPS Agreement (Agreement on Trade-Related Aspects of Intellectual Property Rights)

artistic works **26, 28, 30–3**; photographs **43–7, 71–3**; sculptures **30–33**

artist's resale right **20**

authors: false attribution, rights against **32, 39**; integrity and reputation **20, 37–9, 40**; *see also* moral rights

automatic rights, copyright and design right **17–19**

biological material, patenting of **115–18**

biotechnology inventions **115–18**

blog, copyright in **69–73**

breach of confidence *see* confidential information

causal connection, in copyright infringement **51**

Civil Procedure Rules **99–100, 194, 197–8**

CJEU (Court of Justice of the European Union) **161**

'classic trinity' formulation *see* passing off, common law tort of

colour marks (colour depletion theory; graphic representation requirement; PANTONE colour system; shade confusion theory) *see* trade marks

commissioner's right of privacy **20**

'commonplace' concept, designs: required not to be 'commonplace' *see* design

Community Trade Mark (CTM) **161**

computer programs *see* computer software

computer software: circumvention of technical devices relating to programs **66–7**; copyright law mechanisms protection **57–64, 74–6**; middleware **75**; patent examination **14–15**; Software Directive (1991) **62–3, 75**

computer technology, and copyright protection (Internet; videogames; websites) *see* computer software

confidential information/know-how: breach of confidence actions **177–89**; defences **182**; elements of the action **178, 179, 181–2**; pros and cons of **183–9**; remedies **179, 183**; types of information **180–1**

consumer protection **4, 6**

consumer's rights **18**

copying *see* copyright infringement

copyright **17**

copyright authorship **17, 49**

copyright defences **17**; fair dealing *see* fair dealing defence, copyright; Internet; *see also* copyright infringement

copyright duration **17, 19, 34**

copyright fixation requirement **35–6**

copyright, incidental inclusion **47**

copyright infringement **41, 43–56, 72–7**; causal connection **51**; exceptions to copyright infringement *see* fair dealing defence, copyright; literal and non-literal **57, 60–2**; look and feel **73–7**; primary **31, 43–8, 49–51**; secondary **31, 43–8, 50–1**; substantial taking **51**; test for **44, 46, 51, 52**

copyright originality requirement **27, 35, 45, 51, 71**

copyright ownership **17, 20, 33–4**; by employer **36, 49–50**; joint ownership **35–6**; first author **34–5, 39, 71**; self-employed **45–6**

copyright, permitted acts **46–58**; quotes and parody **53–6**

copyright, restricted acts **45–6, 50**
copyright, skill labour and judgement
 test **51**
copyright subsistence **26–7, 31, 33–4, 44,
 49–51**
copyright, substantial taking **50–1**
copyright works **4, 19**; artistic *see* artistic
 works; literary work **26, 27, 50, 58–9**;
 typographical arrangement of
 published editions **49**
Court of Justice of the European Union
 (CJEU) **54, 153**
creative commons licence **47**

damages *see* remedies
database right **26, 29**
databases *see* database right
de minimis non curate lex maxim, in
 copyright **26, 28**
derogatory treatment, moral right to
 object to **40**
design **79–96**; commonplace **86, 88–90**;
 copying **89**; European Community **79**;
 online registration **93**; originality
 requirement **87–8**
Design and Artists Copyright Society
 (DACS) **45**
design, registered **77–9**; defences **90**;
 definition **82**; distinctive character **77,
 79**; 'must fit' and 'must match'
 requirements **79**; UK IPO Design
 Opinions Service **90**
design right, unregistered **77–9, 81–2,
 92–4**; commonplace **85–8**; definition
 85, 89; first owner **89**; intentional
 copying **90**; method or principle of
 construction **82–3**; 'must fit' and 'must
 match' requirements **79**; negative
 registration criteria **81**; originality
 requirement **87–8**; ownership **95**;
 subsistence **86–7, 94–5**
Designs Registry, UKIPO **79**
developed countries **8–11**
developing countries **8–11**
digital environment **55**
Digital Opportunity Report (May 2011) **24**
digital works **60**
duration of patent monopoly **9**

economic justifications **4–6**; economic
 rights **17, 39**
*EIPR (European Intellectual Property
 Review)* **13**

employee inventors **131–37**;
 compensation **134–5**; outstanding
 benefit **133–5**
enforcement of intellectual property
 rights **191–200**; Communication on a
 Digital Single Market Strategy for
 Europe **194**; Communication 'Towards
 a renewed consensus on the
 enforcement of IPR: An EU Action Plan'
 193–4; criminal liability **193**; IP crime
 196; pre- and post-trial orders and
 remedies **194–6**; self-help **195–6**; type of
 actions **194–5**
Enforcing Small Firms' Patent Rights
 (2000) **99**
essential medicines **10**
European Court of Justice (ECJ) (now the
 CJEU) **63–4, 68, 77, 153, 165**
European Patent Office (EPO) **14, 106, 115**
ex-employees **186**

fair dealing defence, copyright **17, 21–25,
 43, 49, 52, 57**; acknowledgement **24**;
 exceptions **29**; permitted acts **22**;
 reporting current events **24**; quotes
 and parody **53–6**
false attribution, right against **32, 36, 40**
false endorsement **149–52**; *see also*
 passing off, common law tort of
fixation requirement *see* copyright
 fixation requirement

G20 (Group of 20) **11–12**
global minimum standards **9**
goodwill **135, 149–50**
Gower's *Review on Intellectual Property*
 (2006) **111**
graphic representation requirement *see*
 trade marks

Hargreaves Review of Intellectual
 Property and Growth 2011 **13, 24**
Hegel, Georg Wilhelm Friedrich **4, 6**
HIV/Aids **9**
Human rights, and enforcement of IP
 rights **198–9**

idea–expression dichotomy, copyright
 19–20, 57
image rights **147–52**; goodwill in **151–3**
incidental inclusion, copyright **47**
industrial application *see* patents
infringement, intellectual property:
 copyright **31**

injunctions **139, 142–3, 194–5, 197–200**
integrity, right of **20, 38, 40**
Intellectual Property Enterprise Court (IPEC) **98**
interactive media, definition **70**
interim injunction **139, 142–3, 194–5, 197–200**
interim remedies **139, 142–3, 194–5, 197–200**
interlocutory injunctions **139, 142–3, 194–5, 197–200**
International IP Index **192**
Internet, intellectual property rights in **2**
inventions *see* patents
inventive step *see* patents
IPEC (Intellectual Property Enterprise Court) **99–100, 129–30**
IPQ (Intellectual Property Quarterly) **13**
IRAC method **34, 205**

(JIPLP) Journal of Intellectual Property Law and Practice **13**
justifications for intellectual property protection **4–7**

'Labour Theory' (John Locke) **4–6**
LDMA (literary, dramatic, musical or artistic works) **17, 31**
litigation *see* enforcement of intellectual property rights
Locke, John **4, 6**

mala fides **33**
moral rights **17–18, 21, 31–3, 34, 37–41, 47**; defined **20**
morality and public policy issues, patents **115–17**
'must fit' requirement *see* design right, unregistered
'must match' requirement *see* design right, unregistered

National Endowment for Science, Technology and the Arts (NESTA) **130**
natural rights **4–5**
novelty *see* patents

Office for Harmonization in the Internal Market (OHIM) **79**
olfactory marks *see* trade marks
Olympic symbols **156**
Organization for Economic Co-operation and Development (OECD) **8**

originality requirement *see* copyright originality requirement
ownership *see* copyright ownership
OXFAM (Oxford Committee for Famine Relief) **9**

parody, right to quote **53–6**
partial monopoly, in copyright **22**
passing off, common law tort of **137–52**; 'classic trinity' formulation **139**; defences **142**; enforcing goodwill **142**; extended **145**; false advertising **145**; false endorsement **149–52**; goodwill and reputation **139–6, 143–4**; interim injunction to prevent **142**; likelihood of damage to goodwill **141–42**; orthodox **145**; reverse **145**; unfair competition **146–7**
patent applications **106**; national route **106–7**; regional route **106–7**
patent attorney **100**
patent backlogs **14**
patent claims **128**
Patent Court EU **13–14**
patent cross-licensing **106**
patent enforcement **99, 100**
patent examination **12**
patent filing strategy **106–7**
patent infringement **99, 127–31**; defences to **129–30**; remedies for infringement **130**
patent monopoly **97, 106, 122**
patent opinion service (UKIPO) **13**
patent prosecution **101, 106**
patent revocation proceedings **119–22**
patentability **103–4**
patents **74**; absolute novelty concept **77, 103–4**; advantages of patenting **107–9**; anticipation **119–21**; biotechnology inventions **125**; capable of industrial application **104–5**; contrary to public policy or morality **104**; declaration of validity **122**; definition **124**; disadvantages of patenting **109–11**; discoveries **125**; duration of monopoly **122**; enabling disclosure **119–21**; enforcement **188, 191–96**; employee inventors **131–35**; excluded subject matter **104, 111–14**; first and second medical use **111–13**; grant, requirement for obtaining **103–5**; impermissible amendment **122**; independent inventions **186**;

patents *continued*
  industrial application **103–4**;
  inventive step **102–5, 121**; justification
  for **124, 131**; lapse **122**; medical
  methods of treatment and diagnosis,
  surgery and therapy, patentability of
  111–14, 125–6; morality **115–18**; not
  obvious **104–5**; novelty **104**;
  outstanding benefit **131–33**;
  patentability criteria **103–4, 111–12,
  124–6**; person 'skilled in the art' **104**;
  pharmaceuticals **119–21**; prior art
  102–3, 119–22; priority date **104–5**;
  pros and cons of patenting **183–9**;
  public policy **115–18**; remedies **122**;
  revocation proceedings **119–22**;
  'skilled man' **104–5**; state of the art
  104–5; territorial rights **97, 104**; UK
  Statutory Compensation Scheme **131**;
  Windsurfing test **105**
paternity right **20, 39**
PCT (Patent Cooperation Treaty 1970)
  106, 109
permitted acts, in fair dealing **23, 47–8**
personal rights, in moral rights **32, 39**
personality, notion of protection for:
  personal dignity **148–50**; personality
  theory **4, 6, 148–52**; remedies **151–52**
personality and image rights **69–70, 72**
photographs *see* artistic works
plant breeder's rights **126**
plant varieties **126**
primary infringement, in copyright **31**
prior art *see* patents
priority date *see* patents
public domain **19**
public interest **54, 188**

quotation, right and exception **54–6**

R&D (research and development) **10**
registered design *see* design
registered trade marks *see* trade marks
remedies **129–30, 135–7, 137, 139, 142–3,
  191–202**
reputation **137**
resale right **20**
reverse passing off **137, 145**
reverse-engineering **186**
reward for innovation theory **111**

scent marks *see* trade marks
sculptures *see* artistic works

search orders *see* enforcement of
  intellectual property rights
secondary infringement, in copyright **31**
shape marks *see* trade marks
skill, labour and judgement test, in
  copyright **51**
'skilled in the art' test *see* patents
social well-being as a justification **6**
subsistence, in copyright *see* copyright
  subsistence
substantial taking **51**
sufficient acknowledgement **55**

Taylor Wessing Global IP Index **98**
technical assistance to developing
  countries **11**
technological protection measures
  (TPMs) **64–8**; access to digital works
  65; circumvention of technical devices
  66–7; definition **65**; permitted acts
  67–8
technology transfer **4, 6, 7**
trade marks **72, 74–5, 76–7**; absolute
  grounds for refusal to register **155–6,
  170–3**; applications **154–7**; badge of
  origin **159**; colour marks **156, 158–61**;
  Community Trade Mark **161**;
  composite markets **172–6**; confusion;
  167; definition **155**; distinctive
  character **161–62**; genuine use **175–6**;
  geographical names **169**; grounds for
  infringement **165**; infringement **163–8**;
  knock off brand **163**; Madrid Protocol
  for Registration of Marks **153**; non-
  conventional marks **162, 170–72**;
  Olympic symbols **156**; origin function
  166–7; registration **168–76**; Registry
  154–5; relative grounds for refusal to
  register **154–7**; revocation for non-use
  173–6; scent marks **156, 157–62**; shape
  marks **169, 170–72**; sign **159**; slogans
  157, 167; Trade Mark Directive **153, 155,
  165**; unconventional marks **162,
  170–72**; word mark **156, 169–70**
TRIPS Agreement (Agreement on Trade-
  Related Aspects of Intellectual
  Property Rights): access to essential
  medicines and TAN (TRIPS Action
  Network) **8–12**; copyright **20, 75**;
  design **87**; medical methods **112–14**;
  patents **110–11**
typographical arrangements of
  published editions **49**

UK IPO (UK Intellectual Property Office) **192**; Designs Opinion Service **92**; Designs Registry **79**; Patent Office **105, 110**; Patent Opinion Service (POS) **14–15**; Trade Marks Registry **154**
UK Statutory Compensation Scheme **131**
unfair competition **138, 146–7**
Unified Patent Court (UPC) **13–15, 99–101**
unified patent system **101**
unitary effect, of patents **101**
unitary patent **13–14, 98, 101–102**
unregistered design *see* design right, unregistered
US Chamber of Commerce Global Intellect Property Center **192**

utilitarian theory **4**

videogames, intellectual property protection for **73–7**; confidential information protection for **76–7**; copyright protection for **75–6**; infringement **127–9**; middleware **76–7**; patent protection for **76–7**; trade mark protection for **76**

websites *see* blog, copyright in
WIPO (World Intellectual Property Organization) **13, 106, 110**

YouTube **46**